My money is for __________________________.

moolala

moolala

Why smart people do dumb things with their money (and what you can do about it)

Bruce Sellery

McCLELLAND & STEWART

Library and Archives Canada Cataloguing in Publication

Sellery, Bruce
Moolala : why smart people do dumb things with their money
(and what you can do about it) / Bruce Sellery.

Issued also in an electronic format.
ISBN 978-0-7710-8044-9

1. Finance, Personal. I. Title.

HG179.S434 2010 332.024 C2010-903571-2

We acknowledge the financial support of the Government of Canada through the Book Publishing Industry Development Program and that of the Government of Ontario through the Ontario Media Development Corporation's Ontario Book Initiative. We further acknowledge the support of the Canada Council for the Arts and the Ontario Arts Council for our publishing program.

Typeset in Perpetua by M&S, Toronto
Printed and bound in Canada

This book is printed on acid-free paper that is 100% recycled, ancient-forest friendly (100% post-consumer waste).

McClelland & Stewart Ltd.
75 Sherbourne Street
Toronto, Ontario
M5A 2P9
www.mcclelland.com

1 2 3 4 5 15 14 13 12 11

For Dennis and Abby

CONTENTS

Introduction

This might be the first book about money you've read in a long time, or maybe even *ever.* But if you're willing to put down your Margaret Atwood/Dan Brown/Danielle Steele/Malcolm Gladwell/*Sports Illustrated*/*People* magazine for just a few hours, I know it will be worth your while. How do I know? Because I've worked with thousands of people like you over the years to help them get a handle on their money, and many of them were in way deeper —— than you.

Okay, maybe you're not in deep ——. But you might at least have an inkling that there is more you could be doing with your money. And while I know we've just met, my hunch is that managing your money doesn't trump "raindrops on roses" on your list of favourite things. You don't watch the business news channels obsessively or track your expenses with a missionary's zeal. Even though people are always telling you how important it is to plan for retirement, it just isn't a top priority for you. Besides, there are other things you want to do—and have—*now. Today.*

Still, you have this nagging sense that you *could* be doing more, perhaps *should* be doing more, even though you really, truly don't *want* to be doing more to get a handle on your money.

I get it. I really do.

So, if you don't love working on your money, what *do* you love?

Baking molten chocolate cake for your dishy dinner party guests. Reading *Where the Wild Things Are* to your kids. Taking your Labradoodle to the off-leash park. Sanding the backyard deck you built yourself. Snowboarding off piste. Sleeping in. Shopping. Watching trashy reality shows.

Whatever it is, this is a book about what you love.

Let me say that again.

This is a book about what you love.

You're probably thinking, "What do the things I love have to do with getting a handle on my money?" Well, the better you are at managing your money, the better you'll be able to experience more of what you love. Your money is simply a means to that end. Quite often we disconnect our dreams from the financial fuel that will bring them to life. That is a huge missed opportunity, and one that we'll address throughout *Moolala.*

Often we disconnect our dreams from the financial fuel that will bring them to life. That is a huge missed opportunity.

So here you are reading the introduction to a money book. Wow. Good for you. It takes a certain amount of intestinal fortitude to even consider focusing on your financial situation, and here you are doing something positive and proactive by holding this book in your hands. Many people live in complete denial about their money, some for their entire lives. They close their eyes, cover their ears, and loudly hum the theme from *The Facts of Life*, in the hope that they can block out the barrage of retirement ads, their parents' persistent prodding, and the unopened mutual fund statements cluttering their desks.

For a moment at least, you're not doing that. Again, good for you.

WHY I WROTE THIS BOOK

I spent a decade covering the business news in both Toronto and New York. It was a crazy time, what with the dot-com boom and bust, 9/11 and its aftermath, and the criminal trials of fallen stars like Martha Stewart. But over time I came to realize that our audience was mainly people who really love to work on their money, a fairly small percentage of the population that doesn't include most of the people I know.

So what about these people?

Perhaps you're one of these people who don't love to work on their money. You tune in to discussions about politics, art, sports, or family, but tune out the moment the topic turns to money. Your lips purse with disdain at the mere mention of financial planning and you feel you need *more* than a spoonful of sugar to help the medicine go down.

I thought perhaps that I had something to offer. I had a journalist's perspective on the world of personal finance and had spent many years as a workshop leader facilitating challenging conversations—and certainly talking about money can be a challenging conversation. So I decided to launch a personal finance training company called Moolala. Its mission is to inspire people to get a handle on their money so they can live the life they want.

Moolala's mission is to inspire people to get a handle on their money so they can live the life they want.

I love what I do. I have met many extraordinary people through speaking to large groups and leading small workshops across the country over the last few years. The people are diverse in age, occupation, and the money issues they face, but they are all inspiring. I call them the Moolala Community, and they have been invaluable in shaping the Moolala Method. In fact, seeing the changes that they have made in their own lives to get a handle on their money motivated me to write this book, and their personal stories form an important part of it.

WHY READ MOOLALA

If you're going to invest your time and energy in reading this book, the benefit had better be pretty sweet, right? My mission with *Moolala* is to inspire you to get a handle on your money so you can live the life you want—whatever that life may be. I intend to deliver on that promise by helping you do three things:

Gain new clarity in your thinking about money

Clarity makes a world of difference. But when it comes to your money, gaining new clarity can be tough. Every day we're bombarded by conflicting messages about what to do with our money—some from businesses who want you to spend, and others from businesses who want you to save. There are too many financial acronyms, products, opinions, tips, and techniques to keep straight, and almost all of them are delivered in a way that makes you want to reach for the TV remote or take a nap.

Moolala is designed to help you find clarity, without demanding that you memorize financial definitions or stick to an unachievable or puritanical plan. With clarity comes peace of mind, and that can be inspiring in and of itself.

Develop a simple plan of action you can implement immediately

The key word is *simple.* I am not trying to make personal finance your new hobby. Getting a handle on your money doesn't need to become a hobby, or take much of your time. In this book I will take you through the simplest possible plan for the biggest possible benefit, one that you can get started on right now. Like, immediately.

What this plan won't do is tell you how to get rich quick. If you're looking for one of those plans, simply search the Internet for "Lose 20 pounds in 20 minutes," and I'm sure they will have an equivalent plan for your money.

Be inspired to get off your duff and take action

There is a big difference between knowing what to do and actually going out and doing it. Sure, you need a certain amount of knowledge to get a handle on your money. But way, way, way more important than amassing lots of knowledge is taking action. Knowledge alone doesn't make much of a difference. What is required is insight into what's important to you. With insight comes inspiration. And with inspiration comes action. *Moolala* will focus on getting you inspired so you'll get off your duff and take action.

WHAT THE MOOLALA METHOD IS ALL ABOUT

I'd like to give you a brief overview of how I intend to help you get a handle on your money. I call it the Moolala Method, and it is made up of five simple steps that will take you from wherever you are today to where you want to be.

THE MOOLALA METHOD

Step 1: Lay the foundation

In the first step of the Moolala Method, we'll take a look at a fundamental and confounding question: Why do smart, capable people do dumb things with their money?

I consider you to be a smart person. I know, I know, I don't know you personally, but you're someone who has picked up this book, which of course I think is smart. You have some level of schooling, you've probably held down a job for at least a period of time, and you're someone who has achieved a level of stability and success in life. Yet, like most of us, you've also done a few dumb things with your money over the years. Why this happens is a fascinating question to me, and one I've been interested in for many years, first as a financial journalist and more recently as a financial educator and coach. I have seen time and again how weak the correlation is between smarts and smart money management. So we'll begin with a look at why this happens to so many of us, and what you can do to become a smart person who does smart things with your money a little more often.

Step 2: Determine what you want

Now that the foundation is laid, you can start to think about what you want to set on top of it. What do you want your life to look like tomorrow? Next year? And in thirty years?

Determining what you want is a critical step, yet it often gets missed entirely, leaving you with only the mundane task of choosing where to put your annual RRSP contribution (if you even make a contribution at all), or figuring out the date when you'll be able to stop working. In the second step of the Moolala Method, we'll take the time to discover what you really want out of life and come up with some goals that will help inspire you to get a handle on your money.

Step 3: Develop the plan

Once you know *what* you want, the Moolala Method will help you develop a simple plan to help you *get* what you want. The plan will cover a number of different areas, depending on your own unique circumstances, including such topics as improving your cash flow, finding a great financial adviser, defining your investment plan, and even working on life goals that you might not have considered to be "financial" in nature before now. And don't get freaked out by the word "plan." The focus will be on developing a "simple" plan that you can implement immediately.

Step 4: Take action

Now that the basic plan has been developed, it's time to take action. You'll be ahead of most people on your block just by having a plan to begin with. This step focuses on moving that plan from your notebook (or napkin) and into your real life. I'll identify some of the common pitfalls you might encounter when taking action on the plan—like procrastination, for example—and give you tips for how you can overcome them.

Step 5: Stay engaged

How great would it be if you could take your car in for just one tune-up and then never have to worry about it again? Or paint the house just once? File taxes just once? Sadly, that isn't how things work. The final step of the Moolala Method is about staying engaged with the plan. We'll look at what you'll need to do on an ongoing basis, and I'll provide some advice on how to keep your plan on track, even given the joyous insanity of everyday life.

WHAT'S IN IT FOR YOU

I've talked a bit about what I'm focused on delivering to you and how I'll go about it. So now you tell me, what are *you* focused on? Grab a notebook or use the space below to scribble a sentence or two about what benefit you want to get out of reading this book. What would make it worth your time and energy? Here are examples of what members of the Moolala Community said motivated them to get a handle on their money:

"My first child arrives in three months. I need to get my spending under control before that happens! AHHHH."

"I want to reduce my anxiety level about my future."

"My fiancée and I want to develop a vision for our finances BEFORE we actually get married."

"I want to learn what I need to know and what I don't need to know so I can focus only on what really matters."

"I'm looking for a great financial adviser to help me achieve my goals, but I feel like I should know more first so I can make the most of that process."

"I've just gone through a really expensive divorce and want to start this next chapter of my life on the right foot."

And you? What benefit do you want to get out of reading this book?

I want ____.

Okay, message received. Now, a word about how to get the most out of your time and energy.

HOW TO USE THIS BOOK

The Lonely Planet Guide to Thailand was an okay book to read on its own. I picked it up at the bookstore and was impressed by its historical perspective, really clear how-tos, and fantastic ideas on things to do that I never would have found out about on my own. But what made the *Lonely Planet Guide* an *extraordinary* book was what I discovered when I followed its recommendation for a crazy trek to the hillside villages north of Chiang Mai. The quality of the guidebook was a function of how I used it. The same applies to the book you're now holding in your hands. *Moolala* is a mix of personal stories, financial knowledge, and exercises that are designed to personalize everything to your individual circumstances. Using those exercises is key to shifting your experience from gaining knowledge *about* money to actually *using* that knowledge and insight immediately in your own life. Said another way, the exercises will take you from sitting on your couch reading *about* Thailand to sitting on an elephant *in* Thailand . . .

You're going to be doing some writing as you progress through the book. You can jot notes down in the margins, keep a separate notebook handy, or go to www.moolala.ca to download printable worksheets for the exercises. Don't worry: you won't have to show these notes to anyone. I will be asking you to *talk* with other people about what you're learning, but you won't ever need to show them your notes. And at the end of each chapter you'll notice something called "My One Thing." This is a way for you to choose one thing that you want to highlight from the chapter you just finished—perhaps an insight you had or an action you're going to take.

Oh, and one other note. You might notice that I use the pronoun "you" throughout. For some of you, the "you" will include others—a spouse, kids, other family members. Rest assured that I know your thinking, dreaming, and doing around money might involve other people, and that you might include them in the exercises. For simplicity's sake, I've used the singular "you."

WHY YOUR STATE OF MIND IS IMPORTANT

Now that you have a sense of where we're headed with this book, I want to address something really important: your state of mind.

My what?

Your state of mind: what you're thinking about and how you're feeling as you read this book.

There are a whole bunch of thoughts and feelings you could be having right now, and perhaps others will come up as you go ahead and read the book. I think it would be irresponsible of me not to address them. As I mentioned, money can be a tough topic for people, and I don't want you to get thrown off by wandering into an emotional minefield. Your thoughts and feelings are perfectly normal, common, and valid, even if you wish they would just go away. Just noticing what you're thinking or feeling at any given moment will help you stay on the path of getting a handle on your money.

I am going to highlight three of the many, many potential "states of mind" you might have as you read through this book, using examples from the Moolala Community.

Nervous: You might be feeling nervous as you think about working on your money. Most people are, so you're in good company. You probably have your own particular flavour of nervousness—it could be about admitting for the first time that this is something you need to work on, or that you'll find out you're in way deeper —— than you thought. Or it could be nervousness about the process—that maybe it won't work for you, that you're too deeply in denial about your money, or simply not inclined towards introspection or planning. Maybe you're nervous that you don't have the brains/dedication/time to make changes in this area of your life. Or that reading this book will open up a whole new can of worms, and you'll end up dying your hair purple, becoming vegan, and moving to Togo.

I can relate. Years ago, in the midst of a prolonged period of career angst, I was given a brilliant self-help book called *I Could Do Anything If Only I Knew What It Was.* Of course I didn't find out that it was brilliant for a very long time, because it sat in the trunk of my car, spine uncracked, for almost a year and a half. I was just too nervous to read it, let alone follow the exercises. While I wanted to change careers and knew I needed to make a change, I was terrified that if I read the book I would actually make a change, and I certainly didn't want to do that. Insane? Yes. But this might be exactly the kind of logic that your own brain is trying to sort through right now as it relates to your money. Nervousness, discomfort, whatever it is for you, can manifest itself in different ways. For some people, it means getting sleepy, or feeling sick, distracted, or anxious.

A lot of people want to make a change, know they need to make a change, and yet are nervous about making a change. That could be you. But this isn't a problem, and it's certainly not a reason to put the book down. I've got you covered. And in fact, you're really the type of person this book was written for.

"All day I braced myself mentally, because I was preparing to come out of the session with my head spinning. Usually when someone tries to explain financial concepts and strategies, budgets, etc., I get a headache. But this time was different."

–Jonathan, 38, landscape designer. Married.

Skeptical: You might be skeptical that this book is going to make a difference for you. Aren't there enough personal finance books out there? Does this Bruce guy really have something new to say? Why is he asking me about my "state of mind"? How is that relevant?

So, your state of mind could be somewhat skeptical. That's good. We journalists are a skeptical bunch too. Keep reading, and by the end of the book you might still be skeptical, but I'll bet you the watch on my wrist that you'll have a new understanding about yourself and some new ideas about how to improve your financial well-being.

"I was skeptical that Bruce would be able to pull it off. It was his job, not mine, to make the concept of money simple for me. So I felt the pressure was on him. And I just thought, 'Good luck to you, sir.'"

–Zahir, 33, business owner. Married.

Excited: Your state of mind could also be one of excitement. You could be ready to go and fired up about learning something new. You could be happy to have found a book that you can relate to, that meshes with your values, that has a great recipe for butter tarts in Chapter 15, one that even Oprah loves (okay, that's a bit premature, but I'm definitely sending her a copy). If excitement is where your mind is at, that's great too.

"I was excited to learn some tools that would help me gain practical and emotional control over money. I was also looking forward to getting over that feeling of dread that always erupted in my stomach when I had to deal with finances."

–Andrea, 39, university professor. Single.

There may be other "states of mind" that I haven't included here. But just take a moment for yourself and ponder what you're thinking and/or feeling right now, at this very second, so you're aware of it.

Right now I'm feeling ______________________________.

Okay, I hear ya. Thanks.

You will likely notice that your state of mind will change as you continue through the book. For example, if you love numbers, you might be excited in the sections with numbers. If you don't love numbers, you might be nervous (even really nervous) in those sections. If you love introspection, you might be excited about the exercises that have you think about your past, present, and future. And if you don't love introspection, you might be nervous during those sections (even really nervous). We are all a mix of right brain/left brain; feeler/thinker; word-oriented/number-oriented; introverted/extroverted. You'll probably find some sections harder and some easier depending on your preferences, experiences, and individual comfort zone.

You might be asking yourself, now what are we going to DO about our state of mind? It depends. Sometimes there will be something to do about it—like taking a break until the feeling passes, talking to a friend, or going for ice cream. But often there is nothing to do. It is just a part of the process. I was nervous on the day of my wedding. Most people I know are, but there isn't really anything to "do" about it. I want you to notice your state of mind, to be mindful of it so it doesn't get in your way.

READY. SET. GO.

Wherever you're at, whatever you love, however you're feeling, I know you can do this. I have seen so many members of the Moolala Community take steps—both large and small—to get a handle on their money that I am confident you can too.

It is time for us to flip the page so we can begin with Step 1: Lay the Foundation.

Ready. Set. Go.

STEP 1

LAY THE FOUNDATION

•••Chapter 1

WHY SMART PEOPLE DO DUMB THINGS WITH THEIR MONEY

Have you ever noticed that smart, capable people sometimes do dumb things when it comes to their money?

Smart people can file their own taxes, brew their own beer, teach high school, write a marketing plan, fix the blinking clock on the DVD player, navigate the Métro in Paris, and even raise teenagers. And yet, these smart, capable people often do dumb things when it comes to their money.

I like to think I'm pretty smart. Not Mensa smart. But surely smart enough to have avoided the Nortel Networks debacle.

What was I smoking?

The telecom industry was in disarray, and Nortel had laid off tens of thousands of employees. Regulators were pressing charges against the company's CEO for accounting irregularities, but I thought the stock was a good buy. I really thought that Nortel would be able to weather the storm, beat the odds, and rise again. At the time it seemed to me that buying shares in Nortel was almost a patriotic act, the modern-day equivalent of buying a war bond. I could actually play a part in the company's resurgence by investing in its stock while it was trading for less than the price of a loaf of bread.

Ha. We all know how that turned out. Nortel went bankrupt, and whatever parts of the business that were still left were carved up and served to hungry buyers from around the world, leaving virtually nothing for shareholders. Shareholders like me.

Have you ever noticed that smart, capable people sometimes do dumb things when it comes to their money?

Like millions of other smart, capable people, I have bought shares in companies that imploded spectacularly. I have faithfully held on to mutual funds that underperformed year after year after year, never stopping to compare their performance with those of other funds. I once bought a "tax shelter" that lost half its value in the time it took for me to walk from my financial adviser's office back to my car. I spent years in a warm, comfortable daze, blindly putting money away into my investment account but absolving myself of any personal accountability for how my investments performed once the money got there. And perhaps most damaging of all, I failed to make the connection between getting a handle on my money and achieving my goals in life.

Perhaps you know someone like me. A friend, a family member, a colleague, a spouse? Or perhaps that someone is you.

If so, you're in good company. There are lots of people like you and me who have an education, a stable job, and reasonably good spending habits, but who are not doing all they could be doing with their money. As smart and capable as you are, you've probably done a few dumb things with money in your time. Trust me, you're not alone.

Here are a few examples from the Moolala Community:

"I spent over $4,000 clearing away one year's worth of unpaid parking tickets."

–Todd, 39, MBA grad and mid-level executive. Married, with one child.

"I procrastinated on finishing the renovations to my basement suite and getting it rented. The delay cost me $10,000 in lost income from the year it was vacant."

–Misty, 29, realtor. In a relationship.

"When my mom died I received $30,000 from her insurance company. I paid off some debt, gave to a few charities, and then lived off the money for a year. But I really should have had a plan for the money, investing some of it or using it for a down payment on a house, because now I have nothing to show for it."

–Skye, 33, entrepreneur. Single.

"I have spent ten years with a company that has a matching program for RRSP contributions. I didn't enrol in the program until recently so I missed out on having the company match contributions worth 5% of my salary each year. That works out to about $3,000 a year or $30,000 over the last ten years, not including the increase in the value of the investments themselves. I missed out on a huge amount of money simply because I didn't fill out the @#$#@%^* form."

–Naheed, 42, project manager. Married, with two children.

"I was crazy stressed about my credit card debt, but then I saw a huge sale on hot tubs. I had never really dreamed about owning a hot tub, but I bought it anyway because it was just too good a deal to pass up."

–Colleen, 32, stay-at-home mom. Married, with three children.

"Back in university they were giving credit cards away like Hallowe'en candy. That was great . . . until the bills arrived. I now live under this cloud of debt, just as I'm trying to get established in my career."

–Derek, 24, engineer. Single.

"During university I got involved in multi-level marketing, and started selling home water-filtration systems. I 'invested' $750 to get my entry-level kit, which was huge money for me at the time. I went to the meetings, tortured my family and friends by making them sit through my demos, and had three of the stupid things in storage for YEARS until I finally threw them out to exorcise the demons."

–Lilly, 41, consultant. Cohabiting with her boyfriend.

"We have a great house and a cute little cottage but very little else in terms of retirement savings. We'd like to retire in the next fifteen years, but we really don't have a plan and fear that the only way to afford it will be to sell our homes."

–Jacques, 48, IT professional. Married.

"I haven't contributed to my RRSP in years. I just didn't see the point and spent my money on other things."

–Markus, 43, pilot. Single, with two children.

"A friend at work told me about this junior oil and gas stock that was about to skyrocket. I put in $7,000 when it was trading at $1 a share. It is now worth a dime."

–Adam, 49, consultant. Single.

Why do these things happen? Why does almost everyone I talk to nod their head in agreement when I observe that "smart, capable people are doing dumb things with their money"?

THE C FACTORS

There are people who have gotten a handle on their money and people who haven't. In my experience, the difference between them boils down to four key factors that I call the "C Factors."

1) Context: Smart people do dumb things with their money because they haven't created their own context for money. Instead, they have the context they inherited from their family and/or the one pushed onto them by the society in which they live. Neither of these options help smart people do smart things. When you create a context for money that is relevant and empowering to you, doing smart things with your money becomes a heck of a lot easier.

2) Consequences: Smart people sometimes live in denial about the consequences of their behaviour around money. You might intentionally avoid looking at the impact of the choices you make (or don't make), or simply remain pleasantly oblivious to it all. Addressing the consequences of the behaviours that are not working for you allows you to look at your situation more objectively. Once you do that, you can adjust your behaviour to help you get what you really want in life.

3) Complexity: Smart people often mismanage the level of complexity they need to have with their money. You might have too much complexity (buying the "hot stock" on a tip), or you might have too little (not understanding how your company's RRSP matching program works). Finding the right level of complexity for your circumstances and interests can go a long way towards lowering your stress and increasing your results.

4) Community: And finally, smart people do dumb things with their money because they don't engage the community of people around them. You turn to your friends and family for support in many areas of your life—like raising kids, advancing your career, and having a rich social life. Engaging those same people to help you in getting a handle on your money will increase the probability of you having the life you want.

THE C FACTORS

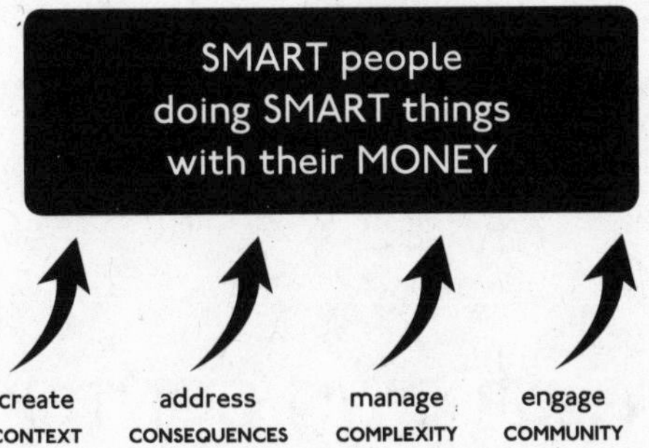

In Step 1 of the Moolala Method, we will lay the foundation by tackling each of the C Factors one by one. We will look at the challenges they present, and then I'll show you some simple strategies that you can use to make the C Factors work for you. You'll learn how to create your own context for money, how to address the consequences of your behaviours around money that are not working for you, how to find and manage the level of financial complexity that's right for your situation, and how to engage your community to help bring what you want to fruition. These strategies are the foundation you need to get a handle on your money so you can live the life you want.

•••Chapter 2

CREATE YOUR OWN CONTEXT
What is your money for?

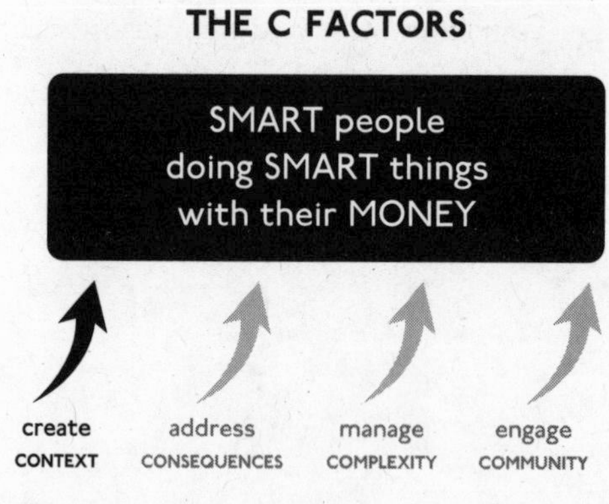

THE C FACTORS

SMART people
doing SMART things
with their MONEY

create
CONTEXT

address
CONSEQUENCES

manage
COMPLEXITY

engage
COMMUNITY

My mother and father were both born in 1936, smack dab in the middle of the Depression. They grew up during World War Two, an era in which oranges were a coveted treat handed out only on Christmas morning. Like most kids of their generation, they were required to help out a lot. My dad collected scrap metal for the war effort and worked at the neighbourhood "Victory Garden" growing vegetables. My mom helped

her mom make laundry soap by hand and spent days over the hot stove stirring jam preserves.

Sure, we poke fun at these tales of woe today, but they were critical experiences for my parents in terms of shaping their context for money, just as my upbringing, in turn, was formative in shaping mine. My mom could stretch a dollar phyllo-pastry-thin. She added water to nearly empty shampoo bottles, extending their use by weeks. And she saved everything: jars, buttons, string, elastic bands, and, of course, wrapping paper. Many of my friends woke up on Christmas morning and ripped open their presents with wild abandon. We Sellery kids had to painstakingly peel back the tape from the wrapping paper with our fingernails, as if we were performing brain surgery on the Queen. We carefully removed the present, set it aside with barely a glance, then flattened, folded, and filed the wrapping paper so that it could be used again. It was many years before I realized that a roll of the stuff could be had for merely $2. My mom had led me to believe it was worth more than the last remaining copy of the Magna Carta.

While my mom had her eye on expenses, my dad was in charge of revenue. He gave us an allowance every week, but it was never paid in cash. The amounts were tallied in a ledger, and we would have to go to him to "withdraw" money from our account. He made an effort to refrain from commenting on the purpose of the withdrawal, but he always asked. I learned that while it was okay to spend money occasionally on things I really wanted, it was far better to save it for the future. I also learned that the only way to get more money was to work for it. No amount of whining, begging, or screaming would ever get my parents to crack open their wallets for a treat at the grocery store. (Now wait, that is not entirely true. Karen Baldwin was a beauty queen from my hometown of London, Ontario. When she was crowned Miss Universe in 1982, my mom bought potato chips to celebrate.)

CONTEXT IS THE BACKDROP FOR EVERYTHING

You could say that my family's context for money was *survival*: "Money is for survival." It was the context that I grew up with, but not one I had created for myself. And this is the point. Smart, capable people do dumb things with their money because they haven't created their own context for money. Said another way, they haven't answered the question: "What is money for, for me?"

Smart, capable people do dumb things with their money because they haven't created their own context for money.

Context, simply put, is *the setting in which an event occurs.* It is the backdrop for everything you do when it comes to your money.

Let's look at context from another perspective first—exercise. People who exercise consistently have a context that keeps them committed to working out even when they don't feel like it. I'm pretty good about exercising regularly, and I exercise because it helps me maintain a pretty good mood.

I know if I don't swim, hike, or go for a run at least three times a week, I will be very, very cranky. Things that wouldn't normally register as remotely annoying will make me crazy: rush hour traffic, the weather, a barista who seems more interested in the ambient Coldplay muzak than MAKING MY CUP OF CAFFEINATED SANITY. NOW. NOWWWWWW!

Sorry.

So I exercise. Regularly. So far, exercise has prevented me from getting arrested for causing a public disturbance at Starbucks, and for that I am grateful.

For other people, the context for exercise is something completely different. Exercise is for *challenge,* for example. Or for *good looks,* the aesthetic benefit. Others would say exercise is for *family;* they want to keep fit and stay mobile so they can play with their grandkids.

People who exercise are clear on what exercise is for, for them. They have a context for it that empowers them and keeps them doing it even when they really don't want to. People who don't exercise regularly still have a context for it, but it could be something like "exercise is *torture.*" If that is your context for exercise, how often am I going to see you at the gym? Try never.

THE DEFAULT CONTEXT FOR MONEY

If you haven't created your own context for money, one that you're excited about and that is meaningful to you, you are left with a few default options. The two most common default contexts are the ones provided by the family you grew up with and the society you live in: your context for money is what your family says money is for, or what society says money is for. Quite often, neither of those two default contexts is particularly empowering or appealing, and they can lead to behaviours that are inconsistent with the life you want for yourself.

WE ARE FAMILY: YOUR FAMILY'S CONTEXT FOR MONEY

As I mentioned earlier, the default context I got from my family was that money was for *survival.* Of course, there were certain things that really worked about that context. I developed a strong work ethic and great saving habits. Like my siblings, I started working at a very young age. First, I helped on my sister's paper route, then I turned to babysitting, and when I hit thirteen I started shovelling driveways and mowing lawns. With the proceeds, I bought Canada Savings Bonds, and the occasional convenience store treat (sometimes a Joe Louis, but more often than not I bought Sweet Tarts because they were only a dime a pack).

But there were also things that didn't work about that context. At eighteen I went backpacking in Europe on my own for six months. I was so intent on spending the least amount of money possible that I basically lived on bread and water, with the occasional slice of *jambon* as a treat. The bread in Europe is really, really good but it does not constitute a well-balanced diet. I lost almost twenty-five pounds during my time away, about twenty pounds of which I actually should have kept. I spent a good many days walking around in a nutrient-deficient daze and almost blacked out at the Louvre. My skinflint behaviour helped me save the money to get to Europe, but because I didn't have a way to modify the behaviour once I got there, I didn't enjoy the trip as much as I might have.

After university, I got a great job in the corporate world. But I had a tough time making the transition to being someone who actually had real money coming in. I showed up for my first day of work in my brother's hand-me-down suit. And while it was a nice enough suit, he was three inches shorter than me, so the cuffs of the pants rose well above my ankles. I looked like a total dork.

Sometimes the behaviour we demonstrate as adults is in defiance of our family's context, which can be just as problematic. My siblings became savers, like me, but one of them could have easily rebelled against the *survival* context and become a major spender.

I'm sure you have your own stories of what money was like in your family. Let's look at what some members of the Moolala Community have said about the default context for money in their families.

Money is secrecy: *"My parents were very secretive about money. I became that way too. When I was in high school, all my friends were a long-distance phone call away in another town. There was no such thing as phone cards back* *then and the rates were high. I was a typical chatty teenager so I would rack up these huge phone bills. I arrived home from school before my parents, so I was able to intercept the phone bill from the mailbox and rip it up before they could see the itemized details. I remember feeling guilty and scared, but felt that secrecy was a better option than the truth. Until I took the Moolala workshop, I had never talked to anyone about money, not even my best friend. What a huge missed opportunity."*

–Devon, 38, entrepreneur. Married, with two children.

Money is for shopping: *"Growing up, I was surrounded by women who loved to shop. Sure, the focus was more on what they were saving than what they were spending. But it was a real treat to stand for a long time in a long line to get in on a good sale. I'm a fantastic bargain hunter and rarely pay full price for anything. But I have purchased many things that I didn't really need because the price seemed too good to pass up."*

–Sue, 51, consultant. Married, with two adult stepchildren.

Money is contentious: *"During the oil and gas boom in the late '70s there was lots of money in my family. We lived in a beautiful house on a small farm. My dad bought motorbikes for me and my brother and even took us to Hawaii for two weeks. But this caused a lot of tension in my parents' marriage because my mom was far more conservative in nature. When the real estate market crashed a few years later we lost our house and my dad had to move to another city to find work. Eventually my parents' marriage ended, and money was certainly a part of the reason."*

–Barry, 42, director. Single, with two children.

Money is magic: *"When I was a kid we used to go to Wasaga Beach. The motel where we would stay was far away from the closest convenience store, but we would still walk there every night to get a treat. We didn't have much money and my mother would always tell us that there wasn't enough for treats, unless we were able to find some change in the sand. We would all look very carefully as we* *walked along the beach, but it was always my mom who would find money in the sand. She said it was magic. It was only later that I found out my mom was hiding the money in the sand herself. But to this day I still believe I'll find money everywhere. All I have to do is to look for it."*

–Debbie, 50, software sales rep. Single mom, with two children.

Money is practical: *"My parents were very practical with money. My dad worked hard and my mom was very careful managing the family budget. As a kid, I was much more interested in instant gratification. When I had money I would immediately spend it, and even now I find myself rebelling against that 'practicality.' For example, if I can't find my utility knife I'll just go out and buy another one, even though I probably have fifteen of them lying around the house."*

–Marnie, 44, artist and renovator. Single parent, with two children.

Money is bad: *"My brother and I were raised by a single mother. She did her very best, but had absolutely no help from family given that our grandparents weren't in the picture. It wouldn't be a stretch to say we were dirt poor. And my mom really believed that anyone with money was bad. As a young adult I started to earn my own money, but I got rid of it as soon as I got it, spending frivolously or giving it away to people I felt needed it more than me. Why? Because I certainly didn't want to be one of those bad people with money."*

–Cynthia, 36, therapist. Married, with two children.

Money is faith: *"Coming from a faith background, if we wanted something we'd talk to God about it. God would provide. As a kindergarten kid I remember putting my very own dollar into the offering plate at Sunday school. The next day my parents found $100 cash on top of the fridge. They told me that this miracle happened because of the dollar I put in. I never forgot that moment and have been of the philosophy that God really will provide."*

–Skye, 33, entrepreneur. Single.

Money is tight: *"Money was always tight in my family. It was the '80s recession and my parents were double mortgaged when interest rates were 22%. I remember my dad yelling at my mom that I needed new clothes, and me being mad at my dad for being mad at my mom. I didn't have new clothes, because we couldn't afford them, but it didn't seem fair to yell at my mom about it. I remember being told to 'tighten our belts,' but never being told to 'loosen them' again."*

–Kelly, 41, learning consultant. Single, with two children.

Now it's your turn to examine your own family's context for money.

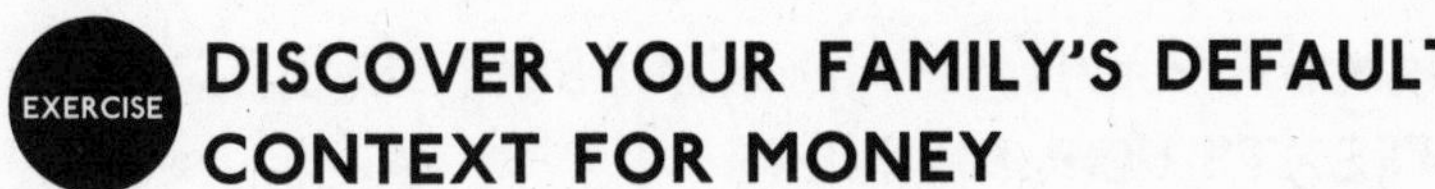

EXERCISE: DISCOVER YOUR FAMILY'S DEFAULT CONTEXT FOR MONEY

PONDER: What is the default context you have as a legacy of your family upbringing? Think through the following questions and jot your insights down in your notebook or in the margins.

- What are some of your earliest memories about money?
- What feelings do you associate with those memories?
- What would you say those memories taught you about money?

IDENTIFY: What is the context for money that you have as a result of growing up in your family? It could be a combination of more than one context, as sometimes different family members can bring different contexts to bear.

In my family, money was for ______________________.

ANALYZE: What about this context works well for you today? What doesn't work so well for you?

Note that these questions are intended to get you thinking about the default context that your family gave you, and not about finding the perfect answer or ascribing blame. There is no right or wrong context, or even a good or bad context. Your family is your family. The past is the past. And you have done what you have done with your money up to this point. The great thing is that by reading this book you're taking an important step in getting a handle on your money so you can live the life you want. And soon you're going to have the opportunity to create your own context for yourself.

KEEPING UP WITH THE JONESES: SOCIETY'S CONTEXTS FOR MONEY

Unless you were raised by wolves or grew up in a remote forest far from cable TV, your family probably wasn't your only major influence in life. The society you live in has a great deal of influence in shaping your context for money: the people you work with, your neighbours down the street, the advertisements you see on television, and the policies of the government of the day. None of this is inherently bad or good. In fact, some of the contexts that come from society can be quite empowering—such as making a difference for others, providing for your family, etc. What is important to understand is that society offers up a variety of contexts for money that can easily become your default context unless you create one for yourself. Here are two of the most prevalent contexts that society offers up.

ONE DAY, SOME DAY, PROVIDED I LIVE TO SEE THE DAY: MONEY IS FOR RETIREMENT

I read a lot of personal finance magazines and am often struck by the homogeneity of the advertisements that fill the pages. It isn't just all those good-looking couples with grey hair, smiling smugly about their good fortune as they walk along the beach. It is the constant focus on one particular life stage.

Retirement.

Sure, retirement is a compelling context for money for some people. But for me it is uninspiring and insufficient. I do plan to stop working one day. But this obsessive focus on retirement implies that I'm going to have a boring life until I'm sixty-five years old, then a great life until I die. What about my life today, tomorrow, next week, next month, next year?

Depending on how old you are, retirement might be so far in the future that you can't possibly wrap your mind around that time ever coming. And because it is a fairly distant and nebulous concept, retirement doesn't inspire action—and taking action is critical for you to get a handle on your money.

Like many people, I know I need to prepare for that future, but I also want to take my daughter to see the Taj Mahal, build a boathouse at the cottage, and volunteer in a Third World country. Some goals I'll accomplish before I stop working full time and some I won't. My point is that while we all need to be preparing for the day when we are no longer drawing a paycheque, retirement as a context for money isn't a great fit for everyone.

BIGGER, BETTER, NEW AND IMPROVED: MONEY IS FOR STUFF

Another major default context in society is that "money is for stuff." You need to buy stuff. More stuff. Bigger stuff. Better stuff. And money is the way to get it. Society has placed a huge value on "new and improved," and the pace of innovation—in every aisle of every store—is staggering: new and improved big-screen televisions, cellphones, granite countertops, moisturizers, and magnetic mosquito catchers. Our economy is built on making stuff, distributing stuff, advertising stuff, and selling stuff, culminating in the International Celebration of Stuff, held every year on December 25. It is extraordinarily difficult not to get sucked into needing the latest must-haves. "Keeping up with the Joneses" is a powerful force. *You* need more stuff because *they* already have it, and you want to be as good as they are. Because it will make your life better. Because you deserve it.

Back when I was in high school I remember that I just absolutely HAD to have a Benetton rugby shirt. All the cool kids had one, and I had no ability to get out from under the default context of "money is for stuff." But as an adult, I have come to realize that I don't have to play that game. Don't get me wrong, I am big fan of my stuff. I own an iPod and love my digital video recorder.

If you love to shop, that's great. There's nothing wrong with wanting material goods; in fact, my stepmother has a black belt in bargain hunting. But it isn't a context for money that I would choose for myself.

Society provides an abundant selection of other default contexts in addition to retirement and stuff, especially when you look at it from the perspective of different countries, religions, and ethnicities. For example, money is for power, for prestige, for keeping score, for making a difference for others, etc. Take a moment to identify a few that you notice in your life.

EXERCISE

IDENTIFY SOCIETY'S DEFAULT CONTEXTS

PONDER: Think about the default contexts in society that you notice most in your life. Are they the ones I've already mentioned? Or are there others that you see based on where you live, what you do, and who you hang out with?

My point is that there are a number of default contexts for money at play, particularly from your family and the society you live in. Getting a handle on your money takes work. One of the key things that will motivate you to do that work is having a context that is relevant to you and inspires you. If it doesn't, you are way less likely to do the work required, no matter how smart and capable you are.

So what do you do now? Well, you have a greater awareness of some of the default contexts for money that you've been living with. Now is the time to unshackle yourself from those, and come up with a context of your own.

Create your own context for money? Yep. That's what I said. You get to choose what money is for, for you. Here is how I came up with mine.

CREATING YOUR OWN CONTEXT FOR MONEY

I came to the question "What is money for?" almost by accident. I was thinking about taking a vacation and noticed that I was really struggling with how to use the three weeks I had accumulated. I was single, with a good job and no debt. From a rational perspective, I really could have gone anywhere in the world. But I was stuck in my "money is for survival" mindset. What I really wanted to do was go hiking in New Zealand, but that went against what I had always thought money was for. It was like the *Clash of the Titans* playing out in my head:

> "I want to go to New Zealand."
> "That's a total waste of money."
> "Come on, live a little."
> "No, YOU live a little."

Then suddenly . . . BANG. I had an epiphany!

I realized that *I got to say* what my money was for.

I found this epiphany was both totally liberating and completely terrifying. If I got to choose for myself, what would I choose?

I didn't call it this at the time, but I realize now that I was creating my own context for money—one that wasn't a product of the family I grew up with or the society I lived in. If I really was able to choose for myself, what would *I* say money was for? Survival? Retirement? Stuff? I don't think so.

I would say that my money is for *adventure.*

My money is for adventure.

I decided in that moment that I would work really hard to earn money and manage it well so that I could have a lifetime of adventure.

I had an incredible time in New Zealand. I kayaked in Able Tasman National Park, hiked both the Kepler and Routeburn tracks, rafted the rivers, flew in a four-seater Piper airplane, and walked across the Franz Josef Glacier. And when I got back home I became really clear on what was in it for me in focusing on getting a handle on my money. Did I like doing the work involved? Not in the least. Was it fun? Nuh-uh. Was I going to Heaven if I maxed out my RRSP contribution and paid off my credit card debt? Nope. The reason I focused on getting a handle on my money was *adventure.* I want adventure now, next year, when I'm fifty years old, and when I'm eighty-five years old. And the way to ensure I continue to live a lifetime of adventure is to get a handle on my money.

THE BENEFITS: WHAT'S IN IT FOR YOU TO CREATE CONTEXT?

Over the years, I have seen three main benefits when people create their own context for money:

Keeps the "why" front and centre: I don't actually *want* to work on getting a handle on my money, and you probably don't either. But if you are really clear about your context for money, and if it is compelling to you, your Moolala Context will increase the probability that you *will* do the work and therefore get the results you want.

A few years ago I was offered a transfer to New York City to take over as the bureau chief for the TV network I worked at. My partner Dennis and I decided it would be a fantastic opportunity and moved down almost immediately, renting an apartment on the fifth floor of a walk-up building on the Upper West Side. We knew Manhattan would be an expensive posting, but at the time the weak Canadian dollar made anything we wanted to buy 30% more expensive than back home. In addition to the currency impact, prices in general were way higher. I remember walking into the Gristedes supermarket across the street from our apartment to buy groceries. A package of bacon was $7.99 U.S., or $10 Canadian. @#$!@#$!

This did not bode well for our ability to live our "adventure" in New York City. But we talked it through and got really clear once again on our Moolala Context: *Money is for adventure.* We didn't want to live in this incredible city and not experience it fully, so that meant we had to get creative.

One of the things we did was sublet our apartment any time we left the city for more than a week. It took time and energy to find subletters and it opened us up to the risk of having strangers in our home. But we were really clear on why we were doing it—for *adventure.* Even after taxes, the money we brought in not only helped us to do more in New York, it also covered our accommodation on a number of vacations: an incredible beach house near Manuel Antonio National Park in Costa Rica, a few nights at Middle Beach Lodge in Tofino, B.C., and a tiny hut on stilts when we went on an elephant trek in northern Thailand.

Provides a check for your behaviour: Your Moolala Context also provides you with something to check your behaviour against. Your behaviour is either consistent with your context for money, or it is inconsistent with your context. If you say money is for freedom and yet you've bought a house that requires two people working full time flat out to pay the mortgage, then your behaviour seems inconsistent. But if you say money is for beauty, buying that big house with its spectacular garden would be behaviour that is more consistent. There will likely be contradictions here and there—some you'll notice right away, especially when you bring a partner into the equation. But creating a context for your money provides a way for you to check your behaviour and talk through some of those contradictions.

Our wedding was a great test for us, given that we were paying for most of it ourselves. Because our money is for adventure, we were focused more on hang-gliding on our honeymoon in South America than on having linen seat covers and a champagne fountain at the reception. Our 140 guests arrived at a theatre we had booked for $1,000, instead of an expensive hall. In place of opulent flower arrangements, we had 140 long-stemmed flowers in big buckets at the entrance. Each guest picked one out, brought it into the theatre, and added it to one of two enormous vases, creating these outrageous bursts of colour. We held the wedding in the afternoon, followed by a stand-up reception instead of a sit-down dinner. That limited the catering bill to about $3,000. The wedding cake came courtesy of my sister-in-law Jackie, who baked and iced 140 homemade cupcakes. They made a grand entrance at the reception—carried in by our siblings lip-synching to "We Are Family." Our parents covered the bar bill and the photographer and that was it.

Our behaviour in planning the wedding was consistent with our context for money.

My point is that by answering the question "What is money for?" we were better able to make decisions about where and how we spent our money. I believe it will make a difference for you, too. You will be better prepared to get creative about your circumstances, stretch outside of your comfort zone, and get a handle on your money so you can live the life you want.

Gives you some language: Finally, articulating your context for money gives you some language that you can use to discuss things with people in your life—your spouse, your financial adviser, or your friends. Of course, sometimes there are conflicts. What money is for, for you, might not be the same as for your spouse. But rather than simply bickering over the bills, you'll have a way to frame the conversations about what you want to spend on and save for in a positive way, so you can set priorities and collaborate on your plans for the future together. When working with your financial adviser, you'll be able to help him or her understand what is really important to you as an individual so they can help you get it.

YOUR MOOLALA CONTEXT: A CREATION, NOT A DESCRIPTION

What is *your* money for? This is your opportunity to put the default contexts of family and society behind you and to create your own context for money. I chose the word *creating* intentionally because it is important to remember that this is a creative exercise, not a descriptive one. For some people, and you might be one of them, the first answer to the question "What is my money for?" is security. Money is for basics, like food and shelter. That's it. Full stop. There isn't anything else to it. And this might be an absolutely accurate *description* of your current context. But does that empower you? Does it excite you? Probably not. If your money is for "security," are you going to be willing to do the work you need to do to get a handle on it? Perhaps, but not likely.

What I have seen really make a difference is having a context that is empowering. For example, think about the context for marriage. If you said to your intended that "marriage is for security," you'd probably get a pillow thrown at you, or worse. Of course, marriage *can* be for security. That's a part of it. But that isn't a particularly empowering context for most people. Another context might be that marriage is for love and companionship. Or for passion. Or for family. Contexts like these are what provide the foundation for those times when the marriage vows of "for better or for worse" really get tested.

So, while "security" might be an accurate description of what your money is for today, I'm going to ask you to look towards the future and get creative. You get to design it; you get to make it up. Here are some examples from the Moolala Community.

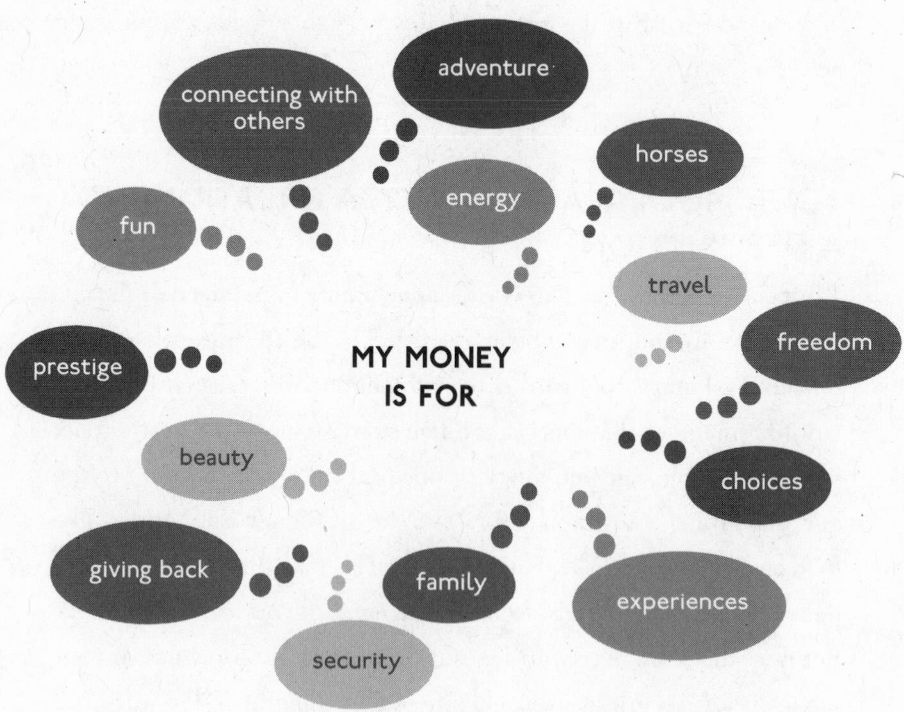

EXERCISE CREATE A CONTEXT: WHAT IS MONEY FOR, FOR YOU?

People come up with an incredible range of responses to the question "What is my money for?" There is no right answer to this question. Now is your opportunity to come up with an answer that empowers you.

PONDER: Take a blank sheet of paper and wander around your home. Look at your books, photos, mementoes. Look out your windows. As you do this, ponder these questions: What do you value? What do you enjoy? What is important to you in your life that money enables? What role do you want money to play in your life? How do you want to use it?

You don't need to think about it too much, and this doesn't need to be THE answer. In fact, the answer might evolve as the circumstances in your life evolve. Keep it simple, and aim for a word or two. If you find that you are struggling with this step, flip ahead a few pages for some ideas to help you answer the question.

My money is for ______________________________.

This is your Moolala Context, unique to you and created by you.

CHECK: Your context for money will be more valuable to you if it empowers you. Why? Because if your context doesn't inspire you, it won't help you to do the things you probably don't want to do: like improving your cash flow, following your investments, and developing a plan for fulfillment of your goals. I recommend that you do a gut check and ask yourself: Does my new context for money empower me? If it does, great. If it doesn't, you might ponder some more.

FIND: Look for an image that represents your Moolala Context. It could be a photo from a photo album or magazine, or an image you find on the Internet. You don't need to spend more than a few minutes finding the image.

REMIND: It will take some effort to keep reminding yourself of your new Moolala Context. Certainly my context of adventure is not what I'm thinking when faced with a bill for $1,000 to fix my brakes. The default contexts from your family or from society can pop up again almost immediately. And it can be VERY hard to keep your context for money front and centre if you lose your job, crash your car, or even open up your credit card bill or mutual fund statement. In an instant, money really is for survival once again.

So stick the image you find in the front of your notebook, on the fridge, or in the file where you keep your mutual fund statements. Write your Moolala Context on a Post-it note and stick it to your debit card, etc. Do whatever you have to do to keep your Moolala Context top of mind. (We'll be talking more about making good use of reminders in Step 4: Take Action.)

As you continue through this book, I will remind you too. I'll ask you to refer to your Moolala Context and the image that goes with it. In fact, you'll notice that I've included a spot for you to fill in your Moolala Context at the very beginning of this book, so whenever you wonder why you're spending the time and energy to work through the book, you'll have your answer handy.

DIFFERENT APPROACHES: WHAT TO TRY IF YOU'RE STRUGGLING TO CREATE A CONTEXT

It is not uncommon for people in my Moolala workshops to struggle to come up with their Moolala Context. It can be really tough. If you are struggling to create one for yourself, remember that you don't need to commit to anything at this point. You might put something down and then come back to it later, after you've read a few more chapters. That said, if you want to do some more thinking now about context, here are some of the hurdles I have seen people face over the years, and what I would recommend you try if you face that hurdle yourself.

You're concerned about your current financial situation: If you've lost your job, have credit card debt, or are going through a divorce, it can be really hard for you to think beyond "money is for security."

- Imagine for a moment that you no longer have this financial pressure—that someone swooped in and found you a job or paid off your credit card debt. Now what would you say your money is for?
- Use whatever you come up with for the purposes of this exercise, even if it seems beyond the realm of the possible right now. This might help you keep the big picture in mind, in spite of your current situation.

You have significant life questions: You might have questions about your career, your marriage, your health, or your future. These can make it hard to focus on the question "What is my money for?"

- Look at the bigger picture by asking yourself "What is my life for?" Then see if you can use or adapt that answer for your Moolala Context.
- You could also focus on the smaller picture by asking yourself "What benefit would I get out of working on my money?" Your answer could be something as specific as a new pair of fancy and impractical shoes, or two nights at the W Hotel in New York. Or it could be as broad as "peace of mind." Whatever it is, use that answer as your context for money for now, and then be open to other thoughts that might come to you as you continue through the book.

You and your spouse have different ideas about what money is for: You might find this to be a tough question to answer because you can't reconcile your answer with that of your spouse. Couples often get stuck debating the minutiae: Pay the credit card bill or go out for dinner? In doing so, you miss out on creating a context that is empowering for both of you.

- Think about your context as a combination of both your needs—freedom and frivolity; home and experiences; family and travel. You will still need to have the discussion as a couple about where specifically the money is going to go, but your decisions will be guided by the context that you came up with together.

You're finding it hard to let go of your default context: Your default context might be too strong to resist, or you might feel as though your real answer shouldn't be your answer. For example, your true answer is that money is for beauty, but in your family money is for saving, and you don't know how to reconcile the two.

There is no such thing as a right or wrong context. But it is important to find a context that will resonate for you as an individual.

- Ask a few of your friends what they think you would say money was for if you were totally unencumbered. Do a gut check on their answers and choose one to use for now. Perhaps another context will pop into your head as you continue to read on.

You can't find the right word to express what you mean: You have some ideas, but you haven't figured out the words. Finding the "right" word is far less important than finding a context that empowers you.

- Use whatever words come to you now and keep reading the book. In all likelihood, the "right" word will find you as you move forward. Or if you're more of a visual person, focus instead on the image you found to represent your new context for money.

Money doesn't matter to you: I often hear people say that money doesn't matter to them, so it's impossible for them to create a context for it. Often what lies underneath the feeling that money doesn't matter is a resistance to the default contexts from society or from family.

- As above, ask yourself the big-picture question, "What is my life for?" Words like *simplicity*, *contribution*, *peace*, *ease*, and *tranquility* often resonate for people who initially say that money doesn't matter to them.

If you find that you still don't have an answer that you like, cut yourself some slack. Let the question sit in the back of your head and see what comes up as you keep reading.

CONCLUSION

The first C Factor that prevents smart, capable people from doing smart things with their money is not having their own context for money. Unless you create your own context, you will be left with the default contexts from your family or from society. Creating a context for money that is empowering, personal, and consistent with your values is critical to getting a handle on your money so you can live the life you want. And in all likelihood, there are some important things you do with your money that you need to get a handle on. These areas will become increasingly clear as we turn to address the second C Factor: the consequences of your behaviour around money.

MY ONE THING

What is one thing I can take away from this chapter that is relevant to me?

____

____

What is one thing I will commit to doing to help me get a handle on my money?

____

____

•••Chapter 3

ADDRESS THE CONSEQUENCES OF YOUR BEHAVIOUR AROUND MONEY

Why do you need to get a handle on your money anyway?

THE C FACTORS

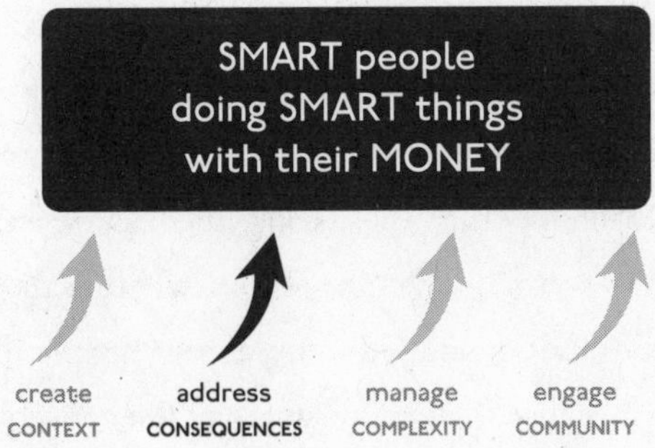

SMART people doing SMART things with their MONEY

create CONTEXT — address CONSEQUENCES — manage COMPLEXITY — engage COMMUNITY

Every weekday at precisely 3:20 p.m. the school bell rang. My friends and I raced out the doors of Clara Brenton Elementary School to catch our ride home. Rob's mom was one of the most dedicated chauffeurs in the car pool and she was always on time, sitting out front in her almond-brown, two-door Oldsmobile Omega. Six of us squeezed into the back seat, packed together like chips in a Pringles can. While there were seatbelts *installed* in the car, not one of us ever *wore* one. It was the early '80s, and even smart, capable people would regularly drive around without their seatbelts on. It wasn't safe, but it was almost universally accepted that you didn't need to wear a seatbelt. That is, until people started to understand the consequences of riding in a car without wearing a seatbelt, namely fatalities and fines.

It took some time for behaviour to change, but it *did* change as people became aware of consequences. Can you imagine a parent today regularly stuffing six kids in the back of a car without seatbelts on? Unlikely. Highly unlikely. Being aware of fatalities and fines as consequences has altered our behaviour, and seatbelt use has increased dramatically.

Smart people do dumb things with their money because they are unaware of the consequences of their behaviour.

The word *consequence* is defined as *the effect, result, or outcome of something occurring earlier.* Consequences can be both tangible and intangible. If you don't wear a seatbelt you face the *tangible* consequences of serious injury or death, as well as expensive fines. You also face *intangible* consequences like the stress and guilt of exposing yourself to serious injury and fines. Taken together, these consequences are enough that most people today wear a seatbelt when they drive, whether they like it or not.

This leads us to the second C Factor: Smart people do dumb things with their money because they are unaware of the consequences of their behaviour.

They are oblivious—sometimes fully aware that they're oblivious, and at other times completely oblivious to the fact that they're oblivious!

In my case, I was oblivious to the fact that I was oblivious. I hired a financial adviser, but I had no idea whether he was doing his job or not. I dutifully transferred my money over to him every month, and just as dutifully filed my statements when they arrived. But I never looked at the performance of the mutual funds he sold me. It turned out that they were real dogs, and I was oblivious to that fact for years. The consequences of being oblivious were that I let thousands of dollars slide down the drain.

My objective in this chapter is to connect your behaviour around money with its consequences, to improve your ability to do more smart things. We have already seen the benefit of making these connections in many other areas of life, in addition to the wearing of seatbelts. Nutritional information posted in fast-food restaurants has made a quantifiable difference in people choosing lower-calorie meals. And warnings about the impact of smoking during pregnancy have greatly reduced the number of women who use tobacco when carrying a child.

Interestingly, addressing the consequences of your behaviour around money will actually allow you to have more of what you really want in life: more freedom, more choices, more experiences, more of whatever it is you've decided your money is for. In my case, I look at the consequences of my behaviour around money because of *adventure*. The better I am at addressing them, the more adventure I will have in my life.

So, what's in it for you?

> Looking at the consequences of my behaviour around money will allow me to have more [insert your Moolala Context here]
>
> ____
>
> ____.

CUSTOMIZED CONSEQUENCES: WHAT FITS FOR YOU?

Now that you've been reminded of what you're working towards, I thought it would be helpful to outline some examples of behaviours around money and its consequences to kick-start your thinking. While your behaviour and its consequences will be unique to you, there certainly are some common themes.

Waiting to start saving: *"I'm thirty-two years old, married, with two kids. I really should have started saving by now. But I just haven't. I know I'm missing out on some serious tax incentives, and I'm starting to get pretty stressed because at this rate I won't be able to retire when I want to."*

–Chad, 32, welder. Married, with two children.

Spending my retirement savings on a couch for my kid: *"We have an acceptable but not abundant amount of retirement savings. I decided to withdraw money from these savings to buy a couch for my son. It was only later that my financial adviser pointed out the consequences: the tangible consequences of not having enough money for retirement, and the intangible consequences of, yet again, failing to teach my adult son about how to save for what he wants and be responsible with his money. This is one of my biggest regrets as a parent."*

–Diana, 56, administrative assistant. Married, with one adult child.

Being unclear about my goals: *"I haven't really figured out what I want for my life and so that means I don't know what I'm working towards, if anything at all. I have a fairly high level of anxiety about the future and feel frustrated that I'm stuck in this rut."*

–Brian, 35, journalist. Single.

Mismanaging my tax bill: *"I worked really hard and earned lots of money as a lifeguard. But I didn't put money aside for income taxes and spent most of what I'd earned. When it came time to pay the tax bill, I didn't have the money. The tangible consequence was that I had to put every single penny towards income taxes. The intangible consequence was that I was completely stressed out about money for six months."*

–François, 38, business owner. Married, with two children.

Honey, I sacrificed the kids: *"As a couple, we have a combined income of about $180,000 a year. We pay $2,500 in rent on our house every month and both drive relatively new cars. And we're carrying about $20,000 in debt. The consequence of living beyond our means is that we haven't saved a penny for our kids' university education. We've missed out on the government grants and don't know how they're going to afford to go to school."*

–Marsha, 51, health administrator. Married, with two children.

Carrying credit card debt: *"I have about $5,000 in credit card debt and am paying 19% interest on it every year. That's $1,000 in interest that I'm paying to the bank. The consequences are that a huge chunk of money is going up in smoke every year, and that I feel really angry with myself for not getting rid of this debt."*

–Nancy, 45, designer. Newly single, with two kids.

Being cheap with friends: *This last example is close to my heart, because it is mine. Based on what you know about me so far, you probably won't be surprised to hear that I used to save almost compulsively. My fear that I was chronically cheap was confirmed by my friend Kurt, when I was in my mid twenties. We went for dinner and he ordered a beer, an appetizer, and an entrée. I ordered only an entrée. When the bill arrived I totalled up only my portion instead of just splitting the bill. He pounced, reminding me that I spent a good deal of time at his house, eating his food and drinking his beer. Splitting the restaurant bill evenly was one of the ways in which all these things just evened themselves out. The consequence of my cheap behaviour was its negative effect on my friendships.*

Rest assured that it will be worth the effort to address the consequences of your behaviour, and it will make a big difference in you getting a handle on your money.

WHY THE EARLY BIRD GETS THE PLUMPER WORM: THE POWER OF COMPOUND INTEREST

When it comes to saving money, the early bird really does get the worm—through the power of compound interest. Compounding means earning interest on your interest, and the longer you wait to start saving, the less time you'll have to make compounding work for you and the less interest you'll earn over time.

In the example below, the early bird saves $100 a month for forty years and the late bloomer saves $200 a month for twenty years. Assuming their money grows at a rate of 7% per year, even though they both contribute $48,000, the early bird's total savings will be $264,000 compared to the late bloomer's $105,000. That is a MASSIVE difference entirely due to compounding: the early bird's money had twice as much time to grow.

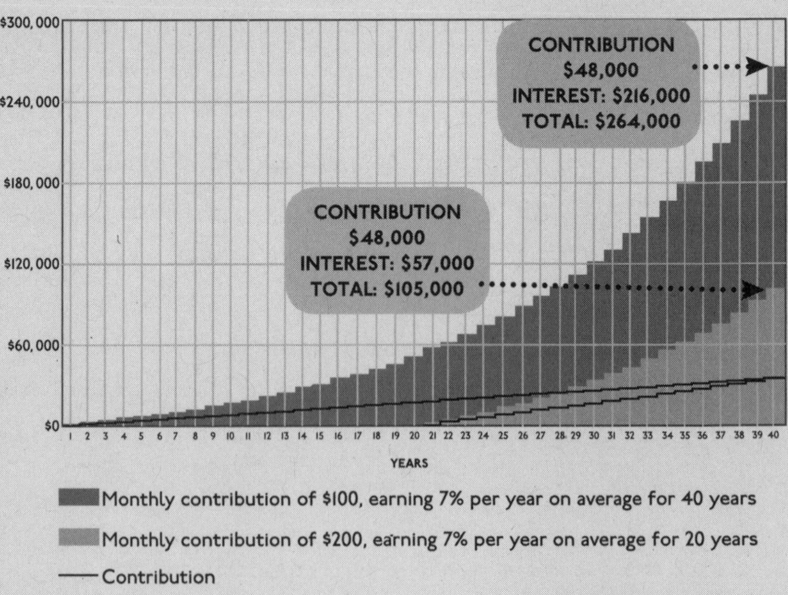

Sure, there are lots of reasons why it is really hard to invest when we're younger. But don't be oblivious to the consequences of starting late.

EXERCISE

IDENTIFY THE CONSEQUENCES OF YOUR WEAKNESSES AROUND MONEY

We all have behaviours around money that we could call strengths, which have positive consequences. And then we have behaviours that we could call weaknesses, which have negative consequences. Given that the purpose here is to get a better handle on our money, we're going to focus on those behaviours that you would say are weaknesses. Let's get started.

BRAINSTORM: Think about some of the behaviours that you have around money that you would say are weaknesses. Look at how you spend money, how you invest money, how you deal with debt, saving for retirement, and working with your financial adviser.

Then, for each of these behaviours, write down in your notebook, the table below, or the worksheet downloaded from www.moolala.ca, some of the tangible consequences, like wasting money, paying big interest charges, not having the money you want for your retirement, etc. Then look at the intangible consequences, like feeling overwhelmed by stress, guilt, conflict, regret, and anger.

WEAKNESS	TANGIBLE CONSEQUENCES	INTANGIBLE CONSEQUENCES

PRIORITIZE: Circle the three behaviours that are most significant for you, so you have a sense of what to focus on first.

THE HURDLES: WHAT GETS IN THE WAY OF ADDRESSING CONSEQUENCES

Trust me, I know it isn't easy to address the consequences of your behaviour. There are a lot of obstacles in your way.

Intelligence ≠ Rational thinking: You can be intelligent without always being rational. One of the reasons why it is so hard to address the consequences of our behaviour around money is that we don't always think rationally about money. If we did, we'd be able to avoid a lot of common mistakes.

Consequences are easy to hide: You can't really hide the fact that you've gained weight. Don't kid yourself, people notice. But few people ever have to know about the sorry state of your retirement savings. When consequences are hidden, they are harder to address.

Consequences are easy to delay: Dog training 101 says that you need to link bad behaviour with the consequence of that behaviour—right away. Your three-year-old Labradoodle pries open the refrigerator while you're at work and sloppily chews through a week's worth of groceries. Is it more effective to discipline dear little Oscar right when you arrive home, or in a week? The negative consequences of our behaviour around money have become quite easy to defer. In the old days, you paid for everything with cash or cheque. Now you have credit cards, overdraft protection, and lines of credit that allow you to borrow against the value of your home. While these innovations alleviate a lot of financial stress, they have also given us a false sense of security, because the link between our behaviour and its consequences has been broken.

We've forgotten we're adults: I'm assuming if you're reading this book that you're at least eighteen years old (or a very mature fifteen-year-old—good for you). One of the things we do as we mature is face up to consequences. We wouldn't be surprised to hear a six-year-old deny breaking the heirloom vase, even while holding a basketball and standing amidst the broken glass. But that wouldn't be acceptable for an adult. An adult would need to face the consequences of breaking the vase, or at least have the wherewithal to hide the ball. And yet, we often forget that we're adults and that we've made *many* of the choices that lead to the circumstances in which we find ourselves. We'll talk more about some of the trade-offs we make (and don't even know we're making) when we talk about improving your cash flow later in the book.

Later in the book, we'll look at how to address the consequences of your behaviour, so that you have some specific strategies to help you overcome the hurdles and get a handle on your money.

CONCLUSION

The second C Factor that prevents smart, capable people from doing smart things with their money is not being aware of the consequences of their actions. Addressing the consequences—both tangible and intangible—of your behaviour will help you to get a handle on your money so you can live the life you want. It is easier than you might think, provided you don't make it too complex.

MY ONE THING

The one weakness around money that I'm committing to dealing with now that I have read this chapter is ______________________________

____.

•••Chapter 4

MANAGE COMPLEXITY
What's the right level of complexity for you and your money?

THE C FACTORS

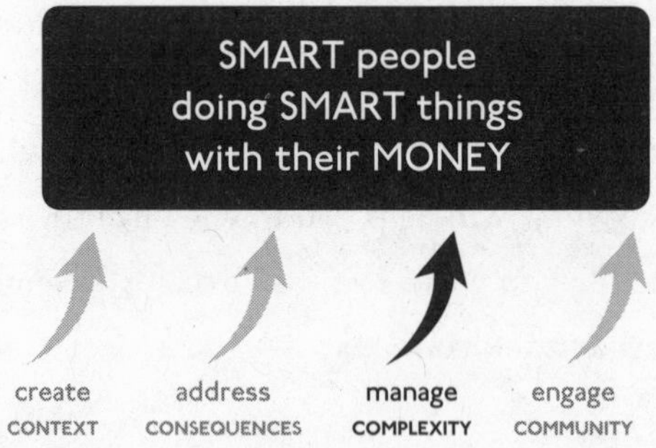

SMART people doing SMART things with their MONEY

create CONTEXT | address CONSEQUENCES | **manage COMPLEXITY** | engage COMMUNITY

I like watching *The Amazing Race* on TV, and reading Dr. Seuss with my daughter, Abby. I like to go hiking in the mountains and running along the river. And I like to travel, throw dinner parties, and talk on the phone. I have a whole bunch of hobbies, but managing my money isn't one of them.

For other people, like my dad, money is a hobby, an activity from which he derives great pleasure. Last Christmas, during some quality father-son bonding time, he took me over to his computer to look through his stock portfolio. A generation ago he might have tinkered with model trains in retirement. Instead, he loves to watch the business news and tinker with his investments.

My mom is more like me in this regard. She doesn't view money as a hobby, and so I was really quite surprised to hear that she had joined an investment club. Her group met regularly, researched stocks, and talked about the pros and cons of high-tech versus commodities. About a year after she joined her investment club, I had the following conversation with her on the phone.

Bruce: How are things going with your investing club?

Mom: Pretty good. We've been reading some great books lately. We just finished *Life of Pi*.

Bruce: In your investing club?

Mom: Yes.

Bruce: That sort of sounds like a book club, doesn't it?

Mom: Yeah, well, we got bored with the investing stuff and we weren't doing very well so we decided to read books and discuss them.

Bruce: But you still call it your investing club?

Mom: Of course.

My mom probably shouldn't have been in an investment club in the first place. It was too much complexity for her—not because she wasn't smart enough, but because she wasn't interested in it. Which leads us to the third C Factor: Smart, capable people do dumb things with their money because they haven't found the right level of complexity for their money.

Complexity refers to *something that is composed of many interconnected parts.* Certainly your financial situation fits that definition. Some people have *too much* complexity when it comes to their money—too many interconnected parts that they either don't understand or have a tough time keeping on top of. Or they have *too little* complexity and aren't sufficiently engaged in what needs to be done to get a handle on things.

Smart, capable people do dumb things with their money because they haven't found the right level of complexity for their money.

Here are some common examples from the Moolala Community of how people can have too little or too much complexity when it comes to their money. As you read through them, think about where you might have too much or too little complexity in your own life when it comes to your money.

Scattered accounts: Too much complexity

"I have moved around a lot and worked for a number of different companies. Every few years I'll open up a new RRSP account for reasons I can no longer recall."

–Kira, 42, accountant. Single.

Kira wouldn't dream of spreading the contents of her spice rack around the house, but that's what she's done with her investments. Her situation is so complex she finds herself either getting overwhelmed by it all or ignoring it completely.

Oblivious about investments: Too little complexity

"I have an RRSP account and deposit money into it every year. But I don't know any more than that. I really have no idea what my money is invested in or how it's doing."

–Owen, 48, real estate agent. Single, with three kids.

Owen never thought much about what he was investing his money in or how it had been performing. When he did start to look into it he found out that the investments he'd chosen were not doing well at all, and hadn't been for years. But he had been oblivious to it. You don't need to go over your mutual fund statements with an electron microscope every month, but you will benefit from having a basic idea of how your investments have performed over the past year.

Tracking every cent ever spent: Too much complexity

"I track everything. Clothes, rent, car maintenance, magazines. I can tell you how much I paid in cosmetics for each of the last five years."

–Misty, 29, realtor. In a relationship.

"We used to have one of those software programs for budgeting, and we'd get bogged down each month trying to rectify the last $50.25. It was the cause of major frustration in the marriage!"

–Kelly, 41, learning consultant. Single, with two children.

Misty and Kelly both spent hours every month tracking their spending. For Misty, that work had no impact on her spending patterns. She didn't review the fancy reports that were available to her and she wasn't aware that she was spending more than she earned. She tricked herself into believing she was doing the right things with her money because she was so busy doing "things." For Kelly, the complex tracking process caused fights with her now ex-husband. Tracking your spending can be helpful if you use it to analyze your behaviour and make changes based on the numbers. But tracking in and of itself isn't a very useful task, and it presents a level of complexity that most people don't need.

Abdicating to a financial adviser: Too little complexity

"I met him once in his office about two years ago. We talk on the phone every year around RRSP time, and he'll make some suggestions about things that I don't really understand. It is basically a quick chat about where my contribution should go and that's it. Honestly, I don't even know what we would talk about if I did make the effort to meet with him."

–Kareem, 35, civil engineer. Single.

Kareem has a financial adviser, but he rarely talks to him or follows the advice he's been given. He treats him like a gardener who will come by when he's away and keep his lawn looking good. But that level of complexity is insufficient for Kareem to get what he wants in life. Financial advisers often tell me that they wish their clients were more engaged in the process: returning phone calls, coming prepared to meetings, and doing what they say they'll do to get a handle on their money. Most of us have a more complex and in-depth relationship with the person who cuts our hair, cleans our teeth, or serves us lunch every day in the food court than we do with the person we pay to work on our money.

Information overload: Too much complexity

"I love the news. I watch, surf, and read tons of it throughout the day. Even though I far prefer celebrity gossip, I feel like I should keep on top of business news."

–Ingrid, 33, marketing coordinator. In a relationship.

Ingrid should stick with celebrity gossip. She doesn't need to know what the stock market did five minutes ago or how the banks fared in Q4. Unless it is your passion or your job, you don't need to know whether the market went up or down a hundred points on any given day. This level of complexity is simply too much for Ingrid and, frankly, for most people.

Information underload: Too little complexity

"I couldn't tell you if I'm spending more than I earn. I really don't know."

–Pat, 28, personal trainer. In a relationship.

Pat knows far too little about her own financial situation. She doesn't know if she is spending more than she earns, or how much she owes on her credit cards. She doesn't know what she'll need to retire or how her investments are performing. She has too little complexity in terms of the information she has about her money.

Playing hot tips with serious money: Too much complexity

"I love playing the market. My brother-in-law has some really good tips, and so do those call-in shows on the business channels."

–Neil, 47, restaurant manager. Married.

Neil loves the "hot tips" he gets from his brother-in-law. He started buying and selling stocks on those tips, but got his head handed to him on a silver platter. Investing more than just fun money on hot tips is too much complexity for most people. I'm not talking about holding shares of boring old dividend-paying stocks. I'm talking about being seduced by the "hot tips," something I see in my workshops all the time. Aside from a few exceptions I mention in the sidebar below, most people should stick to hobbies like scrapbooking, building model trains, running the Ironman, or even extreme ironing: all great hobbies that won't put their financial future at risk.

Which examples sound as though they could be you? Where do you have too little complexity? Where do you have too much? Coming up a little later in the chapter, we'll look at how to find the right level of complexity for your particular situation. But first I'm going to address why complexity is so hard to master in the first place.

STICK WITH SCRAPBOOKING: WHY STOCK PICKING SHOULDN'T BE A HOBBY FOR EVERYONE

Sure, buying and selling stocks can be fun. But there are a number of reasons why you might try to find your fun somewhere else.

The professionals will almost always win: I was in New York having dinner with an old friend who now works for a major hedge fund. He has a Ph.D. from Cambridge University and spends a hundred hours a week analyzing stocks. The CEOs of all the companies in his sector are on speed dial and he's playing with hundreds of millions of dollars, most of which belong to someone else. Do you really want to go up against him?

When you go to Las Vegas, you know that the house will win. But it doesn't really matter because you had some fun at the slots, saw a Cirque du Soleil show, and watched the incredible water fountain in front of the Bellagio. The stakes are higher when you're playing individual stocks, and the consequences are greater.

The work involved to win the stock-picking game is immense: Keeping on top of corporate news and economic trends takes a ton of time and energy. You might make the brilliant "buy" decision, but do you know when to sell? And are you tracking your performance to see if you're actually winning the game? The bottom line is that most people aren't willing or able to do the work required to profit from buying and selling individual stocks; it is too much complexity for them.

Playing stocks can distract you from what really matters: You heard earlier from a recent workshop participant who was hit hard when a small oil and gas stock he bought fell from a dollar per share down to a dime. He had got in on a "hot tip," with money he couldn't afford to lose. Worse yet, focusing on stocks was a distraction that took his attention away from the basics, like reducing debt and contributing to an RRSP, the stuff that would really make a difference to his quality of life.

There are three main exceptions to my "no individual stocks" rule:

- **You are working with a great financial adviser:** If your adviser has a great track record of investment performance, and you're clear on the strategy he or she is pursuing, then individual stocks might make sense. Double check that the recommended stocks fit with your needs and risk tolerance. (We'll be talking more about developing your investment plan later in the book.)

- **Your employer makes buying company stock compelling:** Many employers have stock purchase plans to provide an incentive for you to invest in the company. These can be a very good idea if, for example, the company matches part of your contribution. But it is very important to keep an eye on the stock and the percentage of your portfolio it represents. It doesn't make sense to just own company stock forever simply out of loyalty to the firm. Ask a former Nortel employee who didn't diversify out of the company's stock what it feels like to get burned.

- **You're playing for fun:** Some people really do love the game of playing individual stocks. If you're one of them, go for it and have fun. But limit what you take to the table to 5% to 10% of your portfolio, and ensure that it is money you are prepared to lose.

THE HURDLES: WHY COMPLEXITY CAN BE HARD TO MANAGE

Finding the level of complexity that fits you and your circumstances can be hard, for a number of reasons.

We have more choices now than ever before: Every day we're faced with a tsunami of choices about what we could spend our money on: big-screen TVs, granite countertops, adventure travel. And there are a huge number of choices when it comes to financial products, too. There is more stuff to buy, and more sources of information to consider than ever before, and this overwhelming number of choices can leave you feeling anxious, annoyed, and even paralyzed. Behavioural economists use a term called "bounded rationality" to describe how people behave rationally, but only within certain limits or boundaries. We can't possibly understand everything, because of limitations on our time and our cognitive ability. The bottom line is that it can be brutally hard to determine what we should really pay attention to, and so we end up with either too much complexity or not nearly enough.

We don't focus enough on financial literacy: I memorized the Pythagorean Theorem in math class and later learned how to use interval notation in calculus. But I was never taught how to read a credit card statement or told the difference between equities and fixed income. While there is more and more being done to improve financial literacy today, I would argue that it isn't enough. When you don't know much about personal finance, it can be very difficult to find the right level of complexity for your situation because you don't know what you don't know. What's encouraging for you is that you're reading *Moolala*. This is a great step in finding the right level of complexity for your circumstances, and it will certainly juice your level of financial literacy, too.

Managing your money is boring: Let's face it, for most people, this stuff is pretty deadly. I can jazz it up only so much. The benefits that you get out of working on your money are fantastic, but the tasks themselves are booooooorrring. If you don't have a context for the work you need to do, it's no surprise that you haven't found the level of complexity you need.

The taboo around money is pervasive: Very few people talk about money with any degree of comfort. It is easy to fall prey to the feeling that "I *should* know this," and then because of embarrassment not actually find out what you *need* to know. In some ways, we think money should be complex, because it is important. I think it is helpful to shift our thinking from "I *should* know this" to "I *need to* know this." That would increase the chances that people will actually go and find out what they need to know. Imagine, for example, if you received a diagnosis about your health. In all likelihood, you wouldn't know much about your affliction until it was diagnosed. But you would move fairly quickly to "I need to know this" and go and find out. We're going to talk more about having money conversations with friends and family in the next chapter.

THE PRIORITY PYRAMID

Finding the right level of complexity for your financial situation isn't an easy task, but it is a worthwhile one. As it becomes clearer what you need to do first, and what you don't need to do at all, you'll notice an improvement both in your results and in your peace of mind. To help you find the right level of complexity for yourself, I have developed something called the "Priority Pyramid," inspired by a popular model from the field of psychology.

In the 1940s, American psychologist Abraham Maslow proposed the "Hierarchy of Needs," a model for understanding human behaviour.

Maslow asserted that an individual would have to meet her needs at the lower levels of the hierarchy—like having enough food and water to meet her physiological needs—before she could think about spending the day engrossed in art and poetry, activities that would meet her self-actualization needs at the peak of the pyramid.

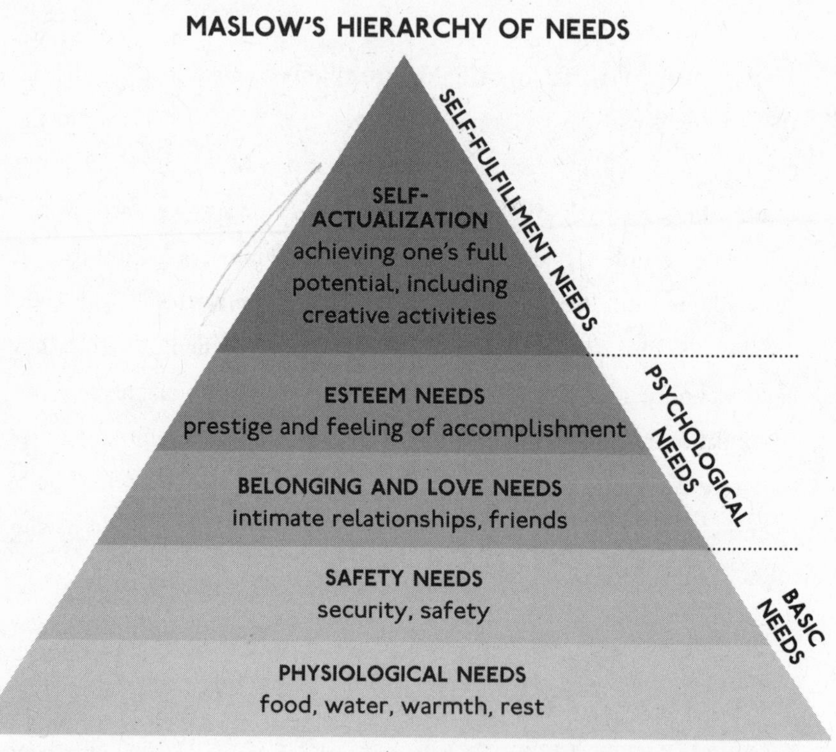

I always face a barrage of questions from workshop participants that are too complicated for their circumstances. For example, they might be spending more than they earn, and yet what they want to know about is how to short-sell stocks. That is a great question for some people, but it is only really relevant after you've answered some more basic questions first. It struck me that we could also talk about a "hierarchy of needs" when it come to managing our money, so I came up with what I call the Priority Pyramid.

At the foundation of the pyramid are basic elements like cash flow and debt. As you address the elements at the lower levels, you move up to the higher levels, where you can focus on optimizing your investment returns. Working your way up the pyramid in this way allows you to focus on what is most important to your individual financial situation and helps you avoid getting distracted by things that are too complex for where you are at the moment.

THE PRIORITY PYRAMID

OPTIMIZING RETURNS	Are there other strategies you could employ to maximize your goals?
INVESTMENT PERFORMANCE	Are your investments matching performance of their benchmark index over time?
TAXES	Are you taking advantage of tax saving vehicles?
SAVINGS	Are you regularly contributing to your savings?
DEBT	Have you eliminated credit card debt?
CASH FLOW	Are you earning more than you're spending?

We'll be looking at the individual layers of the Priority Pyramid in more detail later, when we take a closer look at your cash flow. But here are the basics on how the Pyramid actually works.

Focuses on priorities: The Pyramid is designed to help you prioritize the areas that will make the biggest immediate impact on your finances, so you can focus on what you really need to know and really need to do. For example, it's important to focus on fundamentals like eliminating credit card debt before you get into the complexity of buying individual stocks.

Acknowledges life's fluidity: You might move up and down the Pyramid several times over the course of your life as your circumstances change. For example, having a baby can really impact your spending. So even though you've been focused on savings, you might need to go back and look at your cash flow to ensure you're spending less than you earn now that diapers and Valium are on your weekly shopping list. (Kidding about the Valium . . . sort of!)

Illustrates interconnections: The levels of the Pyramid are interconnected. What you do at one level impacts other levels. For example, as you improve your cash flow, you'll also be better able to reduce credit card debt. Once that's eliminated, you'll have more room to save. As you accumulate savings, you'll be in a better position to take advantage of tax savings vehicles, like RRSPs. Once you have an RRSP, you'll want to focus your attention on how those investments are actually performing over time. And so on.

FINDING YOUR PLACE ON THE PRIORITY PYRAMID

Where you find yourself on the Priority Pyramid is mainly a function of three things: your current circumstances, your risk tolerance, and your interest level.

Circumstances: What is going on in your life today?

Your current circumstances have a significant impact on where you find yourself on the Pyramid. If you've just graduated from university, you might still be at the debt level of the Pyramid. This means that you really need to repay your debts before you start looking at making investments, despite the temptation to do otherwise. If you have a stable job and are contributing regularly to your RRSP, you might be focused on investment performance.

Your circumstances in life will change—you could be getting married or getting divorced; raising kids or about to become an empty-nester; in great health or poor health; celebrating career success or dealing with a job loss. Your circumstances will influence your place on the Priority Pyramid.

Too much complexity: *"As is my personality, I have been trying to do everything at once: contribute to RRSPs, invest in stocks, and budget for a home renovation. The springs are popping out of my head and I'm not doing anything well. This exercise really clarified for me that I need to focus fiercely on debt repayment right now, because that is what is going to make the biggest difference. Once I have done that, then I can move up the Pyramid again."*

–Garret, 53, electrician. Single, with one child.

Too little complexity: *"I realize that I need to move up the Pyramid. I have done everything up to tax vehicles. But in order to get what I want I need to get more involved with my money. The next thing for me to do is to look at investment performance."*

–Christopher, 51, sales representative. Married, with two children.

Risk: What is your tolerance?

Your risk tolerance when it comes to money affects where you are on the Pyramid. This includes not only your *ability* but also your *willingness* to take financial risks. If your portfolio were to drop by 20%, what would the tangible consequences be? Would your retirement be delayed, or would you have enough time and money to buffer the big swings in the market? What would the intangible consequences of a big decline be? Would you suffer sleepless nights from the stress, or would you be able to shrug it off and easily turn your attention back to the reality TV show *du jour?*

Often the types of investments at the top of the Pyramid—at the level of optimizing returns—will be higher risk. If you have a high tolerance for risk, it might make sense for you to buy on margin, trade commodities, and short stocks. If you have a lower tolerance for risk, it doesn't make sense for you to pursue those kinds of strategies.

Too little complexity: *"After my husband died it became pretty clear that I had too little complexity with my money. We had a life insurance policy, so we were okay on the lower levels of the Pyramid, like cash flow and savings. But this money is for my future and for my children's future, so I really can't take big risks. At the same time, I don't want it to just sit there under my mattress. I went out and found a financial adviser who could help me make some decisions about how to make the most of the money while still keeping it safe."*

–Marnie, 44, artist and renovator. Single, with two children.

Too much complexity: *"I wish I had seen this Pyramid years ago, before I joined my investment club. We were eight 'risk-averse' women and we decided to learn more about the financial world. We researched companies and accumulated a warehouse full of printed material—without the faintest inkling of what was really going on. At one meeting we actually brought in a very well-spoken investment manager (a woman, of course . . . who can trust a man???) to enlighten us with her vast reserves of knowledge. We were all enthused about her up-and-coming sure-bet wonder stocks, and we actually put a fair bit of our collective stash into her favourite pick of all—an airline. Before you could say 'fasten your seatbelts,' the stock had crashed and burned."*

–Lisa, 48, stay-at-home mom. Married, with two children.

Interest level: How do you like to spen

If you're someone who loves, loves, loves to play … might really want to get to the top of the Pyramid so … optimizing returns, either with a great financial adviser o… But if you don't love playing the stock market, why bother? … have an interest in what is at the highest level of the Pyramid, an… see a benefit, you don't necessarily need to go there.

Too much complexity: *"I'm seventy-three years old. I still work, but mainly for the fun of it. I have done very well for myself financially, but don't really have an interest any more in managing a complex portfolio. I realized that I want to reduce my complexity and simplify my portfolio by selling out of individual stocks. I'm going to put my energy into travel and the arts, things I love."*

–Margaret, 73, finance executive. Married, with three adult children.

Too little complexity: *"I like numbers and have a bit more time on my hands now that I'm separated. I am looking at how to reposition my finances in a more structured, goal-oriented manner. I would actually enjoy gaining more knowledge about investing strategy."*

–Brad, 34, project manager. Separated, with two children.

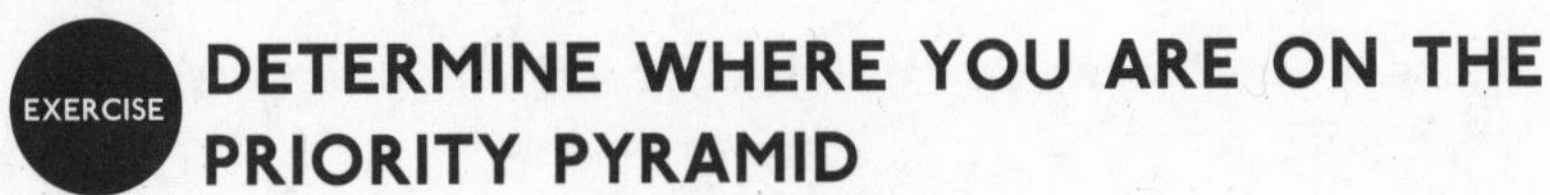

EXERCISE

DETERMINE WHERE YOU ARE ON THE PRIORITY PYRAMID

REVIEW: Have a read through the Priority Pyramid questions below. There are some terms that we haven't referenced yet, so you probably won't be sure where, exactly, you fit. Don't worry. At this point we're just having a first look. It might make sense to bookmark this exercise, because in Step 3 of the Moolala Method we'll cover these topics in more detail, and I'll give you what you need to know, when you need to know it.

- Ask yourself the following questions from the Priority Pyramid and answer with a "Yes," "No," or "Not Sure" on each. You will likely have a number of "Not Sure" answers, either because you simply don't know the answer right now, or because we haven't covered that topic yet.

→ **CASH FLOW:** Are you earning more than you're spending? Over the course of a year, does your income exceed your expenses?

Yes / No / Not Sure

→ **DEBT:** Have you eliminated credit card debt?

Yes / No / Not Sure

→ **SAVINGS:** Are you regularly contributing to your savings?

Yes / No / Not Sure

→ **TAXES:** Are you taking advantage of tax saving vehicles? First and foremost is the Registered Retirement Savings Plan (RRSP). Second, if you have kids, is the Registered Education Savings Plan (RESP). The new kid on the block is the Tax Free Savings Account (TFSA). We'll cover these in more detail in Step 3.

Yes / No / Not Sure

→ **INVESTMENT PERFORMANCE:** Are your investments matching the performance of their benchmark index over time?

Yes / No / Not Sure

→ **OPTIMIZING RETURNS:** Are there other strategies that you could employ to maximize your goals? (If you're reading this book, the answer is likely "No." For example, sector-specific mutual funds, individual stocks, buying on margin, trading commodities, trading currencies, investment real estate, etc.)

Yes / No / Not Sure

WRITE: Jot down a few notes on any insights you have about where you might be on the Priority Pyramid. Specifically, answer this question: "My current level of complexity is too low / too high / just right."

CONCLUSION

The third C Factor that prevents smart people from doing smart things with their money is not having the right level of complexity for their circumstances, risk tolerance, and interest level. You might have either too much complexity or too little. Managing the balance is critical to getting a handle on your money so you can live the life you want. The good news is that you don't have to do it alone. That is where your community comes in.

MY ONE THING

The one area where I need to increase my level of complexity is

____

____.

The one area where I need to decrease my level of complexity is

____

____.

•••Chapter 5

ENGAGE YOUR COMMUNITY
How can personal finance become a team effort?

THE C FACTORS

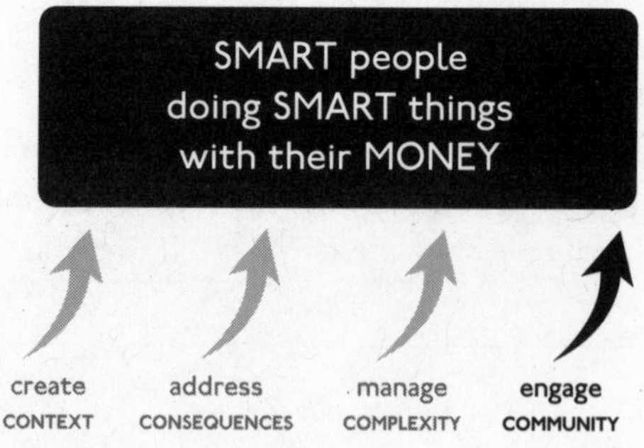

SMART people doing SMART things with their MONEY

create CONTEXT | address CONSEQUENCES | manage COMPLEXITY | **engage COMMUNITY**

"Waddles."

That was my nickname in grade six, bestowed upon me with a great flourish by my soccer coach. It was in reference both to my pear-like shape and my utter disinterest in sprinting down the field after the ball. I'm sure he thought it would stir a competitive instinct deep within me that would make me run faster. But instead it stirred a *revenge* instinct deep within me. What my coach didn't understand was why I played soccer: It wasn't for the thrill of victory. It was to hang out with my friends. I was much more interested in the socializing part than the running after the ball part.

So it came as a bit of a surprise to most people who knew me when "Waddles" decided to run a marathon.

I started telling some friends about my outlandish plan, and despite their surprise, a few of them signed up to take a marathon prep course with me. Then I found a group of guys who were training for a spring race, and we committed to doing our long runs together on weekends. I asked the manager of the gym at work for some strength-building exercises, and I told all my colleagues that I had registered for a marathon coming up that May, in Buffalo, New York. And even though it was only January, I asked my parents to book the day off to come cheer me on at the finish line.

For the next five months I trained hard, even when I didn't want to, which of course was most of the time; through crushing boredom, through wild winter weather, and through persistent injuries, I stuck with it.

Why?

I stuck with it because I had to drive Dan and Dave home from the marathon prep course. Because Guy and Bruce were waiting at the street corner every Sunday for our group training runs. Because Karen, Lori, and Liz, and my other colleagues at work, kept asking how it was all going, especially concerned when they saw me hobble around on Monday mornings after my Sunday long run. And I stuck with it because my parents had promised to be there to cheer me on at the finish line.

On May 5 of that year I laced up my shoes and waddled my way 26 miles from the starting line to the finish in 3 hours, 47 minutes. It was an incredible experience, and the joy I felt totally overshadowed the pain.

But how was I, the consummate non-athlete, able to complete a marathon? It was because of my community. My family, friends, colleagues, marathon coach, sports doctor, and new running mates were fully engaged in supporting me as I worked to achieve my goal.

Communities are a powerful force in our lives. Yet, strangely enough, they are mostly absent when it comes to our finances, so much so that many people don't even talk to their closest friends about their money issues. Which leads us to the fourth C Factor: Smart, capable people do dumb things with their money because they haven't engaged their community to help them get a handle on their money.

COMMUNITY: THE GREAT UNTAPPED RESOURCE

A community is *a group of people who have something in common.* In the case of my marathon community, the thing they had in common was me: the community of Bruce's friends and family. A family is a community. A group of friends is a community. A physical neighbourhood is a community. There are communities of people that you meet, and those who you never meet, including online communities of every imaginable description.

Smart, capable people do dumb things with their money because they haven't engaged their community to help them get a handle on their money.

Communities make almost everything easier and much more fun. And in most areas of life it is pretty easy to get our communities onside. Take parenting, for example. The moment our daughter came into our lives, our communities were engaged. Family members flew across the country to do the laundry. Friends showed up with casseroles, and those with kids provided both solicited and unsolicited advice. Gifts arrived by the armful, and we became overwhelmed both by the generosity of it all and by the quantity of pink everythings that infiltrated our home. And if we had been so inclined, we had access to other, more formal communities available to new parents—classes in baby sign language, Kindermusik, Mom and Baby salsa dancing, Strollercize workout groups. You name it, it's out there.

In fact, in most areas of your life that are important to you, communities are easy to find and often already in place. To wit:

HEALTH	Weight Watchers, hockey team, dragon boating team.
SPIRITUAL GROWTH	Meditation class, Bible study group.
ENTERTAINMENT	World of Warcraft teammates, community theatre, belly dancing.
SOCIAL LIFE	Book club, cooking classes, basketball & beer buddies.
RELATIONSHIPS	Singles clubs, match.com prospects.
HOME	Neighbours, parents with same-age kids, fellow gardeners.

THE HURDLES: WHAT PREVENTS US FROM ENGAGING OUR COMMUNITIES ON THE TOPIC OF MONEY?

Money is most certainly an area that is important to the quality of our lives, yet there is relatively little community support available. This has always struck me as kind of odd. Why is it that we shy away from engaging others about money?

Talking about money remains a cultural taboo: There still is a strong cultural taboo around the topic of money. It can be more embarrassing and upsetting to talk about money than sex. And I'm not talking about asking how much salary someone makes. The taboo around money extends far beyond that, to talking about your goals in life, how you work with your financial adviser, things you've learned about investing, etc. There are some exceptions, of course—we'll talk about money when we can brag about the fantastic bargain we just got. But that isn't because we are particularly proud of being frugal. It's because we think it makes us sound smart. We'll buy things we don't really want or need so that we can sound smart. But smart people, even when they sound smart, still do some dumb things with their money.

We're worried about what other people will think: We like to sound smart and are worried that we'll sound stupid if we talk to people in our life about money issues. We think we *should* know it all, and that other people already *do* know it all, and that we *need* to know it all before we can talk to other people about it or else we'll look stupid. Yet parents with a brand new baby in their arms certainly don't know it all, and they (mostly) don't pretend they do. This allows them to talk to their friends, family, and health professionals to get the benefit of that community support when they really need it. Here's the irony: the fear of sounding stupid could actually prevent you from becoming smarter about money.

Talking about money itself isn't much fun: Most of us would rather watch surveillance video of an abandoned parking lot than talk about the minutiae of RRSPs, GICs, TFSAs, and the rest of the alphabet soup of personal finance. When the context for money is survival or stuff or retirement, of course, the content of this financial alphabet soup isn't very appetizing. But when the context is personal, empowering, and consistent with your values, talking about money suddenly becomes more palatable. Who doesn't want to talk about adventure, creativity, beauty, experiences, and freedom, or whatever it is that inspires you? As I said earlier, we often disconnect our dreams from the financial fuel that brings them to life. And not talking about money with the people in our lives is a huge missed opportunity.

THE BENEFITS: WHAT'S IN IT FOR YOU TO ENGAGE YOUR COMMUNITY

Your community can play an important role in helping you get a handle on your money—whether it is saving for your first house, investing your retirement savings, or planning a trip with your kids to the Galapagos. Here are three key benefits of engaging your community.

Communities provide support: Talking to other runners who had suffered injuries made a big difference when I was schlepping off to physiotherapy to treat my own. They understood how hard I had worked and could empathize with my fear of not being able to complete the marathon. They also provided practical support—by picking up race bibs and sharing the driving, among other things. The bottom line was that they supported me as I worked to reach my marathon goal. It is exponentially easier to achieve your money goals when you have a community you can count on for support, both emotional and practical. You'll be able to talk to them about the goals you want to achieve, the challenges you face paying off debt, or your confusion about the world of investments.

"We call ourselves the 'Dollar Divas'—a group of thirtysomething urban professional women who want to learn more about personal finance. We get together every six weeks or so to talk about money. And eat. We always eat, and eat well. We gossip a little about boys too, but it always leads back to finances: Do you need to disclose if you just bought a fabulous pair of $450 leather boots? What about debts from business school? Should your partner help you out? What do you do if you are madly in love with an expensive lighting fixture and he couldn't give a rat's ass about it? Questions, questions. It really struck me how differently people decide to negotiate financial matters. One of the best things we did was develop and share with the group our own Personal Mission Statement (PMS for short. Perfect, right?). Sharing our hopes and ambitions with each

other was an incredible process, and led us to create a peer coaching component to support each other in achieving our goals."

–Julia, 37, teacher. In a relationship.

Communities come up with ideas: Other people think of things that you never would have come up with on your own: try this running route, call this sports doctor, test these shoes. A community of people can also be a community of problem solvers. When you have questions or are feeling stuck about what to do, you can turn to your community for solutions and ideas that will help you achieve your goals.

"For me, getting a handle on my money was really about getting a handle on my career. Jobs had always fallen into my lap and I had never really had to go looking for one. But then I hit a career plateau and really wanted to be more strategic in my choices, instead of just taking what was easy and accessible. I started to talk to people in my field about international opportunities and they had the most incredible ideas. And at the end of every conversation I asked them who else I should talk to. I ended up meeting with people all over the world and eventually landed an awesome job in the Middle East."

–Marge, 42, film industry executive. Single.

Communities hold you accountable: My friends were always waiting for me at the street corner so we could do our long training run together. Left to my own devices I never would have gotten out the door, especially in the middle of February with minus-thirty Celsius temperatures. Left to your own devices, you might not follow through on making the changes you want to make in the way you behave around money. Having a community onside to hold you accountable and remind you of why you're making changes will make a huge difference.

"I have been talking about increasing my income for a long time. But I finally made a promise to one of my good friends that I would be earning significantly more money by the end of the year. I developed a plan and sent a weekly e-mail update to him on my progress. Some days I hated him for it, but he kept me on track, asking me how it was going and keeping me honest about doing the things I said I would do. I am astounded to see how effective it was to have someone else hold me accountable. I may not double my income by the deadline, but I think I'm way further ahead than I would have been without this process."

–Kelly, 41, learning consultant. Single, with two children.

And a bonus: Communities make any task way more fun: Completing a three-hour training run is exhausting and time consuming, and, in itself, not so much fun. But we had lots of great conversations on those long runs, and as you know, "Waddles" likes the chat, so that made the runs fun. Some of the actual work you'll need to do to get a handle on your money will be pretty boring. Sorry, but it's true. It's way more fun to have a friend who's going through it at the same time. Or at least someone to dish with or vent to about how it is going for you.

TALK TO MY COMMUNITY? I'D RATHER SLEEP ON A BED OF NAILS

Some people have a harder time than others engaging their community. You might be a private person by nature, or you might simply not be interested in talking to other people about what's important to you. In your case, I know it will push you outside your comfort zone just to have one conversation. But I am confident that whatever steps you take in this area, be they big or small, will make a difference in allowing you to get a handle on your money.

THE PITFALLS: WHY IT AIN'T ALL ROSES AND PUPPY DOG KISSES

For all the good that communities do in areas of life that are important to us, sometimes they don't provide the support we want and need as individuals. The communities we live in can put pressure on us to "keep up with the Joneses." ("Oh. That's your *real* stroller? Are you sure your kid is going to be safe in that thing?") Or the friends and family that we surround ourselves with can actually reinforce behaviours that don't work for us in the area of money. ("Come on, it's only $100. And it looks great on you!") But you're a smart, capable person. You can do this. I'll give you some ideas on how to deal with challenging communities—and the individuals who populate them—in the sidebar below.

SUMMONING YOUR STRENGTH: HOW TO DEAL WITH CHALLENGING COMMUNITIES

Here are some tips for dealing with communities that reinforce money behaviours that don't work for you.

Notice what is going on: The first step is to notice how you behave with money when you're with a specific community. For example, when you go out for lunch with your friends from work, do you tend to spend more than you want to? The following exercise will help you identify which communities might be reinforcing or discouraging behaviours you want to change.

Make requests of the people in your community: You might be able to alter how the community operates with a simple request. For example, "Hey, I'm trying to really cut down on how much I spend on lunch. But I still want to hang out with you. Could we plan on bringing our lunches and eating in the lunch room a few times a week instead of going out?"

Practise the new behaviour: It might take some intestinal fortitude on your part to alter your behaviour even if your community does not. But if you keep practising the behaviour, they'll see that you've really decided to change and will likely get used to it over time.

Find new communities: You might want to find or create a new community that supports the behaviour that you want. For example, form a lunch swap group at work—five people each make lunch for the group one day a week. Join a monthly clothing swap. Start a Moolala Money Group.

EXERCISE

UNDERSTAND HOW YOUR COMMUNITIES IMPACT YOUR BEHAVIOUR AROUND MONEY

IDENTIFY: Jot down a list of some of your communities. The list could include your immediate family, high school friends, Ultimate Frisbee friends, colleagues at work, people who work in the same field as you, the community in which you live, etc.

REVIEW: Go back to the exercise on page 51 and reread the list of behaviours around money that you would say are "weaknesses." List them in the table below, in your notebook, or in the worksheet from www.moolala.ca.

CATEGORIZE: For the top three behaviours that you prioritized earlier, scroll down your list of communities and then categorize each community depending on whether they "reinforce," "discourage," or have a "neutral" effect on the behaviour. For example:

BEHAVIOUR	REINFORCE THE BEHAVIOUR	DISCOURAGE THE BEHAVIOUR	NEUTRAL
HONEY, I SACRIFICED THE KIDS: "We haven't saved a penny for our kids' university education."	**NEIGHBOURS:** "The kids want what their friends have, of course. But we're out of our league in this neighbourhood and it is hard to keep up."	**FAMILY:** "My mom squirrelled away my baby bonus cheque for years so I'd have tuition money for university."	**COLLEAGUES:** "I don't really connect with the people at the work, so don't see how they figure in to this."
CARRYING CREDIT CARD DEBT: "I have about $5,000 in credit card debt and am paying $1,000 in interest every year to the bank."	**UNIVERSITY FRIENDS:** "They all use credit cards just as much as I do. And none of them seems at all worried about the interest charges."	**COLLEAGUES:** "I'm part of an entrepreneurs group, and they definitely discourage credit card debt."	**SPORTS FRIENDS:** "We don't really talk about this stuff."
SPENDING RETIREMENT SAVINGS ON A COUCH FOR MY KID: "It was only later that my financial adviser pointed out the consequences of not having enough money for retirement."	**FAMILY:** "This is how we've always done things, and now it's expected that we'll always be there with our wallets to save the day."	**FRIENDS:** "I have a good group of old friends who all have kids. I'm the oddball here in terms of bailing out my son."	**COLLEAGUES:** "We never talk about money at all. Ever."

BEHAVIOUR	REINFORCE THE BEHAVIOUR	DISCOURAGE THE BEHAVIOUR	NEUTRAL

WRITE: What insights did you have in doing this exercise? What did you notice about how your communities reinforce behaviours or discourage behaviours?

REACHING OUT: START THE CONVERSATION ABOUT YOUR MONEY

We are going to take a few baby steps in engaging your communities in the area of money. Don't worry. You're not going to be asking them about salaries or other specifics, or firing friends who reinforce behaviours that don't work for you. But I am going to ask you to start talking to people you trust about money. This might be a difficult part of the process for you, especially if you don't talk to your friends and family about other personal things. So it might be an opportunity to stretch a little bit outside of your comfort zone.

"I started talking about money with one of my oldest friends in the world. We had never discussed money at all within my circle of friends, except for maybe how much our houses were worth. She and I made a concerted effort to talk about money, which has really taken the weight off it and normalized something that was like the boogeyman before."

–Devon, 38, entrepreneur. Married, with two children.

EXERCISE

START TALKING TO YOUR COMMUNITY ABOUT MONEY

WRITE: Jot down the names of two or three people who you feel you can trust: a friend, spouse, or family member. They don't have to be people that you believe have expertise with money. They just need to be people that you trust.

FIND: Find a few minutes to talk to each of them. I've found that most of the time the conversations occur organically, such as when you're having lunch, or going for a walk together, or whatever. Sometimes opportunities don't present themselves immediately, or you find yourself procrastinating. If that happens to you, I recommend that you schedule the conversations.

Here is just one example of how you could begin the conversation, although of course you can use your own words:

> → **SAMPLE SET-UP:** "Hey, can I talk to you about something? I'm reading a book about personal finance and one of the exercises is to talk to people I trust about money. I know this isn't something that everyone talks about, but it would be really helpful to me if I could ask you some questions. You won't have to share anything you don't want to, and I can go first answering the questions if that's easier."

ASK: You can ask them some of the questions I have included below, but really, the intention is just to get you talking. In the example, you'll notice that I have referenced the other C Factors, as this is really the point at which all four of them come together.

- What are some of the things you're excited about that are coming up in the next few years?

This is a non-threatening way to start the conversation. It also sets up the idea that goals are holistic in nature. (Create context)

- Who do you talk to about money?
- Do you talk about your financial goals for the future, your investments, your career?
- What is your comfort level in talking about money?

These questions lay the foundation for you to talk to them about different aspects of money. (Engage community)

- What are some of your first memories about money?

This question will give you a sense of their default context for money. And it opens up the opportunity for you to talk about your own family upbringing and default context. (Create context)

- What are some behaviours (or things you do) around money that you would say work well for you?
- And what are some that don't work for you?

These questions will help you start to identify where you are similar and where you are different from others when it comes to your own behaviour around money. It creates an opportunity for the conversation to include topics that people might not usually talk about. (Address consequences)

- How do you figure out what you need to focus on when it comes to money?

This will give you someone to bounce ideas off as you start to figure out the level of complexity for money that works for you. (Manage complexity)

WRITE: Jot down a few insights. What did you learn from having these conversations with people in your communities? How did it feel? Who else do you think it would be helpful to talk to?

CONCLUSION

The fourth and final C Factor that prevents smart, capable people from doing smart things with their money is a failure to engage their communities. You rely on your community for support, ideas, and accountability in other important areas of your life, so why wouldn't you draw on them to help out here?

In the chapters to come we will address each of the C Factors and turn them from weaknesses into strengths. You'll learn how to make good use of your Moolala Context to come up with goals that inspire you. You'll develop a plan that addresses the consequences of your behaviours around money with the least amount of complexity possible. And you'll learn how to ignite the power of your community to help you get a handle on your money so you can live the life you want.

This completes Step 1 of the Moolala Method. We have done much of the hard work in laying the foundation for Step 2. Now we get to look ahead to the future, dream a little, and determine what you want that future to include.

MY ONE THING

The one person who I'm committing to talking to about money, now that I have read this chapter, is Gord ____________________________________

____.

STEP 2

DETERMINE WHAT YOU WANT

•••Chapter 6

COMING UP WITH YOUR MOOLALA GOALS

What do you want for your life?

I wanted a boombox. Desperately. It was the mid '80s and I was fifteen years old. Back then the boombox was *the* music player of choice. Post eight-track. Pre Discman. I wanted one really badly. In fact, I had to have one. Had. To. Have. One.

Christmas was just one month away and a boombox had to be under that tree or my entire year would be ruined. But growing up as the youngest of five children, I had learned from painful experience that a full-blown campaign would be required if I was to have any hope of getting what I wanted. You see, I had had some serious disappointments in the past. My ten-year-old heart was crushed when the treehouse I longed for did not arrive on Christmas Day. At thirteen, I was crestfallen again when I opened up my big gift. After painstakingly removing the wrapping paper and setting it aside, I was devastated to find . . . a power drill. *A power drill?* I had, to date, shown absolutely no inclination towards any project that would ever require a power drill. But that is what I found under the tree.

Determined to prevent a similar disaster, I set about planting multiple seeds for my dad and stepmother, Cathy. In the weeks before Christmas, I clipped out every photo of every boombox I could find, added a few very subtle captions ("Here's a great idea for Bruce!!!"), and set about papering the house, affixing photos to the ice cream in the freezer, the TV remote control, the underside of the toilet seat lid, and inside the cutlery drawer, the medicine cabinet, and the glove compartment of my dad's car.

And guess what? Under the tree on Christmas morning was my boombox.

My point is that I determined what I wanted and then came up with a plan to get it. Over the years I've learned this approach works just as well for life in general as it does for Christmas presents.

As a child, you likely had a pretty good idea of what you wanted most of the time—whether it was what you wanted to have (an Easy-Bake Oven, a Hot Wheels car wash), or what you wanted to learn (how to ride a bike, how to build a rocket). But once you became an adult, like most people, you probably found it more difficult to be sure about what you wanted. Should you go to university? What should you study? What career should you choose? Where should you live? And once you had the career, and the mortgage, what then? What did you want then?

Some of us lost sight of the difference between what we *should* want and what we *actually* wanted. The default contexts of family and society began to dominate. Money became something we *needed* to survive out on our own. Or it was just for stuff, or for some far-off retirement. All of this was happening as life became increasingly busy—with school, work, marriage, kids, elderly parents, renovations, volunteering, a health scare, etc.—and as a result, many of us got caught up in dealing with our day-to-day concerns, good or bad, instead of thinking about what we *wanted* for the future.

Fast forward to today, and you might not have a clear idea of what you want for your life. Trust me, this is very common. But the fact of the matter is that it can be tough to come up with a plan to live the life you want when you don't know what that life is.

In Step 1 of the Moolala Method, we looked at how the 4 C Factors can prevent smart, capable people from doing smart things with their money. Now, in Step 2, you'll determine what you want out of life so that you can develop a plan to get it.

It can be tough to come up with a plan to live the life you want when you don't know what that life is.

MOOLALA GOALS: THINKING HOLISTICALLY ABOUT WHAT YOU WANT

Most personal finance books focus on achieving specific financial goals, like saving for your retirement or sticking to a budget.

Yawn. Boring.

Yes, those things are important, and we will talk about them—but we'll be talking about other things, too. That's because, in my experience, financial goals alone are not enough to inspire people to take action. What will really motivate you to get a handle on your money is to think about what you want in all the areas of life that are important to you, even if there isn't an obvious flickering dollar sign attached to attaining them. I call these your Moolala Goals, and they are holistic in nature, covering areas like your passions, family and friends, career, contributions, experiences, health, and home. These Moolala Goals are much more expansive than the financial goals that are usually discussed in the context of money, which often comes as a surprise to people. But I think it's a big mistake to separate "life goals" from "financial goals," because they are inextricably linked.

BECOMING A PARENT: A GOAL THAT DOESN'T REALLY FEEL LIKE A GOAL

As I write this, our baby daughter Abby is taking her afternoon siesta. Her arrival in our lives is the fulfillment of a dream my partner and I has had for many years to become parents. Like everyone who pursues an adoption, we jumped through many hoops and waited years for it to happen. Now that we have her in our arms, it seems really odd to think of her as a "goal." The word seems crass and oversimplified, even though it fits the definition. A *goal* is *the result to which effort is directed,* and certainly our adoption took effort.

You might be thinking, "Why on earth is he talking about his daughter in a personal finance book?" Thanks for asking. Here's why:

Many life goals have a price tag attached: Just as our adoption cost money, so, too, do goals like volunteering in Africa, going skydiving, and spending your summers by the sea. To achieve goals like these, you'll likely need to think about how you're going to pay for them.

Life goals are inspiring and motivating: Life goals tend to inspire people in a way that pure financial goals do not. And if you're like most people, the goals that make your heart race with excitement are the ones you're more motivated to work towards. A financial goal of "retiring at age sixty-five with income equal to 70% of my prior salary" probably won't do much for the racing of your heart, and so you're less likely to work towards it. But a goal of "having the freedom to travel the world when I'm no longer working" or "making my baby laugh uncontrollably as I tickle her frenetically" might just do the trick, and give you the motivation you need to get a handle on your money.

Financial advisers can help: Broadening out what counts as a "financial goal" allows you to work with a financial adviser in new ways.

The great advisers out there have the knowledge and ability to help you work towards lots of different goals—not just the "retire at sixty-five" ones. You just need to ask.

Now that Abby has arrived, it doesn't feel as though we "achieved a goal." It feels as though we have created a family. Any way you look at it, we're thrilled she's here and excited to dream about the future.

IT'S JUST A PHASE: A NEW WAY TO THINK ABOUT YOUR WORKING LIFE

I have never been a big fan of the traditional notion of retirement. As we discussed in the chapter about context, retirement is a common default context that implies to me that I'm going to work incredibly hard and have a boring life until I'm sixty-five years old. Then, *shazam,* I'll stop working and my great life will begin.

Now don't get me wrong: saving for retirement is an incredibly important goal. Unless you win the lottery, have a trust fund, or are willing to subsist on a very low government-supplied income, you will need to think about how you're going to handle your expenses in the twenty, thirty, or forty years after you stop drawing a paycheque. But there are reasons why retirement goals should be to financial planning what pasta and olive oil are to Italian cooking: *key* ingredients, but not the *only* ingredients.

You have goals you want to achieve now: As I said above, saving for retirement isn't a goal most people find inspiring, especially early on in a career. You have goals you want to bring to fruition long before you hit age sixty-five, like buying a house, going skydiving, living in the south of France, restoring classic cars, or taking your kids to Machu Picchu.

People want more from retirement than simply the ability to stop drawing a paycheque when the time comes: To focus solely on the mound of cash you'll need means you're not dreaming about the fun stuff, like becoming a certified reiki master, joining your local Rotary chapter, or reducing your golf handicap.

Retirement doesn't look the same as it did for our parents: Most of us will not be able to draw a lucrative pension, like many of our parents did. That means we're more likely to be personally accountable for the amount of income we'll have in our retirement. And we may be faced with more expenses, too, in large part because of predictions that we're likely to live longer lives than our parents did.

I'd like to propose a new way of looking at retirement. Instead of working until age sixty-five, then retiring cold turkey, consider that you may have a number of different phases throughout your career:

- **Full-paycheque phase:** This is the time when you're earning a full income. You might have a salaried job or regular contract work, but for the most part you'd consider yourself fully employed. Rather than see this as a permanent stage, think of it as a time for you to save, both for when you're no longer working and for your Moolala Goals. For example, I saved for two years during a full-paycheque phase so that I could afford to work full time writing this book.

- **Partial-paycheque phase:** This describes those periods of time when you have a partial income. You might be working part time while you're changing careers, or so you can spend more time with your kids while they're young. Or you might have left full-time work for good, but want to stay engaged in your chosen field and pull in a few bucks at the same time.

- **No-paycheque or Post-paycheque phase:** The no-paycheque phase would describe those times when you're not earning an income from work; perhaps you've saved enough to allow you to go back to school, stay at home with your kids, or backpack around the world for a year. Then there is the post-paycheque phase, which is what most people call retirement. It could occur at the end of your career, when you decide that you have enough money to live off for the rest of your life and you don't need to work any more. This post-paycheque phase is the most critical phase in your life to prepare for financially, for one simple reason: duration. While other no-paycheque phases might last only a few years, this post-paycheque phase could last more than twenty or thirty years, and so it is absolutely crucial to plan for it.

Rather than simply earning a full paycheque for forty-five years, then no paycheque for another thirty-five years, most of us will flit in and out of these phases over the course of our lives. And we can choose to deliberately move from phase to phase as we pursue our Moolala Goals.

This way of thinking about your future can be more challenging, but for many it is also more rewarding, because it allows you to sample from the entire all-you-can-eat buffet of life instead of just eating what's on the salad table. Sure, the salads are fantastic. But what about the prime rib? The custom omelette station? The desserts? Are you kidding me? I don't get any of that? The buffet of life is bountiful, and most of us want to sample more than one thing. So grab a plate. It's time to start loading up.

DIGGING DEEP: WHAT WILL IT TAKE FOR YOU TO DETERMINE WHAT YOU WANT?

It might take something on your part for you to determine what you really want out of life. It might require you to muster the *courage* to admit what you want, even if it is only to yourself. It might require you to *believe* that you can actually get what you want in life, a challenge kids don't usually have but adults very often do. Or you might need to *let go* of something that happened in the past, or of a paralyzing need to "get it right." It might require some *creativity* to dream a little without constraints about what you want for yourself now and in the future. It could take you setting aside some *time* specifically to think about what you want. Or it could simply take some *practice*. You're probably used to writing lists for groceries or household tasks, but you might not be practised in articulating what you want in life.

If you're like most people, it might take something for you to determine what you want. What will it take for you?

For me to determine what I want in life, it is going to take

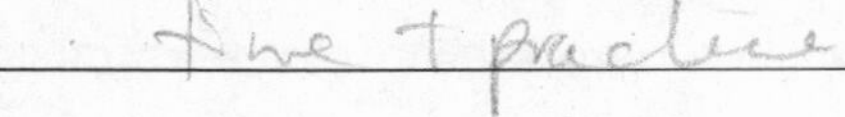
__________________________________.

EXERCISE BRAINSTORM YOUR MOOLALA GOALS

Let's get to it and brainstorm some potential Moolala Goals. At this point, you are simply coming up with ideas and not committing to anything.

This is about what YOU want for your life. Now is the time for you to let yourself dream.

RELAX: Find a quiet place to do this exercise. Somewhere without too many distractions. Once you've settled into your chair, take three deep breaths.

REMIND: It will help to have your Moolala Context top of mind. What is your money for, for you?

My money is for ______________________________.

PICTURE: Now I want you to picture yourself in your favourite place in the world. It could be on a beach somewhere, a mountaintop, a cabin or cottage, your backyard, or your living room couch. The sun is warm and there is a bit of a breeze in the air. And you have your beverage of choice in your hand . . .

ASK: Below is a series of questions to help you start thinking about what you want for your life. I have included a few examples for inspiration. For each category, picture what you might want now and what you might want in the future, and write your ideas down in the table below, in your notebook, or on the worksheet from www.moolala.ca. You might add some outlandish ideas in there, too, a few that you have no intention of actively working on. For example, I'd like to be the Governor General of Canada one day. Outlandish, and not something I'm actively working on, but totally inspiring for me to have on my list. If you find yourself getting stuck, I have included some things to try below.

Let's get started.

→ **PASSIONS:** What do you love? What are you passionate about? What do you love spending your time doing?

- "Wandering through chaotic markets in far-flung countries."

- "Having big dinner parties. Eating and drinking just a little too much with my close friends."
- "Seeing the world through the eyes of my kids."

→ **EXPERIENCES:** What are some things you've always dreamed of doing? How would you finish the sentence, "The one thing I want to do before I die is ________________________"?

- "Attend all the major sporting events in North America, starting with the U.S. Open."
- "See Mick Jagger perform live. And yes, I know my time is running out."
- "Spend six months in Antigua, Guatemala learning Spanish."

→ **HEALTH:** Do you have any goals that relate to your mental, spiritual, or physical health?

- "Attend a ten-day silent retreat (without completely losing my mind)."
- "Run my first Ironman."
- "Take a long bath at least once a week."

→ **FAMILY:** Do you have any goals that relate to your family?

- "Become a parent."
- "Camp out under the stars every summer with my kids."
- "Take my parents back to the village they were born in."

→ **FRIENDSHIPS:** What do you want from your social life? Do you have any goals that include your friends?

- "Hike Baffin Island with my two oldest friends in the world."
- "Develop new friendships, and get together in person versus on Facebook."
- "Start a book club that focuses exclusively on romance novels."

→ **HOME:** Where would you like to be living in five years? What does it look like? Do you want to be mortgage free? Do you want a second home somewhere? Where?

- "Downsize to a smaller, simpler condo."
- "Buy a cottage on a lake with great wind for sailing."
- "See my living room on the cover of House & Home magazine."

→ **CONTRIBUTION:** What are some ways you would like to make a contribution to society? Is there a charity you'd like to work with? Are there family members or friends you'd like to contribute to?

- "Volunteer for Médicins sans Frontières in Africa."
- "Host a conference for teenage girls."
- "Contribute to my nephew's post-secondary education fund."

→ **THINGS:** What are some of the things you'd like to have? Or would you like to simplify and have fewer things?

- "Own a vintage MG convertible."
- "Buy a proper clawfoot bathtub."
- "Purge my stuff. Have a garage sale and get rid of all the junk."

→ **CAREER:** What do you want for your career? Do you want to double your income or work part time? Do you want to become the CEO? Do you want to stop working at fifty-five years old? Do you want to change careers, or work overseas?

- "Win a Grammy award for Best New Artist."
- "Work only ten months out of every year."
- "Enjoy my time when I'm at the office."

→ **NO-/POST-PAYCHEQUE PHASE:** Do you want to take time for a sabbatical? Do you want to phase out work gradually or stop cold turkey? What do you want your life to look like after you stop working?

- "Consult part time until the day I die."
- "Explore South America on a motorcycle."
- "Live two months of every year in New York City."

→ **WILDCARDS:** What do you want that you haven't felt entitled to want before? What would the people who know you best say if you were to ask them what they thought you really wanted? What have you never wanted before, but right now in this moment have decided you do want? Is there something that you wanted in the past, but gave up on?

- "Have my own studio so I can paint anytime I feel the need."
- "Try out for So You Think You Can Dance."
- "Meet the Aga Khan."

CREATE YOUR MOOLALA GOALS

AREA	GOAL
Passions	
Experiences	
Health	
Family	
Friendships	
Home	
Contribution	
Things	
Career	
No-/post-paycheque phase	
Wildcard	

Remember that this list is intended to inspire and guide you, not to control you. As I said earlier, some of these ideas you might never actively work towards. You don't have to decide anything now, as we'll be looking at these goals again more closely later. But you might notice that a picture is starting to emerge as you continue reading. You might also notice that new ideas come to you, when you're driving your car, taking out the garbage, or watching a movie. Keep your list handy so that you can add to it when you have an idea.

SHAKE IT, SHAKE IT UP, BABY: HOW TO GET INTO THE GOAL-SETTING GROOVE

It is not uncommon for people to get stuck during this exercise. Here are a few ideas to get you moving again:

- → **Seek out inspiration:** Flip through magazines, peruse the biography section in the bookstore, pick up a brochure from a travel agency.
- → **Start small:** Focus on a very specific area, like your home. Remember, these don't have to be revolutionary "change the world" goals. Start with something small, like "install a spice rack."
- → **Dream big:** Dream about ideas that might seem outlandish but are nevertheless inspiring or fun for you to imagine. It could be running a scuba school on the Great Barrier Reef, building a self-sustaining hobby farm off the grid, or getting married to the Sultan of Brunei.

→ **Ask a friend:** Reach out to someone in your community and ask them a few questions, like, "When in the past have I been happiest? What are some goals I've talked about that you remember? What do you think I want in life?"

→ **Determine what you don't want:** Where do you *not* want to live or work? What do you *not* want to have in your life? What financial constraints do you *not* want to have?

→ **Take a break:** Put the questions down for a while. Go for a run, watch a classic movie from your youth, eat ice cream. Then, when you're ready, come back.

→ **Carry a notebook:** Jot down ideas as they come to you. Just write anything down, even if it doesn't inspire you right away. You can always go back.

SOMEONE TO LEAN ON: CALL ON YOUR COMMUNITY TO HELP YOU ACHIEVE YOUR GOALS

I am a huge believer in the power of engaging your community to help you get what you want. But first they need to know what you want in order to provide the support, accountability, and ideas that will be so beneficial. Now is a great time to start talking about some of the goals you're excited about with the people in your community.

As you share your goals, you might start to ask what others want for themselves. They might not have had the experience of going through the visioning exercise that you just did, but in all likelihood they will be able to come up with a few things that they want for their lives. I recommend that you find out what some of those things are. What does your spouse want? What does your mom want? What do your siblings want? What does your colleague at work want? I make it my business to want for my friends and family what they want for themselves. You never know how you might be able to help someone else achieve their goals, or how they might help you achieve yours.

Now, sometimes you'll notice conflicting goals, especially within families. What you want could conflict with what your spouse, your parents, or your kids want. You want to travel around the world for a year, while your spouse wants to start having kids right now. You want to stop working at age sixty, but your kids want you to fund their graduate school education. So be aware that as you open up the lines of communication there might be conflicts that will need to be resolved.

EXERCISE TALK TO YOUR COMMUNITY ABOUT YOUR MOOLALA GOALS

In the chapter about community you started to engage others in your Moolala Context, and in talking about money in general. Now I want you to take it a step further.

TALK: Talk to two or three people and tell them about your Moolala Context and some of your Moolala Goals. Share with them whatever you feel most comfortable sharing—it doesn't have to be the whole list. You might find it easier to talk about goals from the perspective of "some things I'm excited about."

> → **SAMPLE SET-UP:** "I'm reading a book about how to get a handle on my money. I want to talk to you about some of the things I'm excited about and maybe ask you a few questions about what you're excited about, too. Are you up for that?"

LISTEN: Ask each individual if they have any comments, feedback, or ideas on anything you said, and then listen to what they have to say.

ASK: Ask them what they want for themselves. It could be as simple a question as, "What are some things you're excited about as you look into the future?"

CONCLUSION

In Step 2 of the Moolala Method, you built on your Moolala Context by dreaming about some goals that you want to achieve. You covered a lot of ground—from passions, experiences, family and friends, to career, contributions, things, and home. You now have a full set of Moolala Goals—life goals and financial goals that have come together like peanut butter and chocolate.

Wow. I've got to tell you, I love what you wrote down. Seriously. It's fantastic.

Okay. I have no idea specifically what you wrote down. But it is a virtual guarantee that I would love it if I could read it, because I always love what people come up with during this process.

Now that you know what you want, your incentive to move on to the next step of the Moolala Method should be pretty clear. Step 3 is all about developing the plan to *get* what you want.

MY ONE THING

The one goal that makes my heart race more than any other is

____

____.

STEP 3

DEVELOP THE PLAN

•••Chapter 7

GETTING WHAT YOU WANT IS EASIER WITH A PLAN

How do you come up with one that will work for you?

I used to be the brand manager for Royale facial tissue. That's the one that had the cute white kittens and the regrettable slogan, "Soft on the Nose. Strong for the Blows."

At the time I had been with Procter & Gamble for just under five years, and I felt like I had a great gig, at a great company. I was challenged, well paid, and worked with bright, fun people.

But something was missing, and I just couldn't put my finger on what it was.

One day, while I was sitting in a meeting with our packaging people, in a windowless conference room on the fourth floor of the office tower, it all became clear. We were discussing the results of research into new designs for our tissue boxes. Facial tissue consumers had been divided into different groups based on their preferences. The "contemporary" consumer was pitched a very "Paris Fashion Week" design—an all-black tissue box with silver accents. Those with "classic country" tastes were offered pink picket fences and turquoise ducks. Staring at a wall of facial tissue boxes covered with paisley swirls, vibrant plaids, and, of course, those damn turquoise ducks, I was struck by a thunderbolt. It was an insight that would have significant repercussions.

I was in the wrong job.

It wasn't a bad job. But it was the wrong job for me.

In that moment, I knew I had to make a change. My time pushing plush paper products was up.

Had I been reading *Moolala* back then, there is no question that one of the Moolala Goals I would have put down in my notebook was "change careers." And if I had been really, really honest with myself, I would have whispered softly what that new career would be.

The secret truth was that I wanted to be a TV news reporter. I had *always* wanted to be a TV news reporter.

It started when I was ten years old and I raced home from school to watch live coverage of the assassination attempt on Ronald Reagan. When I was thirteen I covered my elementary school's basketball games and delivered a live report the next day over the public address system. Throughout high school I devoured the biographies of all the broadcasting greats—and quietly read the newspaper aloud to myself while standing in front of the bathroom mirror. I almost studied journalism in university, but decided that a business degree would be a more practical career choice. During my first week at school, I auditioned for the TV news program on campus, and over the next four years I spent most of my extracurricular time working on the show.

I loved every minute of it.

However, after graduation, instead of following my dream path, I took the path of least resistance and accepted a good job in the corporate world. It was a hugely valuable experience and I was grateful for it, but five years in, I knew I needed a change.

"I'm a smart woman in most other areas of my life, but before I went through the Moolala process I felt guilty, ignorant, and scared about what I was not doing to ensure my financial future. After Moolala I felt hopeful, clear, and eager to take charge of my money. Beyond having had fun and learning something, I feel relieved for having a simple plan to follow."

–Marty, 49, consultant, with two stepchildren.

But how? How does someone make the rather unconventional move from facial tissue to TV news? Clearly, I needed a plan.

What does all this have to do with you? Well, in Step 2 of the Moolala Method, you took some time to determine what *you* wanted. Whatever it is you want—whether it's a job in TV news, the down payment on a condo, a cycling trip through Bordeaux, or five minutes of peace and quiet every day, you will likely need a plan to get it.

And that's where Step 3 of the Moolala Method comes in: developing the plan to get what you want.

This next step looks at a number of topics, each of which is covered in its own chapter. By the end of this step you'll have a plan for what you need to do, based on your own individual situation. You'll come up with some ideas on how to deal with your weaknesses around money, improve your cash flow, and start the ball rolling on achieving your Moolala Goals. Plus, you'll have a super-simple plan for your investments that will help to ensure you won't be selling pencils on the street in your old age.

Here is a preview of how we are going to do just that:

DEVELOP THE PLAN TO GET WHAT YOU WANT

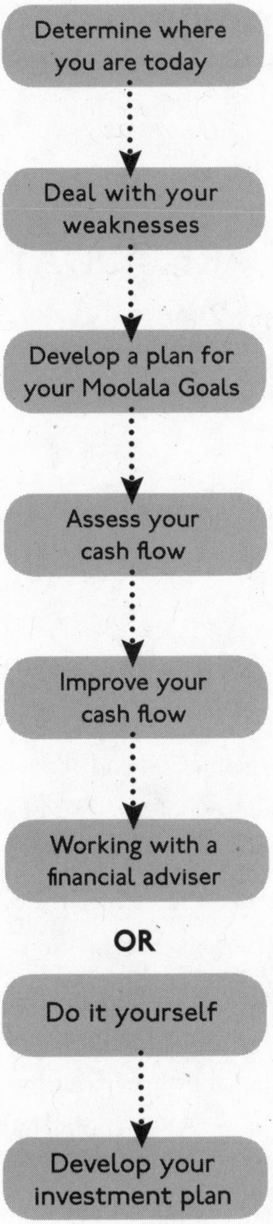

Determine where you are today • • • We'll start, in Chapter 8, by determining where you are today. Because you can't get to where you want to go if you don't know where you are. Right?

Deal with your weaknesses • • • When it comes to money, we all have strengths and weaknesses. In Chapter 9, we'll come up with simple strategies for overcoming some of our weaknesses.

Develop a plan for your Moolala Goals • • • Now that you know what you want, it's time to look at how to get it. In Chapter 10, you'll develop a plan for your Moolala Goals.

Assess your cash flow • • • Most of the goals that we have in life have a dollar sign attached. In Chapter 11, we'll determine if you need to improve your cash flow to achieve your Moolala Goals.

Improve your cash flow • • • In Chapter 12, we'll look at what you can do to either increase your income or reduce your expenses so that you have more money to put towards what you really want in life.

Working with a financial adviser • • • You don't have to do it alone. In Chapter 13, we'll consider how to get the most out of working with a financial adviser.

OR

Do it yourself • • • Some of you will consider a do-it-yourself approach. Chapter 14 will take you through what that entails and how to get started.

Develop your investment plan • • • Chapter 15 will show you a simple recipe for creating your own investment plan, either in partnership with your financial adviser or on your own.

Sound good? Let's get started with determining where you are today.

•••Chapter 8

DETERMINE WHERE YOU ARE TODAY
What's your starting point?

Naples, Italy, was a pretty intimidating city for an eighteen-year-old back in the 1980s. I had never travelled to a place with a language barrier before, and so I was understandably overwhelmed when I arrived by myself at the train station with only the address of a friend of a friend scribbled into my travel journal. The directions they provided at the information desk were in English, but that didn't mean they made any sense to me. I traipsed around the narrow streets with my daypack for what seemed like hours until someone took pity on me. I showed her the soggy piece of paper with my destination on it and she beckoned for me to hop onto the back of her Vespa. It turned out that I was just two hundred metres away. My epic journey was completed in minutes.

That situation could be avoided entirely today. For the directionally challenged, the invention of Google Maps and the like has been nothing short of miraculous. Rather than suffer the frequent blows to your credibility and self-esteem that come with getting lost, you can simply enter your Point A, where you are today, followed by your Point B, where you want to go. The website will then give you *directions* for how to get from Point A to Point B.

GOOGLE MAP FOR THE CITY OF NAPLES

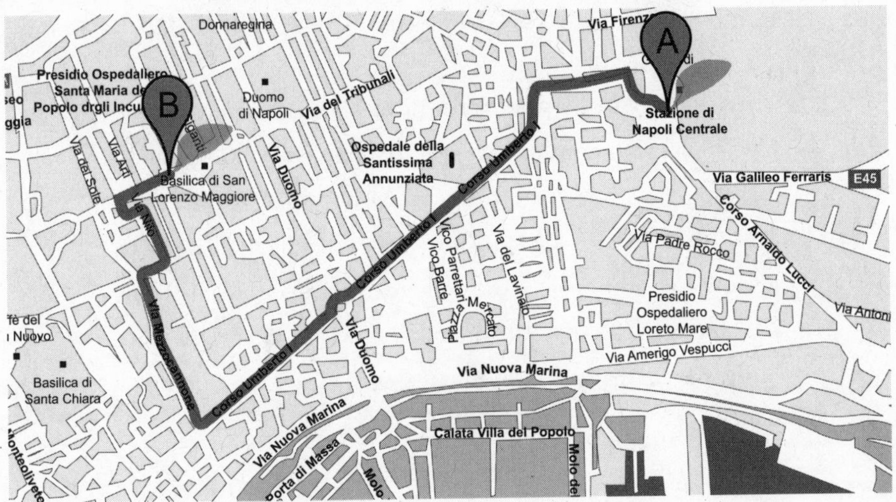

© 2010 Google-Mapdata © 2010 Tele Atlas

Getting a handle on your money works much the same way. In Step 2 of the Moolala Method you determined what you wanted in life. That is your Point B. Now you need to find out where you are today, your Point A, so that you can find the right directions by developing a simple plan or road map to get you there. Because you can't get to where you want to go if you don't know where you are starting from.

You can't get to where you want to go if you don't know where you are starting from.

POINT A: FIRE UP YOUR FINANCIAL GPS

Your very own personal Point A is essentially made up of three parts:

- **Your net worth:** This is a snapshot of your current financial situation. Calculating your net worth is a low-complexity task, and one that will help you address the consequences of your behaviour around money. What you find might surprise you.
- **Your investment performance:** Like many smart, capable people, you probably have investments—like mutual funds, for example—but don't really know how they measure up. We'll take a closer look at how your investments have been performing over time. Now, some of you might not have any investments yet, but stick with me—this is an important piece of the puzzle that you'll need later, even if you can't do much with it now.
- **Your strengths and weaknesses in dealing with money:** When it comes to how we behave with our money, most of us have both strengths (behaviours that work well for us) and weaknesses (behaviours that don't work so well for us), some of which you identified in Chapter 3. To really get a handle on your money, it is important to make the most of your strengths, and to minimize the impact of your weaknesses. And to do that successfully, you first need to know what they are.

YOUR NET WORTH: A SNAPSHOT OF WHERE YOU ARE TODAY

The first part of determining where you are today is estimating your current net worth. This is something you can calculate on your own or as a couple, whichever works best for you. Your net worth is a snapshot of your current financial situation on a particular date in time. Over time, it is the best way to gauge whether or not you are getting a handle on your money. It is calculated by adding up your assets and then subtracting your liabilities.

Assets are the things you own that have economic value. This could include your house, car, mutual funds, or the cash in your bank account. (Your grandmother's costume jewellery, your Smurf collection, and your 62-inch flat-screen TV might have huge value to you, but in the spirit of simplicity, I'd recommend leaving that stuff out.) Don't worry if you don't have a lot or any of these things. You can still do the exercise if your assets are zero, goose egg, nada.

Liabilities are what you owe to another person or company. This includes your mortgage, a car loan, a student loan, a line of credit, credit card debt, and money you owe the Mafia.

Depending on your life stage and circumstances, your net worth could be a positive number, or it could be negative. Maybe really, really negative, especially if you are a relatively new homeowner with a whopping mortgage.

Depending on your life stage and circumstances, your net worth could be a positive number, or it could be negative. Maybe really, really negative.

The financial snapshot you get when you calculate your net worth is accurate only for the *specific date* on which you calculate it. This is different from your cash flow, which looks at your income minus your expenses over a *period* of time, say a month or a year. The connection between the two is that a positive cash flow—more income than expenses—will help increase your net worth over time. In fact, the direction of your net worth is as important as the amount itself. Is it increasing over time? Here's an example:

NET WORTH

ASSETS		
Chequing account		$2,000
RRSP account		$30,000
Car		$15,000
House		$350,000
	TOTAL ASSETS	**$397,000**

LIABILITIES		
Credit card debt		$2,000
Line of credit		$3,000
Car Loan		$5,000
Mortgage		$280,000
	TOTAL LIABILITIES	**$290,000**
	NET WORTH	**$107,000**

CALCULATE YOUR NET WORTH

First and foremost, I want to reassure you that you will NOT be asked to show your net worth to anyone, except perhaps your financial adviser, if you have one. And I recommend that you do as much of this exercise as you can and not worry if it's not 100% complete. It is better to have a first draft than no draft at all. You can always update it later with better information as you get it. Finally, note that it's not uncommon for people to feel anxious while they work on this exercise. But trust me, it's worth it. Remember that you need to know where you are today to figure out the best way to get to where you want to go.

Here we go:

CREATE: Create a table in your notebook or a spreadsheet on your computer, or use the one below. You can also download the template from www.moolala.ca.

FILL IN: This table includes some common assets and liabilities. Fill in those areas that are relevant to you, and add in any others that I haven't mentioned here. Here are a few tips:

> **ASSETS:** To find the balance on your chequing account, go online or grab your latest statement. You can approximate the value of your home by looking at a recent property tax statement to see what the assessment was, or you could go to a real estate website and check what houses in your area are selling for. You can also go online to find an estimate for the resale value of your car.
>
> **LIABILITIES:** Your most recent mortgage statement will tell you how much you still owe. For credit card debt, pull out the latest bill for each of your cards, and pop in the amount of debt outstanding. Some of you might be wondering where you would include your rent in this calculation. You wouldn't. Rent isn't a liability. It's an expense, and so it goes into your cash flow, which we'll be looking at a little later.

MY NET WORTH

ASSETS

Chequing account	$__________
Other investment accounts	$__________
RRSP account	$__________
Current value of company pension	$__________
Money owed to you	$__________
Car	$__________
Principal residence	$__________
Second home or rental property	$__________
TOTAL ASSETS	$__________

LIABILITIES

Credit card debt	$__________
Student loan	$__________
Car loan	$__________
Other loans	$__________
Line of credit (debt incurred)	$__________
Mortgage	$__________
Mortgage on second home/rental property	$__________
TOTAL LIABILITIES	$__________

NET WORTH $__________

CALCULATE: Total up your assets, and do the same with your liabilities. Then subtract your total liabilities from your total assets. At this moment in time, this is what your net worth is. Ta da! That's it.

It could be a positive number or it could be a negative number, but whatever it is you now have a gauge of your current financial situation.

Your net worth will change with time as your house and your investments go up in value (hopefully) and your car goes down in value (inevitably). This is why it is important to calculate your net worth once a year to see what sort of progress you're making in getting a handle on your money. Again, the direction of your net worth is as important as the number itself—you want to see it increasing over time, as a sign that you're moving closer towards your goals. Later, I'll show you a number of ways to increase your net worth over time, such as improving your cash flow and developing an investment plan that will help your money grow on its own.

REFLECT: Jot down any insights you have about your net worth. What did you learn? How did you feel about it? Did anything surprise you?

____

____

YOUR INVESTMENT PERFORMANCE: A REPORT CARD ON HOW YOU'RE DOING

The second part of determining where you are today is assessing your investment performance. This process always reminds me of cleaning out my hallway closet in the spring. Every year I open the closet door and a whole bunch of stuff tumbles out onto the floor. It generally fits into three categories: great stuff, crappy stuff, and surprise stuff. Great stuff is money that I accidentally left in the pocket of my summer jacket. Crappy stuff is the five pairs of worn-out running shoes that I have been holding on to. And surprise stuff includes things like golf umbrellas. Given that I don't golf, I'm always surprised to find golf umbrellas in my closet.

Some of you might not have investments yet. Not to worry. You might ask a family member or friend to use their investments as an example so you can learn how to look at performance.

And some of you might not even know whether you have investments. You know you have an RRSP, but aren't sure if that qualifies as an investment. Here's the answer: an RRSP isn't an investment in and of itself, but it can hold investments. Think of an RRSP as being like a special cookie jar. Inside this jar you can store cash or investments which are shielded from tax. The RRSP jar can have lots of different things inside of it, and it can also be empty, just like a regular cookie jar. Most people usually buy some sort of an investment with the cash they put into their RRSP, so, if you have an RRSP, it is likely that you have investments inside it.

BEER BOTTLES AND THE BASICS OF RRSPs, RESPs, AND TFSAs

Registered Retirement Savings Plan (RRSP): This is the product of an effort by the government to encourage Canadians to save for retirement. It works in much the same way as when my dad encouraged me to clean up our neighbourhood when I was a little kid. I would scour the fields behind our house for the empties left behind after beer-fuelled bush bashes. For every bottle I brought back I would get the ten-cent deposit, *plus* my dad would top it up by another ten cents. My dad provided a financial incentive to encourage my behaviour.

That is just what the government is doing, minus the beer. They are encouraging you to save for your retirement by allowing you to sock money away now in an RRSP. The reason an RRSP is so compelling financially is that you defer income tax on the money you put into it. So if you put $5,000 into your RRSP, it reduces your taxable income by $5,000. Hooray! If you were in a 30% tax bracket, you would have paid about $1,500 in income tax on that money. But because it is safely stored in your RRSP you don't have to pay that tax. And the $5,000 can grow inside your RRSP shielded from tax for years and years. Then, when you're retired, you'll be able to withdraw the money from your RRSP to pay your bills. And while you will pay tax on it then, it will likely be at a lower tax rate than when you first earned it, because your income during your post-paycheque phase will be lower than during your full-paycheque phase.

The amount you can contribute annually to your RRSP is a certain percentage of your pre-tax income, and can change depending on the government of the day. This is called *contribution room*, and you can find out how much you have on the Notice of Assessment you get back from the government every spring.

One other great benefit of building up your RRSP is that you can borrow from it to fund your first home or continue your education. The Home Buyers' Plan and the Lifelong Learning Plan allow you to withdraw money without paying tax on it, subject to certain limits and conditions. You do have to pay the money back, but the plans might give you some wiggle room to fund some of your big Moolala Goals. So if you just can't imagine starting to save for your post-paycheque phase, but could see yourself needing the down payment for a house, or tuition money for an MBA, here is another good reason to sock money away in an RRSP.

Registered Education Savings Plan (RESP): This is the government's way of encouraging you to save for your child's post-secondary education. They give you a grant of 20% on the money you contribute to an RESP, up to a total of $500 per year. So if you contribute $1,000, then they give you $200. Like the RRSP, the RESP is another special cookie jar. In this jar you can hold a variety of investments, perhaps a mutual fund of some sort. The "cookies" themselves are off limits until your child starts attending post-secondary education. If you have a child, in most cases, you should have an RESP.

Tax Free Savings Account (TFSA): This account allows you to save and even invest money without the gains on that money being taxed. Unlike an RRSP, you don't get a tax deduction, but you are able to put the money in and take it out easily. TFSAs are great if you're saving for a big purchase—like a new car—or if you have already maxed out your contribution room on your RRSP and still have money that you want to save or invest.

MUTUAL FUNDS—NOW THAT RINGS A BELL

You could own investments like individual stocks, bonds, GICs (guaranteed investment certificates), or cash inside your RRSP cookie jar, but the most common type of investment is called a *mutual fund*. This is where we are going to focus most of our attention in this chapter.

A mutual fund is a product that pools together the money from thousands of people. Then, a mutual fund manager uses that money to buy stocks or bonds that they believe will increase in value. If you aren't sure if you have mutual funds, pull out one of your old statements and look up a few of the products that are included on it. If you have something that ends with the word *fund,* as in ACME International Equity Fund, it is likely a mutual fund.

You now have a better idea whether you have investments, but you might not be sure whether they would fall under *great, crappy,* or a *surprise*. At this point, everything is a surprise to you. Not to worry. I'll explain as we go along.

MONEY MATTERS: WHY YOU SHOULD CARE ABOUT INVESTMENT PERFORMANCE

Whatever type of investments you have, it is important to know how they are performing. Why? Because it can make a huge difference to you financially. You want to hold investments that go up in value over time so that you can live the life you want. Let's say you saved $300 every month for 30 years and earned 7% on average over that period of time. You'd end up with $368,000. But if you had earned only 5% each year on that money you would have only $251,000. That is a difference of 47%!!! Or a whopping $118,000. Sure, a difference of two percentage points might not seem like a big deal, but it is. It really is.

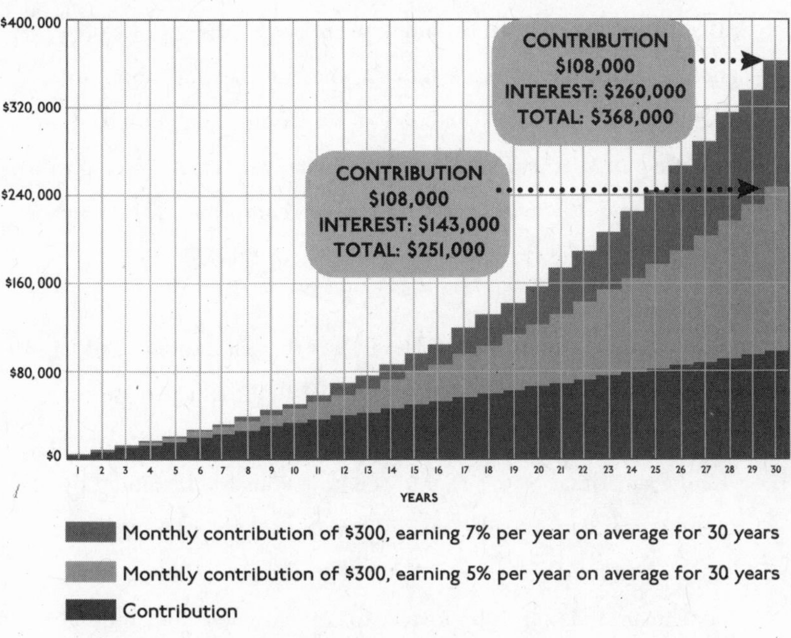

LET'S GET PERSONAL: HOW ARE YOUR MUTUAL FUNDS PERFORMING?

The implicit promise of a mutual fund is that your money will grow, ideally faster than the stock market overall. Even if the fine print in the dense and unreadable prospectus warns otherwise, that is the premise that the sales pitch for most mutual funds is based on. But is it actually so? Before I answer that question, here are a few terms you need to understand:

- **Performance:** When I talk about investment performance, I mean how much the units in your mutual fund increase or decrease in value over time. Performance is expressed as a percentage. For example, your mutual fund could be up 7% or down 7%. You could think of this as being like your performance on your grade ten history test, the one you received a B+ on.

- **Benchmark index:** An index measures the health of a particular group of stocks. In Canada, the one they talk about on the news all the time is the S&P/TSX Composite, commonly referred to as the TSX. The TSX is the *benchmark index* for mutual funds that buy shares in Canadian companies. This is the equivalent of the class average on the history test.

- **Relative performance:** The TSX is the *benchmark index* for the performance of a Canadian mutual fund, and that means that you can measure the performance of your Canadian mutual fund against that of the TSX to see how your fund is doing by comparison. This is called *relative performance* and refers to how the mutual fund you own did *relative* to the performance of its benchmark index. It is important to compare how your mutual fund performs relative to the benchmark index over a period of time so you can judge if it is a good, average, or poor performer. How was your performance relative to the class average on that history test? If the class average was A+, your B+ means you didn't do as well as many of your classmates, so you might be disappointed or annoyed and resolve to study harder for the next test. And if the class average was C+, you might be happy because with a B+ your relative performance was better than the class average.

Relative performance provides context. For example, if your mutual fund rose an average of 7% per year for five years but the TSX rose only 5% per year over the same period, your mutual fund's performance would have exceeded the TSX: its relative performance over five years would have been better than its benchmark index, which is good. However, if your mutual fund rose only 3% on average, while the TSX was up 5%, your fund's relative performance over five years would have been worse than its benchmark index, which is not so good.

Relative performance isn't the be-all and end-all, but it is the starting point. As you saw earlier on the Priority Pyramid, if you're meeting the performance of the benchmark index, and you have the inclination, you can choose to move up the Pyramid to focus on "optimizing your investment returns." This is called *absolute performance*—assessing how your investments are performing in the absolute, without looking at them relative to the benchmark, since the assumption is that your investments are already performing above and beyond the benchmark. Great financial advisers who consistently beat the performance of the benchmark earn the right to move to a focus on absolute performance. These advisers aren't afraid of being compared to the benchmark because they have demonstrated an ability to deliver returns that are better than the benchmark, so they aim higher.

Now you know why it's important to look at the performance of your investments against their benchmark index. But how likely is it that the mutual fund you own will perform at least as well as its benchmark index over a five-year period? Take a wild guess. Is there a 90% chance that your fund will beat the index? Or is it lower, say, only a 50% chance?

The answer might shock you. It is less than 10%.

There is less than a 10% chance that the mutual fund you own will at the very least match the benchmark index over the course of five years.

One way to understand this is to picture one hundred people in a room. If they each owned a different Canadian mutual fund, only ten of them would own a fund that performed at least as well as the TSX. Imagine those ten people standing up while the remaining ninety people stayed seated.

There is less than a 10% chance that the mutual fund you own will at the very least match the benchmark index over the course of five years.

This percentage comes from Standard and Poor's, a credit rating agency that has been tracking mutual fund performance for years. (If you want the latest study, do an Internet search for "Standard and Poor's + SPIVA + Canada.") There has been study after study done for decades that all reach the same conclusion: Most of the time, mutual funds underperform their benchmark index over longer time horizons.

You have probably noticed the rise and fall of your mutual funds over the years. But you might have thought that you were at least doing as well as the stock market overall. You might not have thought you were at the top of your class, but you might have thought you were at least average. Nope. Not likely. When it comes to mutual funds, there is only a 10% chance that you're meeting the index.

COMPETITION AND COST: WHY MUTUAL FUNDS UNDERPERFORM THEIR BENCHMARK INDEX

Why is it so hard for mutual fund managers to perform at least as well as the index? It boils down to two reasons: competition and cost. Let's take the example of a fictional mutual fund manager I'll call Shalima. Investors put their money into her fund, and it's her job to buy and sell stocks to make them money. She is super-smart and has an MBA, a CFA, and a whole bunch of other letters beside her name. She works eighty to a hundred hours a week, analyzing stocks, reading reports, and trying to beat all the other mutual fund managers out there at the game. It is a really competitive, high-pressure job, and with so many people trying to do the same thing—beat the market—it is really hard to do better than everyone else.

And second, the cost to run a mutual fund is high. There is the office space, salaries for Shalima and her support staff, sales commissions to be paid to financial advisers, and marketing expenses for things like websites and brochures. These management expenses can add up. Management expenses are expressed as a percentage of the value of the mutual fund. This is called the *management expense ratio,* or MER.

You might be thinking, "Really? Do I really need to know this? Where is that Priority Pyramid when I need it?"

You *do* need to know this because the MER for your mutual fund effectively comes out of your pocket. Getting a handle on your money includes getting a handle on your MER!

The average MER in Canada is approximately 2.3%. That might not seem like much, but it really has an impact on your returns. The MER is subtracted from the performance of the mutual fund, meaning that the fund has to outperform its benchmark index by 2.3 percentage points, just to match the index. If the TSX benchmark index goes up 7% in a year, the average Canadian mutual fund needs to jump 9.3% just to match the TSX!

But we now know that fewer than 10% of mutual funds beat the benchmark index over time, which is a shocking number. Even though it is a really shocking number, most smart, capable people are oblivious to the fact. They aren't aware of the consequences of investment performance on their money.

Well, you aren't oblivious any more. You are now aware of the potential consequences of holding mutual funds that underperform the benchmark index. There are the tangible consequences of missing out on some big gains on your investments. And there are the intangible consequences of annoyance and helplessness that you didn't even know about it until now. Don't worry. We will do something about that. But first, let's see how your own mutual funds are doing.

EXERCISE ASSESS YOUR MUTUAL FUND PERFORMANCE

FIND: Grab your latest mutual fund statement. I know, you might not have opened one in a while, or maybe you opened it but immediately filed it under "things that make me upset," also known as the plastic bin under the kitchen sink. No hurry. I'll wait. When you find it, look for the names of the mutual funds that you hold.

LOG ON: Bring up the website www.globefund.com. There are other great mutual fund websites out there, such as Morningstar.ca and Fundlibrary.com, but here is one to get you started.

LOOK UP: Choose one of the mutual funds on your statement and enter the name of your fund into the search box near the top of the page, where it says, "Get quote: Enter symbol, fund or company." You might be lucky and find yours on the first go. More likely, the website will turn up a few funds for you to choose from. If the names look similar, refer to your statement for the unit value of your fund. If your statement says it is worth about $8.50 per unit, you can check the online list to see if there is a fund that has that approximate value, and is therefore likely the one you own. When in doubt, call the mutual fund company and ask them.

If you don't own a mutual fund yourself or have a family member with one you could look at, enter the name of one of the big banks followed by the word "fund," and choose a fund randomly from the list that comes up. For example, you could type in "TD fund," "RBC fund," "CIBC fund," "Scotia fund," or "BMO fund."

REVIEW: The website will bring up a table of numbers on the left and a graph on the right. I have included on the following pages an example of the table that the website generates. Flip ahead now so you can see the sort of information that appears. The numbers are real, but I have changed the name of the mutual fund to ACME Mutual Fund.

ASSESS: Coming back to your mutual fund, scroll down the first column of numbers, each of which represents a different period of time, starting at one month and going back as far as twenty years, depending on how long your fund has been around. Select one of the longer time periods—either five or ten years—and scan across that row to see how your mutual fund (second column) has performed over that period of time compared to the group average (third column) and the benchmark index (fourth column). Is it higher or lower? If your mutual fund has the highest number of the three—hooray! You have outperformed both the group average and the benchmark index. This is a rare feat and you should be happy about it. If, however, your mutual fund performance is lower than the group average and/or the benchmark index, you now know its relative investment performance.

ACME MUTUAL FUND

Fund Price: $47.53 (as at January XX, 20XX)

Returns as at November XX, 20XX

	FUNDS	GROUP AVG.	INDEX*
1 month	-15.84%	-5.24%	-4.74%
3 months	-41.27%	-27.32%	-32.08%
6 months	-44.75%	-31.68%	-35.99%
1 year	-52.41%	-30.28%	-30.27%
2 year avg.	-30.68%	-15.22%	-12.42%
3 year avg.	-16.21%	-5.72%	-2.55%
5 year avg.	-6.59%	2.29%	5.71%
10 year avg.	**-3.69%**	**4.37%**	**5.88%**
15 year avg.	4.55%	5.99%	7.54%
20 year avg.	8.22%	6.79%	7.80%
since inception	7.60%	-	-
2007	-3.24%	2.02%	9.83%
2006	23.88%	14.93%	17.26%
2005	14.80%	17.42%	24.13%
3 year risk	24.46	15.87	18.45
3 year beta	1.03	0.80	1.00

*S&P/TSX Total Return

Fund Sponsor:	ACME
Managed by:	ACME
Fund Type:	MF Trust
Inception Date:	December 19XX
Asset Class:	Canadian Focused Equity
Quartile Rank:	4 (3YR ending March 31, 20XX)
Total Asset:	$383.8 million
Mgmt Exp. Ratio (MER):	2.42%
Management Fee:	2.00%
Load Type:	Optional

The performance of your **FUND** is a measure of how well (or not) it has done over many different time horizons.

The **GROUP AVERAGE** is a measure of the average performance for funds that are the same type as your fund. It is important to compare apples to apples here, so if the mutual fund you have invests in Canadian companies, it should be compared to other mutual funds that invest in Canadian companies.

This is the performance of your fund's benchmark **INDEX**. If you have a Canadian Equity Fund (one that invests in Canadian companies), the likely benchmark index is the "S&P/TSX."

This indicates which benchmark index is being used for the comparison. The website will automatically choose the relevant **BENCHMARK** index to compare your fund to.

This is your mutual fund's **MER.**

In our example, when you look at the ten-year period, the ACME Mutual Fund declined by 3.69% per year, on average, compared to the group average benchmark index, which was up 5.88% per year, on average, over the last ten years.

The key comparison is between your fund and the benchmark index. If your fund beats the group average but underperforms the index, that is a pretty weak consolation prize.

CATEGORIZE: Determine whether your mutual funds are Great stuff (✓), performing at least as well as the benchmark index over time; Crappy stuff (X), underperforming the benchmark index over time; or Surprise stuff (?), as in "What the heck is that doing in there? I had no idea I owned a mutual fund that invested in alternative energy stocks." Add a ✓, X, or ? as appropriate.

FIND: Find the management expense ratio for your fund. The average MER in Canada is about 2.3%, but some funds have MERs that are much higher (or more expensive) and some much lower (or less expensive) than that. In our example, the MER is 2.4%, meaning that this fund is a little more expensive than average.

Now, just because a fund has a higher-than-average MER doesn't mean that it will be an underperformer. It means it is a more expensive fund to run, but the mutual fund manager might still be able to beat the benchmark index. Higher MERs are often found on smaller funds that focus on specific niches—for example, a mutual fund that focuses on biotechnology companies.

REPEAT: If, like most people, you have more than one mutual fund, it is worth taking the time to look at all of them so that you can get an overview of your investment performance. You might even print out the one-page summary for each fund so that you can reference it down the road.

PAUSE: Now, the hard part. Don't do anything rash like selling your mutual funds or yelling at your financial adviser. Remember, this step is about determining where you are today so we can figure out your Point A. In Chapter 15, we'll develop an investment plan that will help you get to Point B, where you want to go.

Assessing your investment performance is the second part of determining where you are today. It is critical to address the consequences of your investment performance, so you can develop a plan to get a handle on your money. If your investments are outperforming the index, good for you; later, I'll give you some more tools to work with so you can reach your Moolala Goals even faster. But if your mutual funds are consistently underperforming the index over time, this is costing you money in a real and tangible way.

TAKING STOCK OF STOCKS: CHECKING PERFORMANCE ON OTHER TYPES OF INVESTMENTS

Most people have mutual funds, but you might not be most people. You might, for example, own individual stocks. Whatever investments you have, it really is important to get a sense of how they have been performing. If, for example, you own shares in Canadian companies like Royal Bank, Suncor, and Research in Motion, you would look at how your portfolio of stocks has performed over time, the longer the time horizon the better. Then you would look at how the TSX has performed over the same time horizon and compare the results. If you are working with a financial adviser who is buying and selling individual stocks on your behalf, ask him or her to do this analysis for you. You don't need to do the perfect analysis here; do the *least* complex version possible that will give you an answer to this question: "Are my investments matching the performance of the benchmark index over time?"

YOUR STRENGTHS AND WEAKNESSES: HOW WELL DO YOU DEAL WITH YOUR MONEY?

The third part of determining where you are today is looking at your strengths and weaknesses in dealing with your money.

You have your own unique set of opportunities, limitations, attitudes, habits, and neuroses that will make your experience of dealing with money different from that of others.

How you are impacted by the default contexts from society and the family you grew up with is different. Your behaviour around money is different, and so its subsequent consequences. Where you sit on the Priority Pyramid is different, and the extent to which you talk with friends and family in your community about money is different.

You have your own unique set of opportunities, limitations, attitudes, habits, and neuroses that will make your experience of dealing with money different from that of others.

All these strengths and weaknesses can have a big impact on your ability to get a handle on your money, and understanding them will help you determine what you should focus on first. You might recall that we actually kick-started this conversation back in Chapter 3 by addressing the consequences of your behaviour around money. We are going to revisit your understanding of your weaknesses, and also add in some of your key strengths.

Some of your strengths and weaknesses are tangible, like the amount of money you earn. And some are intangible, like how you communicate

with your financial adviser. Here are some examples of different areas for you to consider.

AREA	STRENGTHS	WEAKNESSES
INCOME: Are you making the money you want to be making?	"I earn a solid income. Not millions, but a good amount."	"I'm not bringing in the amount of money I need to support the lifestyle I want."
SPENDING: Are you spending in a way that is consistent with your income?	"My spending is fine . . ."	" . . . it's my husband who has the spending problem."
DEBT: Do you have credit card debt? Or other debt that feels too high for you?	"I'm religious about paying off my credit card in full every month."	"I rely too heavily on my credit card and often carry a balance."
SAVING: Are you saving what you want to be saving?	"I'm like a squirrel preparing for winter."	"There just doesn't seem to be anything left over at the end of the month."
TAX VEHICLES: Are you taking advantage of a Registered Retirement Savings Plan (RRSP), a Tax Free Savings Account (TFSA), and/or a Registered Education Savings Plan (RESP) (if you have kids)?	"I max out my RRSP contributions every year."	"I have an RRSP set up, but I'm not consistent when it comes to contributing to it regularly."
INVESTMENT PERFORMANCE: Are your investments matching the benchmark index over time?	"My funds are doing well against the benchmark. Woooo hoooo!"	"Nope. Not even close."

AREA	STRENGTHS	WEAKNESSES
RETIREMENT: Are you saving enough for retirement?	"Yes, I've been pretty focused on this, and it helps that my company has an RRSP matching program."	"No, I just haven't been able to find any money over and above my monthly expenses."
ORGANIZATION: Do you have a simple system that ensures bills are paid on time, that allows you to track investment performance, and that doesn't take too much time to manage?	"All my bill payments come out of my account automatically."	"Honestly? My papers are a mess. They are spread around my home office, and I often have to pay late fees."
TAKING ACTION: Are you taking the actions you need to take in the area of money?	"I'm reading this book, aren't I? That must count for something."	"I'm great on the goal-setting part, but not so great on the follow through."
COMMUNICATION: On the topic of money, what is the quality and frequency of your communication with your spouse, family, or financial adviser?	"My husband and I are really great at talking about the future and what we need to do to make it happen."	"I visit my adviser once a year and smile and nod to everything he says without understanding a word of it."

IDENTIFY YOUR STRENGTHS AND WEAKNESSES IN DEALING WITH MONEY

REMIND: Jot down your Moolala Context to remind yourself why you're looking at your strengths and weaknesses.

My money is for ______________________________.

BRAINSTORM: In your notebook, the table below, or the worksheet from www.moolala.ca, jot down in your own words the areas that fit under either "strengths" or "weaknesses." For example, you might say that "income" from your job is a strength, while "spending" is an area that is a weakness, especially when it comes to your wardrobe. Be sure to review the list of areas included in the example on the previous pages. You might also find it useful to refer to the list of behaviours with negative consequences that you identified on page 51.

AREAS	STRENGTHS	WEAKNESSES

PRIORITIZE: Circle what you feel are your three greatest strengths and three most pressing areas of weakness. We're going to look at strategies for overcoming your weaknesses in the next chapter, but in the meantime, take a moment to celebrate your strengths.

CAPTURE: Capture any other insights you had about this exercise. How did you feel doing it? What did you learn? Did any themes emerge for you?

____

____

ENGAGE: Talk to two or three other people in your community and share with them what you noticed about your strengths and weaknesses in how you deal with money. Then, ask them for their perspective on what you said. Does it make sense? Is it surprising?

CONCLUSION

Congratulations on getting to this point, to your Point A. This is a significant milestone, and one millions of people never really reach. Now that you are more aware of your net worth, your investment performance, and your strengths and weaknesses, you have a much better handle on where you are today. This basic overview should provide you with some insight into your current situation with the lowest level of complexity possible.

In the pages to come we'll develop the plan to take you from your Point A to your Point B, by building on your strengths and minimizing your weaknesses, increasing your net worth, and improving your investment performance—all so you can get a handle on your money and live the life you want.

You now have a better sense of your Point A, where you are today. As you move towards your Point B, what you want, there are likely to be a few hurdles to get over along the way to achieving your goals. Up next, we're going to leap right in and look at some of those hurdles and, more importantly, what you can do to overcome them.

MY ONE THING

One thing that really hit home about where I am today is

____

____.

•••Chapter 9

DEAL WITH YOUR WEAKNESSES
What's holding you back from achieving your goals?

It was the second meeting that sealed the deal. I arrived at his very impressive office tower and rode the elevator to its upper reaches. From the mahogany-lined reception area, I was ushered into a corner office with floor-to-ceiling windows that framed an incredible view of the city below. While we had met once before, today was the day my new financial adviser was to take me through his plan for my investments.

Despite my business degree, I knew next to nothing about personal finance, so I was almost guaranteed to be impressed by whatever he said. And I was. I don't remember a thing about the substance of our conversation, but I can still picture the document he put in front of me. It was titled "Bruce Sellery: Personal Investment Plan," and it included a number of pie charts and graphs showing all sorts of who knows what. That he had taken the time to develop an investment plan *just for me!* validated my choice in financial advisers. Clearly we were a perfect match.

My confidence in him allowed me to disengage completely from my investments, and I spent the next few years in a comfortable daze. I contributed regularly to my retirement savings, but otherwise I was oblivious.

It wasn't until I started working as a financial journalist that I realized just how disastrously my portfolio had been performing. When I finally took the time to look more closely at the mutual funds he had sold me, I discovered that they were all close to the bottom of the heap . . . where they had been for years and years.

The consequences of my obliviousness were becoming clear. My investments sucked, and that was costing me big money. Clearly, something had to change. I needed to get moving on this urgently . . .

Sputter. Cough. Cough. Sputter. Stall.

And then I just stopped. I got stuck in the metaphorical mud and was unable to move.

If I had looked at my strengths and weaknesses in getting a handle on my money, "taking action" would definitely have belonged in the "weakness" column. I knew I had to do something, but I wasn't doing it, and I couldn't figure out why.

INSIGHT TRUMPS INFORMATION

You might be at a similar point now that you've identified your weaknesses around money.

What I have found is that before you develop some fancy-dancy plan to get what you want, you might need to deal with some of your more pressing weaknesses around money. Adding more personal finance jargon at this point isn't what will make the difference. In fact, I think that's why some traditional financial literacy programs aren't as effective as they could be. They tend to focus on your understanding of personal finance, rather than on your understanding of yourself. But in my experience, insight trumps information.

Dealing with the weaknesses around money that you identified in the previous chapter will take insight, and that's what we're going to focus on in this chapter.

THE POWER OF PERSONAL ACCOUNTABILITY

There are many different reasons why the weaknesses you have around money stick around for such a long time. It could be that you're stuck in a default context for money that doesn't empower you, or that you're unaware of the consequences of your behaviour. Perhaps you've mismanaged the level of complexity you need, or haven't engaged the community of people around you to help you get what you want in life. Whatever it is, there is one thing that will make the biggest difference in dealing with your weaknesses:

I think that's why some traditional financial literacy programs aren't as effective as they could be. They tend to focus on your understanding of personal finance, rather than on your understanding of yourself. But in my experience, insight trumps information.

Personal accountability.

You becoming accountable for getting a handle on your money so that you can live the life you want.

Now, often when we think about accountability, or, more precisely, a lack of accountability, we think about CEOs who defraud investors, politicians who overspend, or employees who shirk their responsibilities at work. But I'm not talking about that. My definition of accountability doesn't have any judgment or morality attached to it. Being accountable doesn't necessarily make you a good person. And not being accountable doesn't necessarily make you a bad person.

What I mean is this: *accountability is about you being the one to make results happen.*

"Being the one": it really is all up to you. It would be convenient to think that the government should be accountable for your money. Or the banks. Or your financial adviser. Or your spouse, or your parents. But while other people certainly have a role to play, the buck stops with you. (Yes, the pun was intended).

"To make results happen": In Chapter 6 you determined what you wanted for your life. These are the results that I'm talking about. And in order to make these results happen, there are actions you'll need to take.

Most of us have some areas in our lives where we already demonstrate a very high level of personal accountability. Most parents, for example, are accountable for the health and well-being of their children. At the same time most of us have areas where we are not very accountable at all.

In my case, I wasn't being accountable for my investment performance, and my weakness was not taking action. I wasn't doing what I knew needed to be done, and that behaviour was totally inconsistent with my Moolala Context of *adventure*. The question was this: what was standing in my way of taking action?

THE HURDLES: WHAT PREVENTS US FROM BEING ACCOUNTABLE?

It is all well and good to say that personal accountability will make the biggest difference in getting a handle on your money. But you can't just go to Walmart and pick up a box of accountability. It isn't downloadable on iTunes. They don't serve it at Starbucks.

So how do you get yourself some? How do you increase the level of personal accountability that you have with your money?

What you do is get over the hurdles that stand in the way of your being accountable.

My weakness was not taking action on my investment performance. What was the hurdle to my being personally accountable for getting this done? I didn't have to think about it long.

It was fear. I was terrified about screwing it up. I was scared about making a change. And I was afraid of looking stupid—in front of whom, exactly, I don't know, but I was afraid of it anyway.

Fear is a feeling, of course. And feelings are one of essentially three hurdles that get in the way of our being accountable for our money: *knowledge*, *feelings*, and *excuses*. We're going to look at each one individually, and as we do keep your list of weaknesses in front of you so you can start to consider which hurdles apply to you.

Knowledge: The first hurdle you might face in being accountable for your money is a lack of knowledge. It could be knowledge about a specific topic, or it could be knowledge about which action to take.

- **Spending:** "Sometimes I'll look at my bank statement and just wonder, where did all my money go? I really wish I knew the answer to that question."
- **Income:** "Now that I'm divorced, I really need to earn more money. But I don't know how to do that."
- **Consequences:** "I have no idea if I'm on track or not when it comes to saving for retirement."
- **Investing:** "I don't even know what questions I should be asking my financial adviser. I know this sounds defeatist, but it seems like it will be way too much work for me to ever really learn."

Feelings: The second hurdle you might face are your feelings. Unresolved or unidentified feelings could make it very difficult for you to do what you need to do, even if you have the knowledge you need.

- **Fear:** "I am scared to look too closely at my money in case it becomes clear that I'm destined to spend my days selling pencils on the street and my nights sleeping under a bridge."
- **Embarrassment:** "I feel I should have my finances already under control. I have a university degree and I'm successful at work. I really don't want people to know how dire my financial situation is."
- **Helplessness:** "I know I'm totally deluded but I'm waiting for someone to come and rescue me."
- **Distrustful:** "After everything that has happened—the stock market crash, Ponzi schemes, corporate scandals—who can I trust? I feel like I'm better just doing nothing."
- **Laziness:** "I just don't want to work on my money. Really. I just don't feel like it. Someone else should do it for me."
- **Overwhelmed:** "I don't even know where to start. I'm too far behind and there is too much to deal with."

Excuses: I'm willing to bet my house that you have made an excuse at least once in the last three months. I know I sure have. Most people use excuses from time to time to explain why the results they wanted didn't happen. This isn't to say that the excuse isn't legitimate—for example, the excuse that you don't have time to work on your money. It's just that some people use *time* as an excuse to justify their lack of results, while other people who are equally pressed for time don't.

Excuses are the most insidious of the three hurdles, and the most challenging to identify and overcome.

- **Time:** "Honestly, I'm just too busy to focus on my money right now."
- **Blame:** "It isn't my fault. The banks screwed it up for the rest of us. There really is nothing I can do about it."
- **Trust:** "You can't open up the paper without seeing stories about Ponzi schemes and corporate crime. Seriously, who can you trust these days?"
- **Priorities:** "I'm going to start saving, but I have some things I need to buy first."
- **Willpower:** "I just don't have the willpower to do smart things with my money. Other people do, but I just don't, I never have. I want what I want now."
- **Social pressure:** "Everyone at work drives a new car. I'll take too many jabs in the lunchroom if I don't get rid of this jalopy."

MY DOG ATE MY HOMEWORK: WHAT COUNTS AS AN EXCUSE AND WHAT DOESN'T?

I'm often asked how you can tell what counts as an excuse and what doesn't. This can be a hard call to make, because time, willpower, trust, and pressure represent real challenges. Here are a few guidelines:

- **Frequency:** How often do you use it as a justification? Let's say you went into overdraft on your bank account because of unanticipated expenses. Is that an excuse? Well, the first or second time that happens, you might not call it an excuse. But if it happens more often than that, I would make the case that you're not being accountable for your money and using "unanticipated expenses" as your excuse.

→ **Logic:** When you put it under the microscope, does the excuse make sense? To the person using the excuses, all of them sound logical. But sometimes we'll use an excuse to justify something without using our rational mind to check if it makes sense. For example, let's look at the excuse that you can't trust anyone with your money because of Ponzi schemes. Rationally speaking, the risk of you getting caught up in a Ponzi scheme is infinitesimally small—smaller than the risk of you getting killed by a runaway ice cream truck. But the excuse "I can't trust anyone with my money" can absolve you from taking personal accountability for your money, even though it defies logic.

→ **Experiment:** What happens when you treat an excuse as an excuse? Try behaving for a week as though your excuse really is simply an excuse. What would you do? If you frequently use the excuse "I don't have enough time," then book a vacation day from your job, ban TV from the house for a week, or get up an hour earlier in the morning until you get that task done. Try that experiment for a week and see if the excuse sticks around. Remember, it's not as if the circumstances will all go away—they won't. It is just that you now won't have the excuse available at the ready to explain why you didn't get the result you wanted.

EXERCISE

IDENTIFY THE HURDLES STANDING IN YOUR WAY

CHOOSE: Choose one of the most pressing areas of weakness that you identified in the exercise on pages 136–37 and write it down below, in your notebook, or in the worksheet from www.moolala.ca.

Weakness: ______________________________

Hurdles to Accountability:

Knowledge: ______________________________

Feelings: ______________________________

Excuses: ______________________________

PONDER: Ponder the three potential hurdles and think about which might apply to your weakness and how. Sometimes you'll have an insight into how all three hurdles might apply, and sometimes it will be just one. Specifically, ask yourself the following questions:

What **KNOWLEDGE** would help me become more accountable in this area? How might I gain this knowledge? Is there someone in my community who could provide it to me?

____

____

____

What **FEELINGS** come up when I think about this area? Are any of these acting as a hurdle to my being accountable for my money?

____

____

____

What **EXCUSES** am I using to explain why I don't have the results I want? What might someone in my community say is an excuse I use for not getting the results I want?

____

____

____

GET READY TO JUMP: HOW TO OVERCOME THE HURDLES

The exercise above was not a theoretical one. Simply identifying the hurdle isn't enough. You now need to leap over it. Easier said than done, perhaps, but absolutely crucial to getting a handle on your money.

My weakness was not taking action on my investments, and the hurdle in the way of my being accountable for my inaction was fear. What I had to do was take an action, whether I was fearful or not. I had figured out where I was going to move my money to, but I just couldn't bring myself to do it. So I called a friend and made a promise to have the paperwork on the transfer completed within seven days and asked him to check up on me. Then I called the bank and booked an appointment to meet with a real live person to get the ball rolling. The fear didn't really go away, but I finally got off my duff and took action anyway. It wasn't easy, and it wasn't fun, but I got it done.

Here are some other examples from the Moolala Community:

WEAKNESS: "I never talk about money with my husband."

HURDLE (KNOWLEDGE, FEELINGS, EXCUSES)	POSSIBLE ACTIONS
KNOWLEDGE: "I don't know what he's thinking. Is he stressed out about money like me? I don't actually know."	"I could talk through how to have the conversation with my best friend first."
FEELINGS: "I'm fearful about having this conversation. My parents always fought about money when I was a kid and I'm terrified of being just like them."	"I could ask him to have a conversation about money, and give us both some time to think about it first."
EXCUSES: "He's got a lot on his plate right now; I don't want to add something else into the mix."	"I could ask him to have the conversation on the weekend or else schedule a conversation for when his big project is done."

WEAKNESS: "I spend too much money on athletic equipment, like skis and climbing gear."

HURDLE (KNOWLEDGE, FEELINGS, EXCUSES)	POSSIBLE ACTIONS
KNOWLEDGE: "I don't know how much disposable income I really have. That would be really helpful to know."	"I could look at my cash flow so I know how much I can spend without feeling guilty about it."
FEELINGS: "I'm worried that I'm going to live life like it's the Great Depression. I work hard and I like nice stuff and I don't want to have to scrimp on stuff I want."	"I could go on a spending hiatus for 3 months while I figure what I really need instead of just what I want."
EXCUSES: "All my friends live the same lifestyle as me. And besides, it isn't like I'm gambling the money away. This equipment helps keep me healthy."	"I could tell my skiing friends that I'm on a spending hiatus and that I want them to hold me to it."

Some of the actions you take to improve your personal accountability could be really simple, and others could be more significant. Some might be only enough to get the ball rolling, and others might eliminate the weakness forever. It matters less what action you take and more that you just take action. Because when all is said and done, the only thing that is going to make a difference in your dealing with your weaknesses and becoming personally accountable for your money is you taking action.

Now it's your turn.

EXERCISE DEVELOP A PLAN OF ACTION TO DEAL WITH YOUR WEAKNESSES

BRAINSTORM: Choose one of your weaknesses, and think about some actions you could take to get over the hurdle you associated with it, to increase your level of personal accountability in that area. Remember, these are actions you could take. At this point they are just ideas, potential actions that you are not yet committed to taking.

____

____

CHOOSE: Review your list and circle a few actions that you are actually going to tackle. You won't know for certain which actions will give you the results you want, but choose a few that you feel you could accomplish quickly. You just want to get the ball rolling, and sometimes it's more effective to start small than to try and do everything at once. We'll be talking more about how to ensure you actually take the actions you said you were going to take in Step 4 of the Moolala Method: Take Action.

How are you doing right now? It can be a little overwhelming (okay, really overwhelming) to look at your weaknesses around money. You might be nervous about how you're going to tackle the stuff that you uncovered in this chapter. You might be skeptical that it will even make a difference. Or you might be excited that you've come up with some actions to take. It really is an accomplishment to start dealing with this stuff at all. Most people never, ever even take this step. And you have, so good for you. Congratulations! Yes, there is more to do, but for a moment, could you please just bask in the accomplishment of having identified some areas where you can increase your level of personal accountability?

. . . Thank you for basking.

CONCLUSION

Smart, capable people do dumb things with their money; that is clear. But you can deal with some of your weaknesses very quickly, simply by recognizing and being accountable for them. If you choose not to be accountable, don't be surprised if things continue as they are. And you will then have to deal with the consequences of *that*. But you can choose to take on a higher level of personal accountability, and follow up on actions that will get you over the hurdles of your knowledge level, your feelings, and your excuses, so that you can get a handle on your money.

Some of those actions might be related to cash flow—and that is where we are headed next. Cash flow is absolutely critical to getting a handle on your money because the better you are at managing it, the more likely it is you'll be able to achieve your Moolala Goals.

MY ONE THING

The one action that I'm committing to taking to increase my level of personal accountability and deal with my weaknesses around money is

____

____.

•••Chapter 10

DEVELOP A PLAN FOR YOUR MOOLALA GOALS

What are the top three things you need to do?

Parenting is, by and large, unpredictable. Moods can swing from sunny to sour in an instant. Schedules, by necessity, are more malleable than a politician during an election year. And no one can predict when a flash flood of baby puke will ruin the picture-perfect outfit. Because. Parenting is unpredictable.

That being said, our daughter Abby is quite predictable in one very specific way. Every morning when we go into her room to pick her up, she flashes a 50-million-megawatt smile. The kind of smile that says, "My day is made now that I see you!" The kind designed to erase any memory of even the most horrible nighttime behaviour. The kind of smile that makes it abundantly clear why we pursued the goal of becoming parents.

This goal had a plan behind it. As did my goal to move into TV broadcasting. In Step 2 of the Moolala Method, you built on your Moolala Context by dreaming about goals that you want to achieve.

MOOLALA GOAL: "WE WANT TO ADOPT A BABY IN THE NEXT THREE YEARS."

Plan:

- Research potential options: private, open adoption; international adoption; adoption through Child Services.
- Choose best option for our situation.
- Calculate total cost of that option and start setting aside money to fund it.
- Set up a meeting with adoption agency.
- Attend their introductory seminar.
- Complete the home study and paperwork.
- Buy a car seat in case of instant placement.
- Embrace the indeterminate waiting period.

In this chapter, we're going to look at how to develop a plan to bring your key Moolala Goals to life.

Regardless of what your Moolala Goals are, the process by which you develop the plan to achieve them will be pretty much the same. You'll start by prioritizing the goals you want to work on first. Then you'll declare them to someone other than the person in the mirror. And finally, you'll develop a plan to make them happen.

FIRST THINGS FIRST: PRIORITIZE YOUR MOOLALA GOALS

In Step 2, you cooked up your own personal buffet of hopes and dreams, some simple and some fantastical. But just as you can't eat everything all at once, you can't work on all of your goals at once. You can still want everything on your list, but you might only work on a few Moolala

Goals at a time. Remember, one of the reasons why smart people do dumb things with their money is that they mismanage the level of complexity they have. In this case, having too much complexity around your goals can mean that you don't make progress on any of them. So it makes sense to set some priorities.

PRIORITIZE YOUR MOOLALA GOALS

PONDER: Flip back to pages 97–102 or the pages in your notebook and review the list of Moolala Goals you brainstormed in Step 2. Which inspire you the most? Which will improve the quality of your life in the most dramatic way? Which could you complete quickly? Which would leave you with regrets if you didn't pursue them?

____

____

____

CHOOSE: Circle two short-term goals—ones you might complete in the next three to twelve months—and two long-term goals—ones that you'll work on over a longer time span.

MOOLALA GOAL: "I WANT TO GO SKYDIVING WITHIN THE NEXT YEAR."

Plan: "I'm going to start by researching skydiving companies online. Then I'll ask my best friend to hold me accountable for achieving this goal, and maybe even do it with me! Then I'm going to book the jump date in my calendar. And finally, I'm going to jump out of the plane."

–Dawn, 33, plant manager. Single.

PUT A FEW GOALS INTO THE SLOW COOKER

My Tuscan Chicken recipe takes ten hours to cook. After you've put the ingredients into the crockpot, there is nothing to do but wait. Nothing. You don't even take the lid off to stir it, because you'll let the steam out. Some of your Moolala Goals might be like my Tuscan Chicken. You put them in your metaphorical crockpot and let them cook, not just overnight, but for years, even decades. You can have goals that you prioritize and work on actively, and goals that you don't. We have a goal to live part time in New York City during our post-paycheque phase. We talk about it and dream about it, but we're not actually doing anything specific to achieve it. And that's okay. You don't have to work on every goal on your list.

That said, don't put all your goals into the crockpot—that's procrastination, and it will virtually ensure that none of the goals on your list come to fruition.

PUT IT OUT THERE: DECLARE THE MOOLALA GOAL YOU'RE GOING TO WORK ON

Declare sounds like a pretty strong word. You're right. It is a pretty strong word. It means *to state clearly in explicit terms.* Stating your goals clearly and explicitly will go a long way towards motivating you to achieve them.

The most powerful declaration of a goal includes these three parts: *What* is the goal you're declaring? *Who* will you declare it to? And by *when* will that goal be achieved? You could declare that you'll achieve the goal in three months, in a year, or even in fifty years. It doesn't matter what the time frame actually is, but I find that goals bound by time are just more likely to be achieved.

Clearly, my career goal was one of the main priorities for me. Here is what the specific declaration was:

> **What:** Find a job in TV news
> **Who:** My best friend Tammy
> **When:** by October 31

Putting a specific goal down on paper can be both a liberating and a terrifying experience. Liberating in that you're finally getting the ball rolling. Terrifying . . . because you're finally getting the ball rolling. But after I declared my career goal to my best friend, I started to see getting a handle on my money in a different light. It was no longer a series of boring tasks. Instead, it became a means to an end that I was really inspired by: a job in TV news.

EXERCISE

DECLARE THE GOAL YOU'RE GOING TO WORK ON

CHOOSE: Choose one of your key Moolala Goals and complete the following statements.

- → **WHAT:** My goal is ____________________.
- → **WHO:** The person I'm going to declare it to is ____________________.
- → **WHEN:** It will be completed by ____________________.

DECLARE: Now you need to have the conversation with the person in your community you're going to declare your goal to. This will kick-start the support, ideas, and accountability that come with engaging your community, which will make a big difference in your achieving this goal.

SHARPEN YOUR PENCIL: DEVELOP THE PLAN TO ACHIEVE YOUR GOAL

Think of your proudest accomplishments in life. In all likelihood, they were the result of actions you took. Whether you prefer to be methodical or spontaneous, you will need to take action to achieve your goals. Taken together, the actions you identify effectively amount to a plan.

In the business world we spent months developing plans. We did focus groups, crunched numbers, and wrote copious pages, in the most intricate detail, on how to achieve the goal at hand.

You don't need to do that. While some of your Moolala Goals might be complex, I have found that often it's the simplest plan that is the most effective, *provided you take action on it*.

The way to come up with a plan for your Moolala Goals is to answer this question: "What are the actions I could take that would help me achieve my goal?"

Declare *sounds like a pretty strong word. You're right. It is a pretty strong word. It means* to state clearly in explicit terms. *Stating your goals clearly and explicitly will go a long way towards motivating you to achieve them.*

In my case, I knew I needed to do some research first, given that I had no clue how the broadcasting industry worked. I thought it would be helpful for me to take some courses to teach me some of the basic skills. And given that I was quitting a lucrative job, I needed to think about how I would pay the rent during the transition. I initially came up with a pretty rough plan that I refined by talking to other people. Here is what the plan for my career change looked like:

GOAL	STRATEGIES	ACTIONS
FIND A JOB IN TV NEWS BY OCTOBER 31.	1. Get ready for change	• Quit my job • Pay off all debt • Get a line of credit • Buy a couch
	2. Develop an understanding of the broadcasting industry	• Develop questions for informational interviews • Make appointments to talk with people • Read books and websites on the industry • Read the business section of the paper • Watch the business news channels
	3. Improve relevant skills	• Take Broadcast Performance course • Take Writing for Broadcast course • Do writing tests and get feedback on them • Prep for job interviews; focus on skills transferable to TV • Develop list of 10 story ideas to pitch
	4. Engage community	• Declare goal to close friends and family • Develop industry networking sheet and begin filling it in • Determine an accountability structure with key friend

Now it's your turn to take at crack at developing your own plan for one of your Moolala Goals.

EXERCISE

DEVELOP THE PLAN TO ACHIEVE YOUR MOOLALA GOAL

BRAINSTORM: What are the actions you could take that would help you achieve your goal? Is there any research you could do to help you understand how to achieve the goal? Who do you know who could help you in terms of support, ideas, or accountability? Who would you LIKE to know to help you? What is the financial component associated with this goal, and do you need to plan for it?

____

____

____

____

CHECK: Once you have a few ideas on paper, you can ask yourself some further questions to clarify the plan. Start by reviewing the C Factors. These are the factors that can help smart, capable people do smarter things with their money, so it is important to keep them in mind as you develop your plan.

Note that some of these questions will get you to start thinking about the financial component of your plan. Don't worry. In the next two chapters, we'll take a closer look at your cash flow, and I'll give you some ideas on how to find the money to get what you want.

THE "C FACTORS" CHECK

→ **CONTEXT:** What is the context for this plan? Why do you want to achieve this goal?

→ **CONSEQUENCES:** What are the consequences of this plan, positive and negative, tangible and intangible? Is there anything that needs to be built into the plan to address those consequences?

For example, when I quit my marketing job I had to deal with the consequences of a huge drop in income.

→ **COMPLEXITY:** What level of complexity does this plan really need? What is the simplest version that will achieve the goal?

→ **COMMUNITY:** Who in your community can you talk to for their support, ideas, and accountability? These might be people you know, or people that you don't know yet.

THE "4 S" CHECK

This next set of questions is intended to help you see what you might add or remove to make your plan even better.

→ **SUFFICIENT:** Are you taking enough actions to achieve the goal?

→ **SELECTIVE:** At the same time, are you making choices about what you're going to do, and what you're not going to do? This is key, because one pitfall is that you'll try to do too much and end up accomplishing nothing.

→ **SYNCHRONIZED:** Is the plan synchronized with your values, strengths, and circumstances? For example, I could have chosen to go back to school full time to study journalism, but that choice wouldn't have been synchronized with my need to achieve my goal quickly and to do so without incurring more debt.

→ **SUSTAINABLE:** Will you be able to work on this plan over time, or will it prove to be too ambitious to keep up, given the other things you have going on in your life?

Answering these questions and clarifying your plan accordingly will increase the probability that what you've developed will actually be as effective as possible in helping you achieve your goal.

TALK: Take your plan to someone in your community—a friend, a coworker, or an expert in the area where you want to achieve the goal. Talk through what you've developed and ask them what they think. Also, ask what they would do to achieve the goal you have. While you're knowingly asking for feedback, sometimes it can be difficult to receive feedback, so prepare yourself to hear something you don't want to hear. That said, the risk is worth it. In this case, the ideas you get from the conversations can be hugely helpful in your achieving your goal.

WADDLING TO THE MARATHON FINISH LINE: A THREE-PART PLAN

I just wanted to finish. I had no delusions about standing on the Olympic podium holding my gold medal aloft, mouthing the words to the national anthem as I wiped tears of joy from my eyes. I wasn't expecting my photo on a Wheaties cereal box, a Rolex endorsement, or a doping scandal. I just wanted to *finish* the marathon, even if I was the very last person across the line, even if I arrived well after the pylons and banners had been sent back to storage.

But if my goal had been different, if I had really wanted to become a world-class marathoner, my training plan would have been different. I would have needed a plan with a pretty high level of complexity. I would have had a coterie of doctors, psychologists, physiotherapists, nutritionists, and perhaps even psychics attuned to my physical, mental, and spiritual well-being twenty-four hours a day. There would have been a daily workout schedule that combined long runs to build cardio endurance and intervals to build speed, plus an intensive weights regime and a carefully balanced food plan.

But I didn't want to become a world-class marathoner. I just wanted to finish one marathon, specifically the one in Buffalo, New York. I enrolled in the Marathon Dynamics running clinic, and Michael, the coach, told me that my goal was totally achievable. He recommended a low-complexity plan that consisted of just three things:

- **Training runs:** Run four times a week: one long run that increased in duration by 10% each week; then a short "shake it off" run; a hill workout; and finally, a faster-paced tempo run.
- **Shoes:** Get myself checked for orthotics and then buy a pair of good running shoes.
- **Food and drink:** Eat lots of carbs before the long run, and stay hydrated throughout.

Three things. That was the extent of the plan. My point is that Michael helped me to develop a plan that had the right level of complexity to get me what I wanted, which was to cross the finish line in Buffalo.

CONCLUSION

Smart, capable people sometimes do dumb things with their money because they haven't developed a plan for their Moolala Goals. It isn't enough to just have goals. You actually need to develop a plan to make them happen. Setting priorities is an important part of the process to ensure that you don't get overwhelmed. Declaring the goal to other people will start to engage your community in helping you make it happen. And then your initial brainstorming, plus some input from others, will give you a basic plan for achieving your Moolala Goals.

While it should go without saying, I'm going to say it: You now need to take action on your plan. If you don't, you aren't likely to achieve your goals. That is why Step 4 of the Moolala Method is devoted entirely to taking action. But before we get to that, we're going to take a look at the "Moola" in Moolala—what you need to know or do to have the stash of cash to fund your Moolala Goals.

MY ONE THING

The one thing I'm committing to doing, now that I have developed a plan for one of my Moolala Goals, is ______________________________
____.

•••Chapter 11

ASSESS YOUR CASH FLOW
Why can't you just go with the flow?

At first, I blamed the person who did my laundry. Then I remembered that *I* was the person who did my laundry. So there was no disputing the fact that my pants were getting a little tight in the back. I admit that I do have a few vices. Chief among them are my holy trinity of gastronomic delight: beer, beef, and brownies. I ignored the pants problem for as long as I could, until one day I could no longer fit comfortably into my favourite jeans. That was the last straw, and I knew something had to be done—immediately.

I placed a call to a registered dietician at Health Stand Nutrition, pleading for an emergency consultation. Andrea's analysis of my eating and exercise behaviour made one thing very clear: When the calories coming in exceed the calories going out, the result is weight gain.

The focus on this nutritional fact made me think of another simple and undeniable fact about money: When cash going *out* exceeds cash coming *in,* the result is *debt.*

Many smart, capable people hope for, wish for, and sometimes even *plan* for an exception to this fundamental fact about money. We fantasize about a big lottery win, or a forgotten aunt who will leave us her millions. Perhaps a vast oil reserve will be discovered behind our garage, or our home will double in value and the stock market will outpace all reasonable estimates just as we're about to cash out.

But the truth is that most of us will not be blessed with any sort of money miracle. We'll need to get a handle on our cash flow instead.

Cash flow is simply what you earn minus what you spend. It can be either positive (more coming in than going out) or negative (more going out than coming in). You need to have positive cash flow over time in order to increase your net worth, which is why cash flow is at the base of the Priority Pyramid: it is the first area you need to focus on in getting a handle on your money.

The truth is that most of us will not be blessed with any sort of money miracle. We'll need to get a handle on our cash flow instead.

Cash flow is an area where many smart, capable people do dumb things. As we discussed earlier, sometimes they don't have an empowering personal context for money that is consistent with what they want in life, or they fail to address the negative consequences of their behaviour around money. This can lead to problems with their cash flow. Mismanaging cash flow can lead to tangible consequences, like really expensive credit card debt, and to intangible consequences, like feeling stressed and anxious about living beyond your means and not being able to achieve your Moolala Goals.

That's why in this chapter I'm going to ask you five questions that will help you assess your cash flow situation—some of which are also included on the Priority Pyramid. Then, in the following chapter, we'll look at what you can do to improve your cash flow situation, if that's what is relevant for you. And even if you learn that cash flow isn't a big issue in your situation, I recommend that you read this chapter because you might find opportunities to increase your income or reduce your spending that will allow you to achieve some of your Moolala Goals even faster.

Oh, and before we begin, let's remind ourselves why we are doing this.

> My money is for ______________________________.
> And this is why I'm working on my cash flow.

ASSESS YOUR CASH FLOW

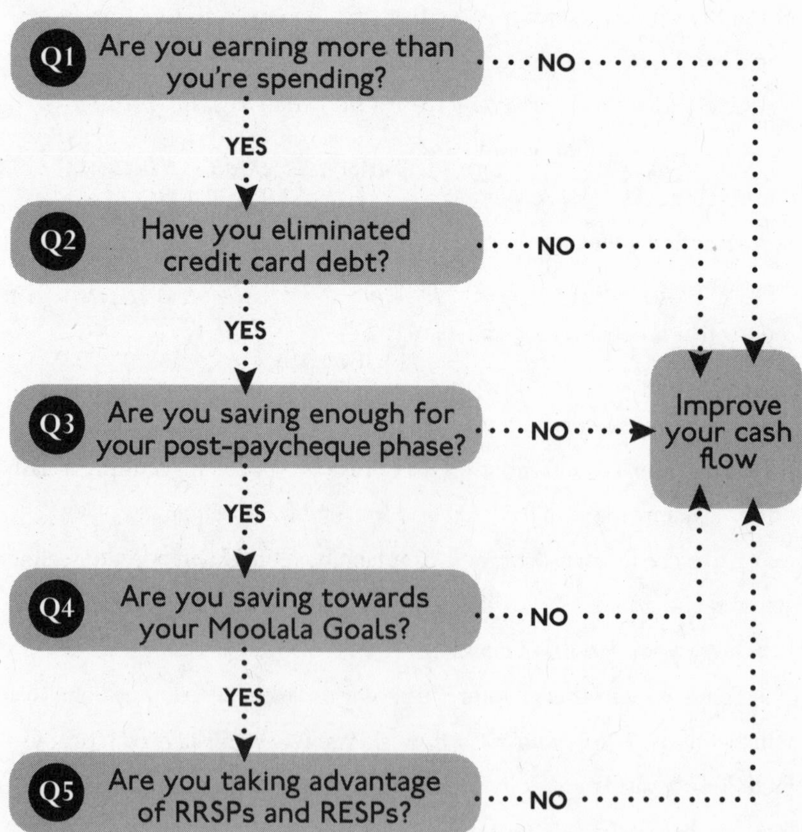

Q1 Are you earning more than you're spending?

I can always count on my favourite jeans to let me know when the calories I'm taking in exceed the calories going out. But when it comes to your money, it might not be so clear whether you're earning more than you're spending. The simple way to find the answer is to look at your last few bank account statements. Do your earnings exceed your spending over time? We'll be looking more closely at cash flow in the next chapter, so don't worry if you don't know the answer to this question right now.

A Are you earning more than you're spending?

Yes / No / Not Sure

Q2 Have you eliminated credit card debt?

This question is important because credit card debt is a huge "goal grabber." You might be spending thousands of dollars on interest payments instead of on what you really want in life. Also, if you have credit card debt, there is a strong likelihood that the answer to Question #1—"Are you earning more than you're spending?"—is also "No."

TRACK YOUR CREDIT CARD DEBT

You probably pulled your out credit card statements when you calculated your net worth a while back. Grab them again and . . .

CHECK: Look to see if you are carrying a balance over from month to month. If you are, then the answer is "No," you have not eliminated credit card debt.

NOTE: Take your pen and circle the amount of your outstanding balance, the annual interest rate that you are being charged, and the amount of interest you paid in dollars that month.

BREATHE: If you do have credit card debt, take a deep breath. At this point we're just gathering the information. And don't worry, we'll talk about how to tackle debt in the next chapter.

(A) Have you eliminated credit card debt?

Yes / No / Not Sure

(Q3) Are you saving enough for your post-paycheque phase?

There might be times in your life when you will move into a no-paycheque phase—for example, when you're changing jobs or raising kids. But, as we discussed in Chapter 6, the most critical of these is the post-paycheque phase, which will likely occur later in life, when you no longer have a full-time job, and last for a period of twenty, thirty, or even forty years.

Your answer to this question is critical when it comes to cash flow. If it is a "Yes," you can move on to Question #4. If it is a "No," you'll want to look closely at how you can improve your cash flow so you are saving enough. Most likely, your answer at this stage is some version of "How the hell would I know?" If that's you, keep reading, and I'll help you find out.

As you'll recall, I'm a big fan of figuring out the level of complexity that best fits your circumstances. Outlined below are a few different ways to find a simple answer to the question "Are you saving enough for your post-paycheque phase?" My recommendation is that

you skim through all the options, then choose the one you're most comfortable with.

Two notes of caution before you begin. First, the estimates that any of these methods produce can swing wildly based on the assumptions you use. And second, note that the answer to this question can be disconcerting. This might be the first time that you have looked at the distance between where you are today and what you want for the future. But it is a fundamental question to answer in terms of addressing the consequences of your behaviour around money. The great thing is that you're asking the question—many people never do—so you're ahead of the pack.

TODAY IN THE FOREGROUND, TOMORROW IN THE BACKGROUND

"Why are we talking about saving for our post-paycheque phase before saving for our Moolala Goals? Are you singing the same old song about retirement that everyone else seems so obsessed with?"

Good question, especially given that I've said the context of "Money is for retirement" isn't a very empowering one for most people.

When it comes to saving, I think about saving for the post-paycheque phase as being in the background, while saving for Moolala Goals is in the foreground. It isn't an all-or-nothing scenario, but rather a continuum that depends on your age and your circumstances. If you're still in your twenties, you might save for shorter-term Moolala Goals first. If you're in your forties and haven't saved a lick for your post-paycheque phase, you might decide to focus squarely on that. But if you've been saving diligently for years, you might choose to make some of your Moolala Goals more of a priority. You are the one who can best determine where on the continuum you are and where your focus needs to be for the future.

Remember that saving for your post-paycheque phase isn't just about saving for the boring essentials. In fact, it is *synonymous* with saving for the Moolala Goals that you'll achieve once you stop working. Keep in mind that your Moolala Context is for the duration of your life: today, tomorrow, and when you're seventy-five. In my case, money is for *adventure:* I want to be able to afford adventure now *and* when my hair turns grey and I dress in Tilley from head to toe. The consequence of *not* saving for my post-paycheque phase is that I *won't* be able to afford the adventures that I want later in life.

Saving for your post-paycheque phase is important because the stakes are high. If you're like me, you plan to stop working one day, which means you'll need some sort of income stream to support you. As you'll learn in this chapter, the amount of money you will need can be significant, so the earlier you start building that nest egg, the easier it will be for you to save what you need.

I know you might be wondering how you could ever save for both your post-paycheque phase and your Moolala Goals. I get it. In fact, for you this might be the next level you choose to address when it comes to dealing with the consequences of your behaviour around money, which can sometimes be a challenge. But by the end of this chapter you will have insight into how much money you'll need for your post-paycheque phase. This is an insight that even smart, capable people don't always have until it is too late for them to do much about it.

In the next chapter, I'll show you ways to improve your cash flow and free up some money for you to put towards both your post-paycheque phase and your Moolala Goals, with the least amount of complexity possible. Sure, it isn't easy, but it *is* possible to save for both, especially if you create the right context, address the consequences of your behaviour, manage your complexity, and engage your community to help you get a handle on your money.

Option 1: The 10% Savings Benchmark

The first way to answer the question of whether or not you're saving enough for your post-paycheque phase is to check your savings against the savings benchmark. Conventional wisdom says that you should save a minimum of 10% to 20% of your gross income every year. Your gross income is how much you earn before taxes have been deducted, so if you earn $70,000 before taxes, you should be saving $7,000 per year at a minimum. I know that might sound like a heck of a lot of money, but you might need a heck of a lot of money for your post-paycheque phase, depending on the lifestyle you're planning for.

EXERCISE: CALCULATE YOUR 10% SAVINGS BENCHMARK

CALCULATE: To figure out your 10% Savings Benchmark, fill in these blanks:

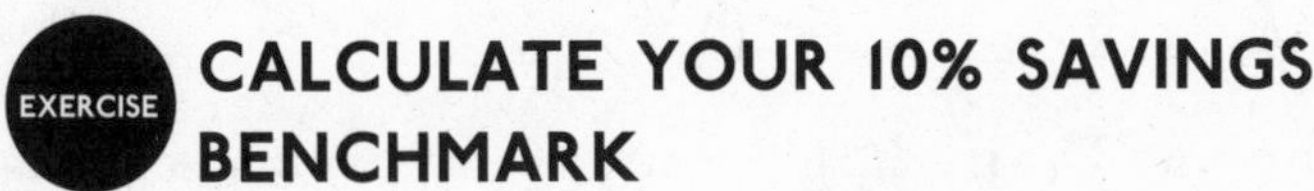

CHECK: Are you saving at least that amount every year? If, like most people, you invest in RRSPs, you can compare how your RRSP contribution measures up to your 10% Savings Benchmark. Flip through your papers to find your "Notice of Assessment" from the Canada Revenue Agency (CRA). This is the piece of paper that was mailed to you after you filed your last tax return. It will tell you what you contributed to your RRSP in the last tax year. If you can't find your Notice of Assessment, go online at www.cra-arc.gc.ca, or give the CRA a call.

A Based on the 10% Savings Benchmark, are you saving enough for your post-paycheque phase?

Yes / No / Not Sure

Option 2: The "Rule of 20"

The second approach is called the "Rule of 20." It says that you should take the annual income you want when you stop working and multiply it by 20. That will give you the lump sum amount you'll need to save in order to generate the income you want. Some, like financial services firm Russell Investments, use the number 20, others use the number 25, but the basic principles are the same. Here's how it works:

Annual Income Desired: How much income you'll need during your post-paycheque phase will depend on what sort of lifestyle you want. Are you planning pricey trips around the world, or are you happy with a simple and inexpensive life in the town where you currently live? The basic rule of thumb is that you'll need between 60% and 80% of the salary you earned in your last year of full-time work to live on during your post-paycheque phase. This is because your costs should be lower—you'll likely have paid off your mortgage and your kids will be out of college or university. So, for example, if you earn a salary of $60,000 in your last year of full-time work, your Annual Income Desired would be $36,000 at the low end of 60%, $42,000 in the middle at 70%, and $48,000 at the high end of 80%. If you are in a couple, you can combine your Annual Income Desired with that of your partner.

Lump Sum Required: Now take the Annual Income Desired and multiply it by 20. This will give you the lump sum amount you will need to save in order to generate the Annual Income Desired for your post-paycheque phase. For example, if your Annual Income Desired is

$42,000, then $42,000 × 20 = $840,000. If you want to have $42,000 coming in each year, you'll need to have saved $840,000 by the time you stop working.

Here are some other scenarios at different levels of income, using 70% of current income and the "Rule of 20."

CURRENT INCOME	$40,000	$60,000	$80,000	$100,000
70% of income	28,000	42,000	56,000	70,000
"Rule of 20"	20	20	20	20
LUMP SUM REQUIRED	$560,000	$840,000	$1,120,000	$1,400,000

APPLY THE "RULE OF 20"

CALCULATE: To calculate your Annual Desired Income, take the salary you predict you will be earning in your final year of full-time work and multiply it by 60%, 70%, or 80%, depending on the lifestyle you want to be leading.

My Annual Desired Income is $________________________.

Now multiply that number by 20.

According to the "Rule of 20," the amount of money I'll need to save for my post-paycheque phase is $____________________________.

CHECK: Are you on track to have that lump sum saved by then?

Do an Internet search for "savings goal calculator" or visit www.moolala.ca for a selection of tools that will help you figure out how long it will take you to save the lump sum you want. Here's one for your reference: http://www.bankrate.com/calculators/savings/saving-goals-calculator.aspx

A Based on the "Rule of 20," are you saving enough for your post-paycheque phase?

Yes / No / Not Sure

"So, Bruce, you're telling me that if I currently make $60,000 and want to have $42,000 a year to live off when I'm done working, I will need about $840,000 in savings?!? Are you kidding me?"

No. I'm not kidding you. And yes, it is a lot of money. But it is doable. If you think back to Chapter 3, where we talked about compound interest, you'll remember that you can build up significant savings over time, but to let the power of compound interest really work for you, you need to start saving now.

"I am sixty-three years of age, and being a procrastinator, and an 'outta sight, outta mind' kind of guy, I have not wanted to deal with money matters. I am now worried about my retirement. For the last four years, I have been financing my daughter at university, and now that she has graduated, I know I need to take care of my finances. I have $100,000 in RRSPs that I have been contributing to for the past ten years, but I fear that this isn't going to be enough. I don't want to wake up when I'm seventy years old and regret that I did not make an effort to figure this out sooner."

–Jack, 63, business owner. Single, with one adult child.

Option 3: Online retirement calculators

The third way to get an answer to the question of whether you are saving enough for your post-paycheque phase is to use an online retirement calculator.

CONSULT AN ONLINE RETIREMENT CALCULATOR

FIND: Go to www.moolala.ca for links to a few online retirement calculators. You can also do an Internet search for "retirement calculators" or choose one that is associated with your bank.

ENTER: Take a few minutes to answer the questions, which will likely include the following:

- **CURRENT AGE**
- **THE AGE YOU PLAN TO RETIRE**
- **THE NUMBER OF YEARS OF RETIREMENT:** This is a polite way of asking the age you plan to die—morbid and mostly unplannable, but still important for the exercise.
- **ANNUAL INCOME DESIRED IN RETIREMENT:** As I mentioned, the rule of thumb is that you'll need between 60% and 80% of the income you earned in your last year of work. If your Moolala Goals include lots of international travel, you might want to err on the high side. And if you're planning on something cheaper, err on the low side.
- **COMPANY PENSION PLAN:** You will be asked if you expect to draw some of your retirement income from a company pension, or if you'll be relying solely on your RRSP and government sources.
- **CURRENT VALUE OF RRSPs:** You'll want to have a recent RRSP statement at hand.

→ **CURRENT AMOUNT AND FREQUENCY OF RRSP CONTRIBUTIONS**

→ **INFLATION:** The calculator might assume a default value for inflation, but it is usually adjustable. It should be around 2% or 3% per year.

→ **INVESTMENT PERFORMANCE:** Again, the calculator might assume a default value, but one that you can change. This variable has a significant impact on your results, so if you want to be conservative, you might use 5% or 6%, and if you want to be more aggressive, you might use 7% or 8%.

CALCULATE: The calculator will use your assumptions to spit out some important numbers. It will give you an estimate of what you will have saved by the time you want to retire. And it will give you an estimate of what you'll need to have saved based on how much you want to spend in retirement. The difference between the two will give you a sense of whether or not you are saving enough for retirement.

A According to the online retirement calculator, are you saving enough for your post-paycheque phase?

Yes / No / Not Sure

Option 4: Your financial adviser

The fourth way to answer this question is to ask your financial adviser, if you have one. Your adviser will have your information in hand already and should be able to talk you through multiple scenarios, based on when you decide to stop working, how much you're saving, and how well your investments perform.

Final Answer Regardless of the method by which you arrive at the answer, are you saving enough for your post-paycheque phase?

Yes / No / Not Sure

Q4 Are you saving towards your Moolala Goals?

In Step 2 we took some time to dream about what you want in life. Experiences you want to have. Goals in areas like family and career. Things you want to buy and what sort of home you want to have. Some of those goals will require cash, so it is important to save for them. How much you need to save for each will depend on how much the goal will cost, but the key is to start saving. Again, it is important to ask yourself these questions because they shed light on whether you need to make changes to improve your cash flow.

As I mentioned earlier, while it isn't easy, it *is* possible to save for both your post-paycheque phase and your Moolala Goals. As you develop the plan to save for your Moolala Goals, keep in mind the idea of having saving for your post-paycheque phase in the background while having saving for your Moolala Goals in the foreground. To keep things as simple as possible, I recommend you set up an automatic monthly withdrawal to sock away money for your post-paycheque phase so you don't have to think about it. Then turn your attention to how you can save for the Moolala Goals that matter most to you.

A Are you saving towards your Moolala Goals?

Yes / No / Not Sure

Q5 Are you taking advantage of RRSPs and RESPs?

The government has a vested interest in you saving money—in particular, for when you stop working full time and for your children's post-secondary education. In order to encourage this behaviour, they reward you for it. We talked a bit about these savings vehicles in Chapter 8, but here's a refresher.

Registered Retirement Savings Plan (RRSP): RRSPs are important because they help you reduce the tax you have to pay and are one of the few tax breaks we have left in Canada. While the specific amounts change, essentially you are allowed to contribute a portion of your gross income to an RRSP up to a certain maximum. If you don't contribute the maximum in a given tax year, the "contribution room" carries over. What that means is that if you can't max out your RRSP one year, you'll have the opportunity to do so in future years when you have additional cash. ("Yeah, Bruce. Like THAT is ever going to happen.") The 10% Savings Benchmark that you calculated earlier should be the minimum you put into your RRSP each year.

It really is important to make the most of this tax break because income from government sources is just not going to be enough for most people to live on when they stop working.

Registered Education Savings Plan (RESP): RESPs help you save for your children's post-secondary education. You can save up to $2,500 per year in an RESP and the government will give you a grant of 20% of that amount, up to $500. The amounts might change over the years, but the basic principle is to encourage you to set aside money now that can grow over the years to offset the huge cost of tuition and living expenses associated with college or university. The RESP is a no-brainer if you have kids. The government grant means that your money automatically increases by 20%. Where else can you get a 20% return guaranteed?

What about the Tax Free Savings Account? The Tax Free Savings Account (TFSA) allows you to save money without having to pay tax on the gain. This is a good place to save for a new car or a big trip, for example. But if you earn more than about $40,000 per year, an RRSP is a better way to save for your no-paycheque phase. For simplicity, I am not covering the TFSA in detail. My belief is that most people need to first focus on the RRSP and RESP, and then look at the TFSA.

EXERCISE: CHECK THE STATUS OF YOUR RRSPs AND RESPs

RECORD: Find your Notice of Assessment again and write down how much you contributed to your RRSP last year, and the amount of "contribution room" you have currently. Also, write down how much you contributed to your child's RESP, if you have one.

A Are you taking advantage of RRSPs and RESPs?

Yes / No / Not Sure

FLIP BACK TO THE PRIORITY PYRAMID

Now that you have answers to the questions about cash flow, you'll be able to more accurately determine where you are on the Priority Pyramid. Take a moment to flip back to pages 69–71 to see which level best describes where you should focus your attention.

PANIC PREVENTION: HOW TO AVOID THE STRESS OF RRSP SEASON

- Find out what your RRSP contribution limit is for this year, which is based on your income last year. As I mentioned, this number is found on your Notice of Assessment from the CRA.
- Divide that amount by twelve to calculate a monthly number.
- Determine if you have enough money to contribute that amount each month through an automatic withdrawal. Note that if you don't start doing this in January, you won't hit the full amount you need to save by the end of December. In that case, what you should try to do is save an additional amount of money to help you meet the full contribution amount by the end of the year.

CONCLUSION

Cash flow is the foundation of the Priority Pyramid. It is the area you need to get sorted out before anything else. The five questions asked in this chapter are intended to help you assess your cash flow, so that you can better understand where you're at.

You now have answers to each of those questions. Some of you will have answered "Yes" to all five questions; if that's you, congratulations, you can move on to Chapter 13, where we address your financial advice needs. But, if you're like most people, a "No" has likely snuck in there, which means you might have some work to do. The very next thing we are going to do is figure out what you can do to improve your cash flow.

MY ONE THING

The most important thing I learned from assessing my cash flow is

____

____.

•••Chapter 12

IMPROVE YOUR CASH FLOW
What does the alphabet have to do with it?

I was not going to give up beer.

I knew that if I wanted to trim down a bit and fit back into those jeans I would need to reduce the number of calories coming in and/or increase the number going out. But my daily libation was strictly off limits. I was very clear about this boundary with Andrea, the dietician, and she wasn't fussed a bit. There are lots of ways to improve the balance of calories coming in and going out, she said. We just needed to find a way to do that that would work for me.

And that is the task that lies ahead for you, except that you'll be focusing on your cash flow instead. Grab your beverage of choice and let's get to work.

THE ABCs OF IMPROVING YOUR CASH FLOW

The Moolala approach to improving your cash flow is as simple as ABC. It goes like this: A is for *analyze,* figuring out where your money is coming from and where it's going to. B is for *brainstorming,* thinking about creative ways you could increase your income and/or decrease your expenses. And C is for *change*; this is where you actually choose the three or four things you are going to do differently, and then change your behaviour.

A diet is to food what a budget is to money, and I've got to tell you, I'm not a big fan of either.

The ABC approach is effectively the same process that Andrea used with me. We analyzed my eating behaviour, brainstormed some potential solutions, and then made some changes. She helped me figure out how many calories were in certain foods so I could find a balance between what I was eating and how much I was exercising. She advocated a way of eating that I could sustain over time, instead of following a strict "diet."

A diet is to food what a budget is to money, and I've got to tell you that with a few exceptions I'm not a big fan of either.

Here's why:

- **High failure rates:** Not many people succeed at following a budget, in large part because it is really difficult to maintain that level of discipline and attention to detail over time.

- **Too much complexity:** A strict budget is often just too complex for most people to manage over time. And it might not even be that helpful. Sure, the $5 lattes you love cost $100 per month. But there is no point tracking them when the real issue is the $500 you spend on clothes and shoes every month.

- **The pitfall of "tracking":** It is very easy to let your budget lapse into merely tracking your expenses. As we've discussed earlier, if you don't use that knowledge to alter your behaviour, then you are wasting your time.

- **Scarcity versus abundance:** A budget can feel limiting rather than liberating, and can quickly create a context of "scarcity." That context just wouldn't empower me to do the work I need to do to get a handle on my money.

Here are my exceptions, two examples where budgeting makes sense. First, budgets can work really well for a specific time period or for a specific event, like saving for your vacation or your wedding. And second, sometimes your circumstances dictate a serious change in your spending habits for a short-term period. If you've lost your job, for example, and need to watch every single penny until you have a paycheque coming in again.

Now, even though I don't budget, it is not as if I'm spending money like a madman. I know that in order to have a *lifetime of adventure*—today, tomorrow, and fifty years from now—I need to get a handle on my money. That means spending less than I earn, eliminating credit card debt, ensuring that my investments meet the performance of the benchmark index, etc. And so I used the ABC method to analyze, brainstorm, and change my behaviour around cash flow. And you can too.

A IS FOR ANALYZE: FIGURE OUT WHERE YOUR MONEY GOES

Smart, capable people often do dumb things with money because they don't know where their money is going. It is time to figure that out for yourself by analyzing your income and expenses in a little more detail. (But not too much detail. I want you to do the analysis that will give you the most insight with the least amount of complexity.) But first, let's take a look at what one of the members of the Moolala Community discovered when she analyzed her cash flow.

SEE JANE DO HER ABCs

Jane is thirty-two years old, single, and has a job in banking. She lives downtown and loves to travel. She wants to own her own condo, but hasn't started saving for it yet. Here is what her cash flow looks like.

JANE'S MONTHLY CASH FLOW

REVENUE MONTHLY		
After Tax Income	**$ 4,500.00**	
EXPENSES MONTHLY		**PERCENTAGE OF INCOME**
Rent	$ 1,700.00	38%
Car insurance	$ 100.00	2%
Car payment	$ 570.00	13%
Car gas	$ 100.00	2%
Groceries	$ 200.00	4%
Restaurants	$ 400.00	9%
Cable	$ 215.00	5%
Parking	$ 300.00	7%
Car maintenance	$ 100.00	2%
Travel	$ 100.00	2%
Piano lessons	$ 90.00	2%
Gym membership	$ 90.00	2%
Charity—foster child	$ 66.00	1%
Clothes and shoes	$ 200.00	4%
Entertainment	$ 200.00	4%
Credit card interest	$ 80.00	2%
RRSP contribution	$ –	0%
House down payment	$ –	0%
TOTAL EXPENSES	**$ 4,511.00**	**100%**
Cash Flow: + or (-)	$ (11.00)	

Analyze: Once Jane did some basic calculations, she began to analyze what her results meant. Here are some of her insights:

- "My rent eats up almost 40% of my paycheque. I've heard the rule of thumb that it should be in the range of 30% or $1,300. Oops."
- "My car expenses account for 26% of my paycheque, which is completely insane given that I live and work on the transit line."
- "I love to travel but feel trapped by all the other expenses I have."
- "I'm paying a lot in credit card interest. I guess that's the consequence of having a $5,000 balance on my card, at a 19% interest rate. Ewwww."
- "I haven't been making RRSP contributions, and while I'd really like to be saving for the down payment on a condo, I haven't started yet."

Now it's your turn.

EXERCISE

ANALYZE WHERE YOUR MONEY IS COMING FROM AND GOING TO

REMIND: Be sure that you have your Moolala Context in mind. Why on earth would you bother to look at your cash flow if there wasn't a bigger benefit to you?

My money is for ______________________________.

CALCULATE: Using the worksheet on pages 187–89 or from www.moolala.ca, figure out what income you have coming in, after taxes, and what expenses you have going out. If you have access to a spreadsheet, it will make things easier. You can also download a template from www.moolala.ca. Feel free to add and/or delete categories for both income and expenses so that this analysis reflects your individual circumstances as accurately as possible.

INCOME: If you have a job where you get paid a regular salary, look at the amount that is deposited into your bank account every month. If you're a contractor, freelancer, or work part time and your income swings up and down depending on the month, total up what you earned over the last twelve months and divide that number by twelve to come up with a monthly number. This will give you a rough starting point.

EXPENSES: The objective is to figure out approximately what you spend on average each month. The easiest way to do this is to take twelve months of credit card statements and bank statements and input the expenses you have incurred over the course of the year. Your credit card statement might already break expenses down into various categories, so you can use those for simplicity. And If you don't know the exact number for something, use an approximation. Total up the month-by-month expenses, then divide by twelve to come up with an average monthly number in each area.

Then calculate how much your three to five biggest expenses are as a percentage of your after-tax income. This will help you better identify the big areas to focus on. Here's the math for your rent, for example:

Rent ÷ after-tax income X 100 = ______ % of income.

ANALYZE YOUR CASH FLOW WORKSHEET

REVENUE MONTHLY

After Tax Income $ ____________________

EXPENSES MONTHLY		**PERCENTAGE OF INCOME**
Mortgage / Rent	$________	________%
Property taxes	$________	________%
Condo fees	$________	________%
Home insurance	$________	________%
Utilities—gas, electricity, water, telephone	$________	________%
Cable TV	$________	________%
Internet	$________	________%
Cellphone	$________	________%
Home maintenance	$________	________%
Public transit	$________	________%
Car payments	$________	________%
Car insurance	$________	________%
Car maintenance	$________	________%
Parking	$________	________%
Gas	$________	________%
Groceries	$________	________%
Restaurants	$________	________%
Clothing (including shoes, accessories, etc.)	$________	________%
Health expenses (prescriptions, dental bills, glasses, massages, etc.)	$________	________%

EXPENSES MONTHLY		PERCENTAGE OF INCOME
Beauty expenses (haircuts, tanning salon, etc.)	$________	________%
Childcare	$________	________%
Kids' activities (hockey fees, Kumon, etc.)	$________	________%
Vacations	$________	________%
Entertainment	$________	________%
Newspaper/magazine subscriptions	$________	________%
Gifts	$________	________%
Credit card payments	$________	________%
Credit card Interest	$________	________%
Loan payments	$________	________%
Line of credit payments	$________	________%
RRSP contributions	$________	________%
Moolala Goals savings	$________	________%
Other investments	$________	________%
Other savings	$________	________%
Other expenses	$________	________%
	$________	________%
	$________	________%
	$________	________%
TOTAL EXPENSES	$________	100%
Cash Flow: + or (-)	$________	________%

ANALYZE: Good for you for getting to this point. Trust me, this is more than most people ever do. If you have a positive cash flow—more income than expenses—keep reading for some ideas on how to improve your situation so you can achieve your Moolala Goals sooner. And if it is negative, don't worry. The rest of this chapter is about how to improve your cash flow.

First, let's take a look at what you learned from this exercise.

What insights do you have about your income?

____

____

What insights do you have about your expenses? Does anything surprise you? ____________________________________

____

What are the consequences of your behaviour around expenses, both tangible and intangible? How does it fit with your Moolala Context? How does it fit with your Moolala Goals?

____

____

Which expenses are habits, like buying lunch at the office every day? And which are choices, like karate lessons for the kids?

____

____

What does a trusted friend or family member see from your cash flow analysis?

____

____

B IS FOR BRAINSTORM: GET CREATIVE ABOUT HOW YOU CAN IMPROVE YOUR CASH FLOW

When I wanted to lose a few pounds, I had three options: Reduce the number of calories I took in by pulling back a bit on the beer, beef, and brownies. Increase the number of calories I burned off by running more frequently or for a longer duration. Or do a bit of both. The same applies to your money. You can increase your income, reduce your expenses, or do a bit of both. Here are some examples of what members of the Moolala Community have committed to doing:

Improve Income

- "Work some additional overtime."
- "Get a second job on weekends."
- "Sell stuff on eBay."
- "Rent out the cottage and use the revenue to pay down the line of credit."
- "Get a roommate to offset my mortgage payments."
- "Rent out my garage."
- "Call my HR manager and find out about the company stock plan."

Reduce Expenses

- "Move to a smaller apartment."
- "Reduce the number of meals I eat out, especially lunch."
- "Sell my car."
- "Cancel cable, gym membership, and piano lessons."
- "Pause charitable contributions for the time being."
- "Get rid of land line at home."
- "Combine cellphone plans among family members."
- "Set up automatic withdrawal from my bank account directly into my RRSP account so there is no way I can spend the money."

- “Put the money I’m spending on rent towards a mortgage instead. I could borrow money from my RRSP under the Home Buyers’ Plan to fund the down payment on a condo.”
- “Put my credit cards in a sandwich bag in the freezer.”
- “Talk to my family about cutting down on gift giving.”
- “Call my credit card company and ask them to reduce my credit limit so I’m less likely to use it.”

There are a few things to remember as you move into the brainstorming phase.

→ **Improving your cash flow is about getting a handle on your money so you can live the life you want:** It isn’t just about raising income and cutting expenses. You might find that you even increase expenses in some areas in order to achieve your goals faster. For example, you may choose to cut expenses by moving to a smaller house, so that you can increase the amount you spend on travel—maybe a big trip to Europe every year.

→ **Remember that you aren’t actually committing to anything in the brainstorming phase:** You are just bringing some options to the table.

→ **It will take some creativity to imagine your life in a different way:** We hold deeply ingrained assumptions about what our life should look like and what we deserve. Those assumptions can make it difficult to even consider different choices concerning income and expenses. For you to get a handle on your money, you might need to consider changing some things that until today were sacred to you, that you couldn’t imagine living without.

HANDS OFF MY CABLE TV!

You didn't throw a party to celebrate the new channels you got on your expanded cable TV package, but does the thought of cutting back on the channels you can have send you into a deep-blue funk? Don't worry, you're not alone. Behavioural economists point to a concept called "loss aversion" to explain why the negative impact of losing something often outweighs the positive benefit of gaining something else. Human beings are more averse to losing than they are happy about gaining.

And it isn't so much about the reality of the loss, but the perception. Loss aversion helps to explain your bias towards the status quo. We have a tendency to want to keep things the way they are, even if they aren't working. That way, at least we won't have to make any changes that might lead us to lose something, even if it's at the expense of what we stand to gain.

Now that you understand a bit better how your brain functions, how do you work around your own loss aversion so that you can align your behaviour around money to support the life you want to live?

KIDS HAVE TANTRUMS. ADULTS MAKE TRADE-OFFS

Three-year-olds want it all, and they want it now. If they don't get it, they have tantrums. Adults can still have tantrums, but more likely they make trade-offs. Consider the idea that everything you spend money on is a trade-off. It sometimes won't feel as though you have any choice in the matter—like when you're paying for heat in the middle of a cold winter. But it can be a liberating perspective to consider that everything you do around money is a trade-off that you have some say in. You are in the driver's seat, and you are trading one thing off for another, even if you're not conscious that you're doing it. Some of those trade-offs work for you and some don't. Here are some examples of areas where people commonly make trade-offs:

Income: By and large, as individuals, we choose what we do to earn money. There might be factors that lead us to a certain choice, or that make some choices very difficult to pursue, but we certainly have influence in terms of how much income is coming through the door. Still, we're often unaware of the trade-offs we make in the area of income.

"I actually know how to earn more money—they are always looking for people to take more shifts at work. But I really like my weekends. What I realized was that I was trading off peace of mind. I was pretty stressed about my credit card debt, so I finally traded off a few months of Saturdays to earn more money and get rid of the debt."

–Howard, 28, technician. Married.

Expenses: When you decide to spend money on one thing, it isn't available for you to spend on something else. We often feel trapped by our expenses, instead of seeing them as trade-offs we're making.

"The thought of selling our second car was really upsetting to us. But the amount we were spending on car payments, gas, and insurance meant that we couldn't save for our kids' education. They are ten and twelve years old, and we hadn't put away a dime in RESPs. I really don't love taking transit, but I'm happier knowing that they'll graduate from university with less debt."

–Jenna, 46, store manager. Married, with two children.

Time: Your challenge might be devoting sufficient time and energy to getting a handle on your money. Certainly the idea of shifting how you spend time is difficult for most people, so it can be really valuable to be clear about the trade-off you're making.

"I have the mental capability to learn more about money. I just don't have the time. But I guess if I'm really honest with myself I know that I could just get up

an hour earlier two days a week for a few weeks to work through this book. I really, really value getting seven hours of sleep, but you're right: It's a trade-off."

–Eric, 40, musician. Single.

Communication: You might be someone who avoids talking about money for fear of looking stupid. A lot of people deal with this, even with their financial adviser, the person paid to answer even the dumbest questions. Is the trade-off of avoiding the hit to your self-confidence really worth not getting a handle on your money?

"I'm a successful lawyer and quite used to feeling confident in my business dealings. It was way more comfortable to pretend that I understood what my financial adviser was saying than to admit that I really had no clue. Yeah, I guess it was a trade-off, and eventually the benefit of being informed trumped the cost of admitting my ignorance to her."

–Megan, 38, lawyer. Single.

BRAINSTORM WAYS TO IMPROVE YOUR CASH FLOW

Now I'm going to have you do a bit of brainstorming. You may come up with ideas about things to STOP doing (stop eating out three times a week), as well as things to START doing (setting up automatic bank withdrawal for your "Volunteer in Africa" account). Your circumstances will indicate where the biggest opportunities lie. And by the way, I don't expect that all these ideas will be as appealing to you as a week at the Four Seasons Resort in Costa Rica in February.

BRAINSTORM: Jot down some ideas below or in your notebook for how you could improve your income and/or reduce your expenses.

What are some ways you could increase your income?

___

___

___

What are some ways to reduce your expenses?

___

___

___

TALK: Have conversations with two people in your community and ask them for their perspective on your ideas. Do they have any other ideas? Which ones do they think will be the most effective? I appreciate that talking to people in your community about your cash flow will take a great deal of trust on your part. But remember, communities provide support, ideas, and accountability. And you might really be able to use some of those right now.

"I keep a wee envelope in my wallet and every time I deny myself a latte, I put that amount of money into the envelope to keep the savings real. Or even better, I leave my wallet in the car when shopping so that I have to go back and get it. It calms the impulses to act when the energy to buy is the highest—at the point of discovery."

–Marty, 49, consultant. Partnered, with two stepchildren.

C IS FOR CHANGE: COMMIT TO CHANGING BEHAVIOURS THAT DON'T WORK FOR YOU

The final component of the ABC model is to actually follow through on *change* by changing some key behaviours. Andrea, the dietician, taught me that it wasn't all or nothing. With her guidance I figured out a short list of things I was going to change about my eating habits. I reduced the amount of protein I ate, increased the fruits and vegetables, and set a limit on my beer, beef, and brownies to 300 calories per day. Change is the hardest part of the ABC model, but it works.

What are the changes you're willing to commit to that will make the biggest difference in your cash flow and improve your ability to achieve your Moolala Goals?

COMMIT TO MAKING CHANGES

CHOOSE: Write down the two or three changes that you will commit to making to improve your cash flow. Keep it simple—don't try to do thirty things at once.

TALK: Have conversations with at least two people in your community to tell them what changes you have committed to making. Ask them to check in with you once a month to see how it is going for you.

CONCLUSION

Improving your cash flow is a critical part of getting from where you are today to where you want to be. It deserves all the focus and attention you can give it, because if you aren't earning more than you're spending, it will be virtually impossible for you to get a handle on your money. But you aren't alone in all this. In the next chapter, we're going to address your financial advice needs. Perhaps a great financial adviser would make all the difference for you.

MY ONE THING

The one thing I'm committing to changing to improve my cash flow is

____

____.

•••Chapter 13

WORKING WITH A FINANCIAL ADVISER

Are you making the most of the relationship?

The water pump looks as if it was manufactured at the dawn of the Industrial Revolution. Manual gauges, a few simple bolts, and a round, grey casing that would not look out of place on Apollo 11. Given its age, and the total absence of anything electronic about it, you would think the water pump would be simple to operate. Sadly, that has never been the case for me. I am just not handy. Every spring at the cottage my shortcomings as a handyman are on prominent display as I try to get the pump up and running. Instead of fiddling, fussing, cursing, and pleading—which I have done my share of in the past—I usually end up calling the plumber. He comes to the cottage and magically makes things work without charging me an arm and a leg.

George, my next-door neighbour, has a different approach. He is much handier than I am and seems to get his water running every spring *without* a mayday call for professional help. We both get to the same result—water flowing from the taps—but using two different approaches.

When it comes to your money, specifically your investments, you have the same choice to make. Do you use the services of a financial adviser, or do you do it yourself? This is a really important question, and one that often stirs a passionate response from advocates on both sides of the discussion.

I am not an advocate of either approach. Rather, I am an advocate of you getting a handle on your money, using whatever approach works for you.

Financial adviser or do it yourself? I am not an advocate of either approach. Rather, I am an advocate of you getting a handle on your money, using whatever approach works for you.

I have seen people do that brilliantly, on their own or working with an adviser. And I have seen people fail spectacularly, on their own or working with an adviser.

DO IT YOURSELF VERSUS WORKING WITH A FINANCIAL ADVISER

Do It Yourself (DIY): Martha Stewart showed aspiring cooks how to torch crème brûlée in their own kitchens. Home Depot made simple tiling jobs accessible to the masses. And over the last decade, the big financial institutions have made it easy for regular folks to manage their investments online. Some DIY-ers are very successful on their own. They are willing to invest the time and energy it takes to manage their portfolios, in exchange for lower costs. Others try going solo but end up getting dismal results because they either do the wrong thing or they do nothing. Without a doubt, these people could benefit from the insight and experience of a good adviser.

Working with a financial adviser: Personal trainers can make a big difference in you achieving your personal health goals. Career coaches, life coaches, and even interior designers all provide professional advice that can help you get what you want in their respective areas. Many people are happy to pay for a great financial adviser who will help them get clear on their goals, create a plan, and ensure they stick to it. They get great results and peace of mind.

And then there are those people who *have* financial advisers but don't get the value for the money they're paying, either because the adviser isn't up to snuff, or because they aren't actually taking the advice they've been given. People in this category often think that simply *having* an adviser = good advice. But it isn't enough. You actually need to cultivate a *strong* relationship with a *good* adviser, and then *follow up* and take the actions that the adviser prescribes.

Whether you do your own financial planning or work with an adviser is a personal choice, and one that can change over time depending on your life stage and circumstances. My aim is to help you make that choice for yourself and then show you what you need to do to get a handle on your money so you can live the life you want—no matter which approach you choose.

In this chapter, we're going to look at the ins and outs of working with a financial adviser. And in the next chapter, we'll talk about the Do It Yourself approach—what it entails, and how to know if it makes sense for you.

GRADING YOUR FINANCIAL ADVISER

If I had my way, I would get my hair cut just once a year. I don't really care what it looks like and I find it kind of annoying that I have to fit the appointment into my schedule when I could be doing something more fun. Unfortunately, my hair is something that requires periodic attention, like my money. Interestingly, many people spend much more time thinking about their hair (or their car or their golf swing) than their money. So let's start there. Here are my criteria for a good hairstylist:

- **Haircut:** Good-quality cut, done the same way every time.
- **Location:** Near my work or home.
- **Price:** Under $40.
- **Magazines:** A supply of celebrity magazines, preferably *People*. This isn't a must, but it's certainly a bonus.
- **Communication:** No interruptions while I read said magazines, and no sales pitch for products like pomegranate pomade.

Your criteria for a good hairstylist will likely differ from mine. And in all likelihood, your criteria for what makes a good financial adviser will differ from mine, too.

Whether you already have a financial adviser or are thinking about using one, the first step for you is to determine the criteria that matter most to you. And once you're clear on what's important to you, I'll show you how to give your financial adviser a score based on that criteria.

DETERMINE THE CRITERIA

Here are the criteria that I use to assess a financial adviser.

Delivers performance that meets the benchmark index:

In my view, this is fundamental—as fundamental as a hairstylist delivering a good haircut. Your financial adviser should deliver performance that, at a minimum, meets the benchmark index over a period of time. A financial adviser can give great customer service, host spectacular client appreciation events, and know the names and birthdays of all your children, but does he deliver performance? Or does she take the time to help you understand the numbers?

✓ *"Quite frankly, I'm not really interested in my money. But every year I go in for a meeting with my adviser and she shows me how my money did over the last twelve months, and how the relevant benchmark indices did by comparison. There are blips above and below over the years, but even with the fees she charges, I'm doing better than the benchmark index."*

–Nancy, 53, marine biologist. Married, with two children.

✗ *"I have no idea how my investments have done versus the benchmark index. The only information on my statement is how the funds themselves performed, so I have nothing to compare it to."*

–Markus, 33, customer service rep. Married.

Communicates in a way that works for you: I sometimes hear people complain that they are intimidated by their advisers and don't feel they can ask them questions. This is an issue, because it's tough to get "advice" if you don't feel as though you can talk openly with the person you're paying to provide it. You want to feel as comfortable discussing sensitive personal issues with your financial adviser as you would with your family doctor. A great financial adviser is someone you feel comfortable talking to, who listens to your needs, and who stays in contact as frequently as you wish and in the way that works best for you. Do you want to connect in person every few months? Or would you prefer phone or e-mail? How often do you want your adviser to provide a perspective on market events: Monthly? Annually? Never?

✗ *"I always seem to leave her office feeling stupid. She constantly talks over my head, and I've just given up trying to get her to explain things to me simply."*

–Michelle, 43, event planner. Married.

✓ *"Our teenage son went into rehab to deal with an addiction. We felt we could trust our adviser with this news, and he was able to help us navigate the financial implications of what was a really tough time for us."*

–Andrew, 50, systems analyst. Married, with three children.

Provides solid advice and doesn't just sell products: An accountant makes her money by offering advice. So does a lawyer. Generally speaking, it is a transactional relationship—they give you advice and you pay for it. But most financial advisers work on a commission basis. They make their money by building up a large roster of clients and by selling them financial products like mutual funds, from which they earn a commission. (See "Checking the price tag" at the end of this chapter.) Great financial advisers are able to deliver solid financial advice and sell products at the same time. They adjust what they provide based on your needs, which will evolve over time depending on your life stage and circumstances. The not-so-great ones sometimes focus too much on the sell and too little on the advice. Has your adviser taken the time to get to know you? Or to develop a written investment plan based on your goals? Do you feel as though you've been getting good advice over time?

✓ *"My elderly mother recently had her driver's licence revoked. Our financial adviser helped us formulate ways to keep Mom mobile and to use income from her portfolio to fund things like in-home care, the use of a car service, etc. We weren't sure how we could afford these things until she showed us the math."*

–Moira, 45, fundraiser. Married, with one child.

✗ *"I don't think I have ever really received any financial advice. Every year she tells me which mutual fund to put my money into, but that's the extent of it."*

–Derek, 45, sales rep. Married, with two children.

Understands and works on all of your goals: Great financial advisers understand the big picture and can think holistically about goal-setting. Their primary focus is likely going to be on planning for your post-paycheque phase, given its importance to your future. But great advisers will also provide financial advice for how you can achieve your goals in other areas, whether it's *experiences* you want to have (cycling in France), *contributions* you want to make (volunteering in Africa), *career* goals you want to achieve (becoming a VP, working part time), or *things* you want to buy (a new car, Wimbledon tickets). Has your financial adviser asked you about your life goals? Did she engage in the conversation? Do you feel like she has a sense of the big picture?

✘ *"I have tried to talk to our adviser about other things—setting up a charitable foundation, financing the addition on our house, etc.—but he just didn't seem interested."*

–Sanjay, 53, lawyer. Married, with three children.

✓ *"I have three goals that I'm working towards: saving for the down payment on a house, saving to take time off to travel, and investing for my retirement. My adviser came up with a plan to support all three goals in a way that still allowed me to splurge on the occasional pair of shoes."*

–Maxine, 36, marketing manager. Single, with one child.

Holds you accountable for achieving those goals: If you pay a personal trainer $90 a session, she'll make sure you complete the prescribed number of push-ups. You're paying a financial adviser a whole lot more than that, so he should not only provide you with ideas and support, but also hold you to account, to ensure you do what you need to do to get a handle on your money. The great financial advisers will follow up with you on your goals to ensure you're on track and give you the support you need to achieve them. Does your adviser do that? Does your adviser follow up when you don't do something you agreed to do?

✓ *"We have been with our adviser for about three years but hadn't been great at sticking to our financial commitments. We were addicted to a few financial vices and were not saving what we had agreed to save. She booked an appointment with us and pointed this out—graciously, but firmly. And she said she couldn't continue to provide advice to us if we weren't going to take it. I was shocked at first, but then incredibly impressed that she would consider losing our business to hold on to her own integrity. It was a wake-up call, and we decided to shape up and do what she recommended, as painful as it was."*

–Shannon, 38, consultant. Married, with three children.

✗ *"Accountability? My guy just sells me a mutual fund every winter. That's it. That's all."*

–Casey, 34, graphic designer. Single.

EXERCISE GRADE YOUR FINANCIAL ADVISER

PONDER: Think about the criteria above. Which are relevant to you and your situation? Are there other criteria you would add to help you assess a financial adviser? Even if you don't have one currently, doing the first part of this exercise will highlight what would be important for you, which will be useful if you ever do start looking for one.

CHOOSE: Write down below five criteria you would say matter the most to you in your relationship with your financial adviser. They can appear in any order you like.

CRITERIA	SCORE (1 TO 10)
1.	
2.	
3.	
4.	
5.	
TOTAL	/50 %

SCORE: Give your financial adviser a score between 1 and 10 based on how well he or she does on each criterion, with 1 = low and 10 = high. Before you write anything down, I recommend that you choose a number that represents the minimum acceptable score a financial adviser should meet for you to be satisfied. The minimum acceptable score for most people seems to be around 35/50 or 70%. But this is entirely your call, and you can set the bar higher or lower.

CALCULATE: Add up the numbers to determine your financial adviser's total score. Did your adviser score above or below your minimum acceptable number?

WRITE: The assessment above might have captured most of your feelings about your financial adviser, or you might have other thoughts. Take a moment to identify any other aspects to that relationship that you would say are strengths or weaknesses.

____

____

____

SHARE: Discuss the results of this exercise with someone in your community. Ask them if your results are similar or different from their experience, and how their relationship with their adviser works. Sharing it out loud will crystallize what you noticed and also increase the chances of you doing something to improve the financial advice you get.

MAKE IT WORTH EVERY PENNY: FOSTERING A GREAT RELATIONSHIP WITH YOUR FINANCIAL ADVISER

You now have a better sense of how your financial adviser is doing on the criteria that matter to you. If the score you came up with exceeded your minimum acceptable score, you should call him or her and lay on the kudos. Clearly, your adviser deserves it. And consider sharing your good fortune by referring a friend or two.

If your financial adviser failed to meet your minimum acceptable score, you have three options. You can rejuvenate the relationship with your adviser, find a new financial adviser, or choose the Do It Yourself approach, which we will cover in the next chapter.

My view is that you should make an effort to rejuvenate your relationship with your financial adviser before you try to find a new one. Sometimes people get frustrated and move on without really making an effort to help the current relationship work, and then they face the same issues with their new adviser.

Let's start with that option first.

OPTION 1: REJUVENATE YOUR RELATIONSHIP WITH YOUR CURRENT FINANCIAL ADVISER

I talk to financial advisers all the time who wish their clients took more personal accountability for their financial situation and were more engaged in the process. So, in all likelihood, your adviser will welcome your efforts to rejuvenate the relationship, especially when the alternative might be that you decide to walk away and find a new adviser.

Rejuvenating your relationship with your financial adviser is about clearing up any issues that might exist between the two of you, and then setting expectations for how you're going to work together successfully in the future. To help guide the conversation I have outlined some questions below. You can ask them in whatever order makes sense to you, and add a few of your own if you feel like it. And remember—you are paying for the services of a financial adviser, and you are the one who is accountable for getting your money's worth, not them.

QUESTIONS TO HELP YOU REJUVENATE YOUR RELATIONSHIP WITH YOUR FINANCIAL ADVISER

Performance:

- How has my portfolio performed versus the benchmark indices over the past year? Over the last five years?
- Can you help me understand what these results mean?

It is critical to talk about investment performance because it can make a huge difference to your financial health, and it can affect your ability to pursue your Moolala Goals. This topic will also prompt your adviser to explain why your portfolio performed the way it did, which is good information for you.

Strategy:

- What is the strategy of each part of my portfolio?

REJUVENATING THE RELATIONSHIP: CLEARING THE AIR

"I think my financial adviser was just as relieved as I was to have the conversation. I've been her client for many years now, but definitely not a very involved one. When the stock market hit the skids a few years ago, I was really upset. We had a few very terse conversations, but didn't really resolve anything. Since then there was this polite distance whenever we spoke, which was infrequently. The thing is, I like her and believe she really is committed to doing a great job. That was enough for me to book a meeting with her and go through some of the 'rejuvenate' questions. We started with the one about the relationship and all my angst poured out. She wasn't at all defensive, and after clearing the air we talked about how we were going to work together in the months ahead. I feel like my confidence in our relationship has been restored."

–Simon, 45, university professor. Married, with one child.

It is important for you to get a sense of whether your financial adviser can explain to you why each investment product is included. If you have fifteen different mutual funds, for example, it is appropriate to ask why. This topic will also open up the lines of communication and demonstrate your interest in becoming more engaged with your money.

Relationship:

- What are the strengths of our relationship?
- What are the weaknesses of our relationship?

This is an opportunity for you both to address what has and hasn't been working for you in your relationship. You can use the criteria in your assessment above as a starting point. This might be new territory for you to discuss with this person, so don't be surprised if it is a tough conversation to have.

The Future:

- How are we going to work together in the future?
- How are we going to make sure we check in on how the relationship is going?

Assuming that you do want to continue your working relationship with this adviser, this is the time to set some expectations for how you're going to work together in the future.

How are you going to achieve performance that meets the benchmark over time? How do you want to communicate? What advice do you want? What support do you need on your other Moolala Goals? What do you want your adviser to hold you accountable for?

It is also important that you build in a few checkpoints down the line—perhaps once every three months, to see if you're on track in rejuvenating the relationship.

BOOK: Pick up the phone, dial the number, and say, "Hi there. I would like to book a time for us to talk about a few things. When might work for you?" You could also send the same request via e-mail.

PREP: Bring the results of the "Assess your mutual fund performance" exercise you did on your investment performance in Chapter 8 so that you already know whether or not you are matching the performance of the benchmark index. Then take a look through the list of questions above and choose which ones are most relevant to you. Keep in mind other questions that might be relevant to your situation that you could also ask. You might also want to review the questions in the next section, "Option 2: Find a new financial adviser," in case it spurs other ideas. Some people find it helpful to send the questions to their financial adviser in advance, but be sure to bring the list of questions with you when you meet. There is a printable version at www.moolala.ca.

ASK: Now have the conversation. For a lot of people it makes sense to take notes, especially when you talk about how you are going to work together in the future.

CHECK: Listen to your intuition. What was your experience of this meeting with your financial adviser? Did you feel as though he or she listened to you? Did your adviser provide some ideas or solutions on how you could work better together in the future?

CHOOSE: Are you going to make the effort to rejuvenate your relationship with your financial adviser? If your answer is "yes," that's great. Turn back to the questions in the previous section starting on page 208 if you think it might be helpful to have another conversation to set clear expectations. If, on the other hand, your answer is "no," you aren't committed to rejuvenating your relationship, see the sidebar "Breaking up (with your financial adviser) isn't so hard to do," then move on to Option 2, finding a new financial adviser.

BREAKING UP (WITH YOUR FINANCIAL ADVISER) ISN'T SO HARD TO DO

The day you hired your financial adviser, was there a minister present? Was there an exchange of rings? Did you dance to great '80s music and wake up hungover the next day? I thought not. With a few exceptions perhaps, you did not *marry* your financial adviser. It might feel that way, but you didn't actually promise "till death do us part." This is a business relationship, and one you are paying a fair amount of money to maintain. If it isn't working for you, you can move on to someone else.

What might surprise you is that if you do choose to leave, the logistics are fairly easy.

Find a new adviser first: Remember that this is not a marriage. You don't need to leave your current adviser before you find a new one. In fact, it's preferable that you have a new one in place so that your investments can be transferred from one adviser to the other as easily as possible.

Update your current adviser: Let them know that you have decided to change advisers. You aren't under any obligation to tell them why, though it might help *them* a lot to know why you chose to leave.

If your adviser is a friend, the conversation can be tougher. In that case, you might ask them to refer you to someone else because you don't want your business relationship to interfere with your personal relationship.

You might be concerned that the breakup conversation will be stressful, and therefore you have been procrastinating about it. The fact is, you don't actually have to have it. You can sign on with your new adviser and they will sort out the transfer with your current adviser so you don't have to be involved.

Wait out the time it takes to transfer: Changing financial advisers is much harder emotionally than logistically. Your new firm leads the process and will give you some paperwork to sign. They have a vested interest in you transferring your money to them, and so it is generally a fairly painless process from your perspective.

When it comes to moving from one adviser to another, it's usually best to hold on to your investments until *after* you move. The new adviser will have an opinion on any refinements you should make to your investment plan and how to minimize something called *Deferred Sales Charges* (we'll cover this in more detail later). So it is usually best to wait to make changes until after the money has been moved, with a few exceptions that your new financial adviser will tell you about if applicable.

OPTION 2: FIND A NEW FINANCIAL ADVISER

If you have decided that you're unhappy with your current financial adviser, and even making the effort to rejuvenate the relationship didn't work, the next option is to find a new adviser. This is also an option if you're a Do It Yourself investor who wants some more support, ideas, and accountability with your money.

Aside from you yourself, your financial adviser is often the most important person in helping you get a handle on your money so you can live the life you want. And yet often, smart, capable people don't invest enough time and energy in hiring the right person for the job. Like shopping for a new car, or a wedding dress, finding a financial adviser who is right for you is well worth the effort, because of the support, ideas, and accountability they'll provide.

FINDING A NEW ADVISER: A BREATH OF FRESH AIR

"I am so glad I went out on a limb and found a new adviser. It took some work but was totally worth the effort. I feel like I have formed a great partnership with my new adviser—one in which we can both openly express where we're at. When I identify goals, she holds me to them, and if she feels like I'm not pulling my weight she lets me know. She is totally approachable and proactive in her advice.

"The transfer from my old adviser to my new one was relatively easy. He was hurt when I told him about the change, but then my new adviser took over and managed the process completely. It took longer than I expected—over three months—but I am so glad I made the move."

–Sharon, 48, business analyst. Single, with one child.

The first resource I would call on in your search for a new financial adviser is your community. They may be able to supply names of people whom they already work with, whom you could interview. Once you have some candidates I recommend setting up an interview with your top three. Use that time to discuss the questions below, in addition to any that relate to your criteria for what makes a great financial adviser.

QUESTIONS TO HELP YOU ASSESS FINANCIAL ADVISER CANDIDATES

Getting to know you:

- How long have you been a financial adviser?
- Why are you in this line of work?
- What designations do you have, and what does each of them mean?

- How many clients do you have, and what is the average size of their portfolios?
- How would you describe your approach?
- Do you create a written investment policy statement or plan for your clients?
- How do you invest your own money?

These questions are intended to help you learn more about the adviser as a person and about their approach. It is important to see if there is a good fit, both on tangible attributes, like years of experience and professional designations, and intangible ones, like communication style and temperament.

If your portfolio is smaller than that of most of the adviser's clients, do you feel confident that they'll try hard to build your net worth to match the others, or do you fear that you will get less attention because you're a less profitable customer? Also, if you need a lot of advice, knowing how many clients they have might give you a sense of how much attention you can expect from this financial adviser.

I prefer advisers who draft an investment policy statement or written plan, because having it on paper makes it much easier to follow up on.

These questions are also designed to help you gauge the adviser's willingness to disclose information, to give you a sense of their credibility, and to determine if your values fit with theirs.

Fees:

- Can you tell me, based on a portfolio of my size, how much I would be paying in commissions and fees?
- Which commissions are negotiable?
- How are these costs paid? Annually? Quarterly? And do I pay them out of pocket, or from the income of the portfolio?

It is important for you to be really clear on what you are paying, even if it doesn't come directly "out of your pocket," like the management fees (MER) on mutual funds. If they say "You don't pay anything," I would run for the hills. I have never heard of anyone getting great financial advice for free. (Note that there are full details on how advisers are paid at the end of this chapter.) Not many commissions are negotiable, with the exception of front-end loads. That said, firms sometimes have administrative fees that can be waived at the discretion of the adviser.

This part of the interview will also help you to assess how comfortable the adviser is talking about fees and commissions. Great advisers generally have no issue with this conversation.

Performance:

- Will you provide me with regular updates on my investment performance versus the benchmark index?
- Can you show me an example of a statement?

This set of questions has two purposes. First, to see if the adviser's firm is set up to show investment performance versus benchmarks over time. Not all are. And second, to reinforce that this is something that is important to you.

Life goals:

- How do you factor in my life goals that aren't related to retirement or investments?

I would want to know if the new adviser is willing and able to think holistically about your goals. Some are, and love to hear that you are going to engage in the process at that high a level. Others simply aren't. They focus only on investments and don't have the time or inclination to give you advice in other areas. There is nothing wrong with this approach, but it makes sense to know in advance.

After completing these interviews, circle back to your original set of criteria and ask yourself which of the candidates you think will best be able to deliver on your needs. Be sure to factor in your own intuition about who is going to be the best "fit" for you. Then choose.

FIND A NEW FINANCIAL ADVISER

ASK: Put out the request to family, friends, and colleagues for financial advisers they like. Be sure to give them a sense of the criteria you've identified above so they really know what you're looking for.

INTERVIEW: Have conversations with at least three potential advisers so you have a sense of the different personalities and approaches.

CHOOSE: Based on the criteria you outlined earlier, decide which financial adviser you think will be able to provide what it is that you are looking for.

START OFF ON THE RIGHT FOOT: SETTING EXPECTATIONS WITH A NEW ADVISER

Good for you for putting yourself out there and doing the work to find a new adviser. Now that you have made your choice, it is really important for both of you to talk about your expectations and get clear on how the relationship is going to work. The questions above were intended to help you assess potential advisers. Now that you have made your choice, the questions below will help you set expectations and ensure the relationship works effectively.

There are two objectives for any conversation about expectations. First, obviously, is to go over the expectations themselves, both yours and your adviser's. Second, and even more valuable, is to create a touchstone that you can return to over time. If things aren't going the way you want them to, you can refer to your initial conversation about expectations, saying either, "We agreed to do X and we're not doing it," or, "I realize we didn't cover this when we were talking about expectations, but I'd like to add it to the list."

QUESTIONS TO HELP YOU SET EXPECTATIONS WITH YOUR NEW FINANCIAL ADVISER

Context:

- I want to tell you about what money is for, for me, so you understand where I'm coming from.
- Here are some of the goals that I have, some of which I'd like your help in bringing to life.
- I have learned some things about my strengths and weaknesses in dealing with my money. Here are the highlights, so you're aware of them.
- I want to cover off a few other things that you should know about working with me, like key relationships and potential life changes.
- What are some of your goals?

You asked in your interview if your new financial adviser was willing to help you with your holistic list of goals. Now is the time to tell them what those goals actually are, as well as any other details that will allow them to support you in getting a handle on your money. They should also know about your key relationships, like current and former spouses, elderly parents, children, and secret illegitimate children. You should also tell them about potential life changes ahead, like if you are planning on having a baby, getting married, going back to school, or awaiting a big, fat inheritance.

The last question is a bonus. I always like to know what other people are working towards in life because I think it makes for a richer, more interesting relationship.

Behaviour:

- What is your preferred method of communication—phone, e-mail? How often should I expect to talk to you, and for what reasons?
- What should I do when I don't understand something?
- How do we make sure you hold me accountable to my plan?

These questions give you an opportunity to discuss what is expected of each of you. For example, some clients want a lot of contact with their adviser, and others want very little. These questions will clarify what would be best for everyone.

Every adviser worth their salt is happy to take any questions you have. It is often the client who is reticent to ask, because they don't want to look stupid. This sets the expectation that you'll both have questions. It also gives you a chance to talk about what level of complexity you want to get into with your adviser. You might want the details on everything, or you might have more of a "need to know" perspective.

The final question ensures that you talk about accountability.

CHECKING THE PRICE TAG: HOW TO FIGURE OUT WHAT YOU'RE PAYING FOR FINANCIAL ADVICE

You probably know how much you pay for a litre of gas, a movie, your cellphone plan, or a Starbucks Grande Non Fat Tazo Chai Latte. You might not *like* what you're paying, but at least you know *how much* you're paying. Many smart, capable people don't really *know* how much they are paying for financial advice, so they don't understand the *consequences* of not getting value for their money. And some people actually think they're getting their financial advice for free. Yeah, right. Here's a quick look at the various fees and commissions you could be paying.

MANAGEMENT EXPENSES AND THE MER

As you'll recall, if you own mutual funds in your portfolio, you are paying the mutual fund company a fee. It is referred to as the "management expense ratio" or MER. The average MER for a Canadian Equity mutual fund is about 2.3%. So, for every $10,000 you have invested, you pay on average $230 in fees to the mutual fund company every year. These fees can really add up over time as your investment portfolio grows. And obviously the amount you pay goes up the more money you have invested. As you get closer to your post-paycheque phase, you might have upwards of $500,000 or even $1 million in your account, which could mean an average of $11,500 to $23,000 is going out the door in fees every year. As we've seen, management fees are one of the main reasons why many mutual funds so rarely beat the performance of the benchmark index.

COMMISSIONS PAID TO FINANCIAL ADVISERS

In addition to management fees, you might also be paying commissions to your financial adviser, depending on which type of financial adviser you have. There are basically four different compensation models, each with its own own pros and cons.

Commission-based: This is by far the most prevalent model in Canada today. In this model, financial advisers sell investment products on commission. While stocks, bonds, and GICs generate sales commissions, mutual funds usually generate both sales commissions and trailing commissions.

- **Sales commission:** Advisers may earn a sales commission when the mutual fund is bought or sold. There are essentially three different types of sales commissions, which also are called loads. These commissions are in addition to the MERs you pay every year:

  Front-end load: You pay a one-time commission when you buy the mutual fund, also known as paying at the "front end." This commission could range from 0% to 5% and is sometimes negotiable.

  Back-end load or "deferred sales charge" (DSC): You pay a one-time commission when you sell the mutual fund, which is known as paying at the "back end." The amount of commission you pay declines over time, starting at about 7% if you sell the fund within the first year, and declining by 1% for each subsequent year, all the way down to 0% if you hold the fund for seven years. What many investors don't understand is that the adviser is paid his or her commission when the fund is purchased. This commission is usually 5%, making DSC funds very profitable for the adviser.

The DSC is intended to keep you in the fund as long as possible, so the fund company continues to earn the MER. The challenge for you is that it sometimes doesn't make sense to hold the fund for seven years—your circumstances could change, or the fund could perform poorly. However, because the DSC is so steep, it creates a disincentive for you to sell the mutual fund before the seven years are up. For example, if you held $10,000 in a DSC mutual fund and wanted to sell it after only two years, you would have to pay 5%, or $500, as a deferred sales charge.

No-load: You don't pay a sales commission when you buy or sell a "no-load" fund.

→ **Trailing commissions:** These are also called "trailer fees" and they are paid to your financial adviser for as long as you hold the mutual fund. The fee paid is usually about 1% of the value of your investment, depending on the type of mutual fund, and it is already included in the MER. So, for example, if you hold $50,000 in mutual funds, you are paying about $1,150 in management fees, and of that $1,150, just over $500 is being paid to your financial adviser as a trailing commission for as long as you own the funds.

The trailer fee is what really distinguishes financial advisers from other commission-based salespeople. When you buy a car, the salesperson earns a one-time commission and that's it. They don't earn a commission every year for as long as you own the car. But when you buy a mutual fund, your adviser keeps earning that trailing commission every year. The rationale is that your financial adviser will continue to provide you with value-added advice over the course of the year, whereas you won't see your car salesman again until you buy a new model a few years down the road. Hence, my obsession with ensuring that you're getting good value for the fees and commissions that you're paying.

For a financial adviser to make a great living, he or she might aim to have three hundred clients, each with at least $300,000 in investments. Setting aside the sales commissions for a moment, that would generate about $900,000 in trailer fees every year for the firm. The percentage that the financial adviser keeps depends on a number of factors, including the size of the firm and the amount of commission they're generating overall. But a successful adviser who is able to land three hundred clients of this size would bring in about $450,000 and take home about $270,000 per year.

Fee-based: The second compensation model is the fee-based model, in which advisers charge 1% to 1.5% of the value of your assets to manage your portfolio, but generally do not earn the trailer fee offered by the mutual fund companies. This model is generally targeted towards investors with more than $500,000 in investments. At that level, based on a fee of 1.5%, the adviser would bring in about $7,500 in fees from that client per year. You shouldn't have to pay anything out of pocket because a portfolio of that size would generate sufficient income to cover the fee. For a non-RRSP account, this fee might be tax deductible, which is a nice plus.

Fee-only: In this model, financial advisers provide you with financial advice and you pay a flat fee for it. The amount starts at around $1,000, depending on the complexity of the plan. Fee-only planners are tough to find in Canada, in large part because it isn't as lucrative a business as the fee-based or commission-based model. A simple financial plan for a client with $500,000 might earn a fee-only adviser a one-time fee of $3,000, nowhere near what a commission- or fee-based adviser would earn every year on that account.

Salary: There are also some financial advisers who are on salary. Proponents of this model say it allows advisers to be more objective about what they recommend. Investment advisers at bank branches often fall into this category. Their focus is usually on selling products like mutual funds or GICs versus stocks and bonds. The products are most often "no-load"—meaning that there is no sales commission to the financial adviser—but, as with most mutual funds, you would still pay an MER.

The amount of money you pay for financial advice is important for a couple of reasons. First, it is a big sum of money in and of itself. What else would you spend $1,150 every year on? An all-inclusive trip to Cuba? A new couch? And second, it is important because what you pay has a big impact on your investment performance. You can't "control" how the stock market performs, but you can control the fees you are paying. The bottom line is that fees can significantly impact your financial well-being over time, and that is why you need to make sure that your financial adviser delivers the performance, advice, and service you expect.

CONCLUSION

A great financial adviser can be an important partner to have when it comes to getting your finances in order. Your adviser can help you stay focused on your Moolala Context for money and alert you to the consequences of your behaviour. Advisers can greatly reduce the complexity you have with your finances by taking care of details and helping you

determine what you really need to focus on. And, perhaps most importantly, a great financial adviser becomes a key member of your community, ready and able to provide support, ideas, and accountability to help you get a handle on your money so you can live the life you want.

As helpful as a great financial adviser can be, not everyone needs one. Another approach to your money is to Do It Yourself. That is the focus of our next chapter.

MY ONE THING

The one thing I'm going to do to get more for the money I'm spending on financial advice is ______________________________________

____.

•••Chapter 14

DO IT YOURSELF
Is a DIY approach to your finances right for you?

A few years ago, for my birthday, I received a copy of *The Gourmet Cookbook*. It had a bright yellow cover and was four inches thick, 1,039 pages long, and completely intimidating. It featured recipes like "Pistachio Turkey Ballottine with Madeira Sauce" and "Apricot Soufflés with Vanilla Rum Crème Anglaise." There were absolutely no photographs except the one of the author on the inside back cover. Her smile seemed to say, "I dare you. Just try to make the Tatsoi and Warm Scallop Salad with Spicy Pecan Praline." If this was "Do It Yourself cooking" I wasn't having any of it, and I hid the cookbook in a corner cupboard, behind the roasting pan.

The next year I received a second cookbook for my birthday. It was called *The Art of Simple Food*. It had a warm pastel-yellow cover, was under two inches thick, 405 pages long, and completely welcoming. It featured recipes like "Roasting a Chicken" and "Sautéed Shrimp with Garlic and Parsley." I understood most of the words in the index, and I loved the homey, hand-drawn illustrations. The author photo inside the back cover seemed to say, "Come on. Try it. It will turn out just fine." This book gave me the confidence to stretch outside my comfort zone, and I started using it immediately.

The Gourmet Cookbook was way too complex for me. But *The Art of Simple Food* was just right, and it allowed me to make things, inexpensively at home, that I had only ever eaten in expensive restaurants. This may be the case for you, too, when it comes to getting a handle on your money.

The Art of Simple Food *allowed me to make things, inexpensively at home, that I had only ever eaten in expensive restaurants. This may be the case for you, too, when it comes to getting a handle on your money.*

THE BENEFITS OF DIY: WHAT'S IN IT FOR YOU

In the previous chapter, we covered how to rejuvenate your relationship with your current financial adviser (if you have one), and how to find a new one (if that's what you want). Now, some of you may be giving some thought to "Doing It Yourself," even if only for a portion of your portfolio. While Do It Yourself investing isn't right for everyone, many smart, capable people are now taking it on, for two main reasons.

→ **Simplicity:** DIY investing has become much simpler. Investing is following the trend that has unfolded in the travel industry over the last twenty years. You used to have to go to a travel agent to book your flights. Now everyone has access to the same fares online. Don't get me wrong, travel agents still do lots of great work on complicated itineraries. But for a low-complexity international flight, you don't really need a travel agent any more. The same might be true for your money. You now have access to the tools that years ago were available only to the pros. The most significant advance in DIY investing has been the arrival of the online discount brokerage. All the big banks operate them, and they make the logistics of investing online as simple as banking online.

- **Low Fees:** Financial advisers and mutual fund managers deserve to be paid, of course, but as we've discussed earlier, often the fees that they charge to manage your investments eat up any gains your investments have made. Discount brokers charge very low fees, so DIY can be a much less expensive option, which can help improve your investment performance.

"I was really excited to try doing my own investing. I wanted to be more in control of my money, even though I have never really been interested in personal finance in the past. Given that my situation is pretty simple, this approach made sense to me. I just followed the steps as prescribed, and it worked.

"Now, six or seven months into it, I don't even think about it. I can see online that my money is still there—it goes up and goes down every once in while—but I don't freak out about it any more."

–Barry, 42, director. Single, with two children.

DIY VERSUS FINANCIAL ADVISER: THINGS TO THINK ABOUT

There are a number of things I would recommend you think about before you make a choice to Do It Yourself, use a financial adviser, or combine the two approaches.

- **Willingness to do some work yourself:** It will definitely take some time and energy to manage your investments yourself. One of the major advantages of having an adviser is that they have the tools and the time to do much of the work for you. But the trade-off is that you'll be paying for that expertise and convenience. In the next chapter, I'm going to take you through a very simple investment plan that you can put into action really quickly, but you still have to be willing to do some work yourself.

- **Complexity of your finances:** If your financial situation is complex—you have multiple trading accounts, assets in foreign countries, and business investments—it might make more sense for you to work with a financial adviser to help you keep on top of everything. But if, like most Canadians, you have a financial situation that is fairly straightforward—an RRSP and RESPs for your kids—it might be worth it for you to consider doing it yourself to save on the fees.

- **Need for personal service:** For many people, the cost of an adviser pays off because they like having someone who is paid to talk to them about their money. They are willing to live with the higher MERs of mutual funds because they derive a great deal of value from the relationship. This can be a significant benefit, and a compelling reason to work with an adviser.

- **Value of investments:** How much money you have to invest is also a factor. Most Canadians don't have the $300,000 to $500,000 that fee-based advisers require you to have. That's one of the main reasons why most people work with commission-based advisers and pay an average of 2.3% on their mutual

> funds, instead of the 1% to 1.5% they would pay with a fee-based adviser. While you're building your nest egg, especially if you're in your twenties, thirties, or forties, you might consider the DIY approach for now, and then move to an adviser later, as your portfolio grows in value and/or complexity.

Now, if you're thinking about the "Do It Yourself" approach, even for a part of your portfolio, you probably have some questions. First among them: What does this really entail? Is this like buying an airline ticket online? Or is it like making Peking Duck?

Before you get all freaked out about this idea of doing your own investing, let me assure you of two things. First, there are many great advisers out there who can get you solid investment returns and save you time and energy, and if that is the route you want to take, fantastic. Second, the Moolala approach is simple, simple, simple. We'll talk more about the Moolala "Do It Yourself" Investment Plan in the next chapter, but first, here are the basics on getting started.

TAKING THE FIRST STEP: OPEN A DISCOUNT BROKERAGE ACCOUNT

You have a bank account, right? Was opening one a traumatic experience? I thought not. This won't be either. I'm going to show you precisely how to open up a discount brokerage account, step by step. Bookmark this page, bring it with you to the bank, and don't hesitate to refer to it. The bank employee will be curious. Show them the book. See if they can pronounce "Moolala" with a straight face. Here's what you need to do.

- **Call your local bank branch and book an appointment to open a discount brokerage account:** I know, many of you probably haven't seen the inside of a branch in years, but they do still exist. And while you can open a discount brokerage account online, I think you'll appreciate the personal touch. You want to have the name, e-mail address, and phone number of one particular person at the bank that you can contact if you need additional support. And you may need additional support. Allow yourself at least an hour for the appointment because there is a bunch of paperwork to go through.

→ **Get yourself ready for the appointment:** Track down any statements that show investments that you currently have. That way, you can begin the process of transferring your money over right away. Also, bring your photo ID, your bank card, and perhaps a coffee.

→ **Arrive on time and be charming:** Sometimes banks deliver bad service and sometimes they just get a bad rap. Remember that the person serving you can save you a lot of time and aggravation, so arrive on time and be charming. There is often a fee of $100 or so to set up the account if you have less than $25,000 to put into it, but sometimes the kind person will waive it.

→ **Ask the banker to open up two accounts:** The first is an RRSP account, and this is where you'll be investing for your post-paycheque phase. As I mentioned earlier, it is critical that you start saving for this as early as possible, as you'll need a good sum of money to pay your expenses during the twenty to forty years of your post-paycheque phase. The second account to open is a Tax Free Savings Account, if you don't already have one. It can be used to save for some of your shorter-term Moolala Goals or for after you've hit your maximum contribution limit on your RRSP. Even if you think that the likelihood of you ever maxing out your RRSP is the same as Mick Jagger being sainted, a TFSA is worth having. (Note that interest earned on money held in a TFSA isn't subject to tax. But if the sum of money in the account isn't that large, a regular savings account might work almost as well as a TFSA in saving for your Moolala Goals.) Have the nice bank person connect the accounts to your primary bank account so you can easily transfer money into them.

- **Answer a whole bunch of questions:** The bank employee will ask you a bunch of questions, in adherence to the "Know Your Client" regulations. Don't play macho here—this isn't a job interview. If you don't have much experience, say so. The reason they ask these questions is to ensure that beginners don't have access to services that can cause great financial harm if used incorrectly, so it's in your best interests to answer honestly.

- **Optional:** Once the accounts are active, transfer some money over: If you are ready to make an RRSP contribution, ask the banker to transfer money from your bank account into the RRSP, just to get things started.

- **Optional:** If you have a steady paycheque, I would strongly advise you to set up automatic withdrawals from your bank account into your RRSP account. The money goes to the right place automatically and you don't have to scramble during RRSP season in February to find the money to make your contribution. Make sure that you increase the amount of the auto-withdrawal if/when you get a raise at work. To remind yourself of what your monthly RRSP contribution should be, you can refer to the "Panic prevention: How to avoid the stress of RRSP season" sidebar on page 180.

- **Optional:** Transfer existing investments from other places: This is where you ask the banker to begin the process of transferring over whatever accounts you might have elsewhere. For example, if you have decided not to work with your financial adviser any more, then the person at the bank will have you sign the forms to transfer your money over.

- **Thank the banker:** Thank them for their help and ask for their business card with an e-mail address and phone number. Yes, there are call centres, and yes, you will use those call centres at some point, but it is really nice to have a specific, real person to get in touch with if you have questions. They won't be able to provide you with financial advice, but they can answer any "I can't get my account to do this" questions.

- **Log on to your bank's website and check things out:** It might take a few days, but soon you'll be able to see those new accounts live on the Web. How cool is that? If you can't see them, call the nice banker. Tour around the site and see where things are. Make yourself at home.

DISCOUNT BROKERS: FREQUENTLY ASKED QUESTIONS

How do I know which online discount brokerage to use?

Simplicity, simplicity, simplicity. In this case, that might mean opening up a discount brokerage account where you do most of your banking.

That will enable you to easily link your bank accounts together and see them all on one screen. That said, some of the independent discount brokers have gotten really good at connecting their services to your bank accounts, making transfers just as easy. Your call.

But don't some of them offer better products and better deals?

When all you're buying is butter, sugar, milk, and eggs it really doesn't matter which store stocks the organic arugula or sells the rice wine vinegar at a 20% discount. Sometimes one offers a better deal than another, but they are all pretty competitive when it comes to trading commissions. And while some are easier to navigate or provide better investment research, it's more important to get you set up and using the accounts as quickly and easily as possible.

What fees should I expect to pay?

There might be an administrative fee of $100 or so per year, and you'll pay a commission on the transactions you make, though these are usually under $20. If you buy mutual funds through your discount broker you'll also be paying the MER.

How much time will it take to manage my investments?

If you follow the Moolala DIY Investment Plan we'll be discussing in the next chapter, it will take you less than two hours, four times a year. Seriously simple, simple, simple.

Do I need to start reading the business section of the newspaper?

No! You can if you'd like to, but you really don't need to know how the economy or stock markets are performing to get a handle on your money.

CONCLUSION

Whether you work with an adviser or do it yourself, what's important is that you're getting a handle on your money, and doing so at a level of complexity that's right for you. While advisers are a great option, more people are turning to DIY investing because it's simpler than ever before and costs less. Regardless of which option you choose, it is critically important to put your money to work for you.

In the next chapter, we're going to focus on two things: how to develop your investment plan, and how to make butter tarts. I love butter tarts. Do you love butter tarts?

MY ONE THING

The one thing I need to think about to help me make my choice between working with a financial adviser and doing it myself is

____

____.

•••Chapter 15

DEVELOP YOUR INVESTMENT PLAN

What is the simplest way to get a handle on your investments?

AUNT MARG'S BUTTER TARTS

Pastry for 12 tarts, unbaked

⅓ cup butter (softened)

1 cup brown sugar

2 tbsp cream

1 egg, beaten

1 tsp vanilla

Beat all ingredients together and spoon into tart shells. Bake at 450 degrees for about 8 minutes.

I love butter tarts. My mom made them many, many times as I was growing up, and now I make them too. And I love *these* butter tarts in particular because they are runny, delicious, and incredibly simple to make. I use store-bought pastry shells and always keep some in the freezer, at the ready.

The recipe for butter tarts doesn't need to be complex. It is simply a function of three things: what, how much, and how.

- **What:** Pastry shells, butter, brown sugar, cream, egg, and vanilla.
- **How much:** 12 pastry shells, ⅓ cup butter, 1 cup brown sugar, 2 tbsp cream, 1 egg, and 1 tsp vanilla.
- **How:** Beat all ingredients together and spoon into tart shells. Bake at 450 degrees for about 8 minutes.

The recipe for your investment plan doesn't need to be complex either. In this chapter we are going to look at the *what, how much,* and *how* of developing one for you. This is a critical step in getting a handle on your money, so you can live the life you want.

The idea of developing an investment plan might make you uneasy. But the fact is that anyone who would like to stop needing a paycheque one day needs an investment plan. Remember in Chapter 11 we looked at whether or not you were saving enough for your post-paycheque phase? Your investments are what will provide you with the income to live on when you stop working. And in order to build up those investments, you need to have a plan. Investing, as opposed to simply saving, might also be right for some of your longer-horizon Moolala Goals. See the "Save for the short term, invest for the long term" sidebar on page 238 for more details.

Now, some of you will follow a "Do It Yourself" approach, and some of you will partner with a financial adviser on your investment plan. His or her recipe for your investment plan could be more complex

SAVE FOR THE SHORT TERM, INVEST FOR THE LONG TERM

Some of your Moolala Goals have a short time horizon—say, under five years. For example, you might be planning to take time off to travel or have a baby, or build an addition onto your house. For these shorter-horizon goals, you'll want to save your money in low-risk ways, like depositing cash into a Tax Free Savings Account (TFSA), or buying guaranteed investment certificates (GICs). Low risk makes sense because you don't have time to wait for your investments to rebound if they decline in value. For Moolala Goals with a much longer time horizon—say, more than ten years—you can take some more risk because you won't need the money until much further into the future. In fact, if your post-paycheque phase is more than ten years away, you'll need to take more risk to generate a higher return so that your money will grow faster than inflation.

than the one I'm going to take you through here, but it won't likely be fundamentally different. We'll talk about how to work with your adviser to develop your investment plan later in this chapter, but it is probably still worth you reading the section below so that you'll have a better understanding of how your adviser's recipe compares.

Ready? Okay, here we go.

THE MOOLALA "DO IT YOURSELF" INVESTMENT PLAN—THE RECIPE

The recipe for your investment plan certainly *could* be complicated. You could have all different sorts of "what." The amounts in "how much" could vary wildly and change frequently. And you could follow an almost

infinite number of approaches on the "how." But does it really *need* to be that complicated? I would argue no. For most people, a very basic and simple investment plan works really well.

Let's begin with the "what."

TEACHING SHERPAS TO BAKE BUTTER TARTS

Imagine for a moment that you grew up in the mountains of Nepal, in the shadow of Annapurna. In that culture, butter tarts are not on the menu, so it is unlikely that you would ever have made them. You probably wouldn't ever have tasted vanilla, and you wouldn't know what a pastry shell looked like. Aunt Marg's butter tart recipe would be unfamiliar to you in every way. But with some time in our kitchen and a little help from my mom, you could learn to identify and measure the ingredients. In fact, I'm quite confident that you could learn to bake butter tarts quite successfully.

Now, you aren't a Sherpa from Nepal. But you might be someone who has never followed a recipe for an investment plan. So before we bake the recipe (or do the actual investing) I'm going to introduce you to the ingredients.

"WHAT" GOES INTO THE RECIPE

Pastry shells, butter, brown sugar, cream, egg, and vanilla.

There are three basic types of assets (or ingredients): equity, fixed income, and cash. When you put money into any of these different asset types you will have what is called a *portfolio.* Now don't you sound fancy? And you want to have some of each ingredient in your portfolio, for different reasons.

Equity: This refers to stocks, and mutual funds that invest in stocks. With equity investments, you own a little tiny piece of a company. You could own an actual share of a company like Coca-Cola. Or you could own a unit of a mutual fund that owns shares in Coca-Cola.

The first reason you would have some equity in your portfolio is for growth. Provided the company is successful, the value of that tiny piece should earn you a good return on your investment over time. The second reason is that some types of equity investments pay you something called a *dividend*. A dividend is essentially your share of the company's profits, and the amount can change over time. As history has demonstrated, sometimes violently, equity investments are not without risk. Shares in companies can go up and they can go down. But taking some risk is important because you want your money to grow for you, so that you can afford to live off the income during your post-paycheque phase.

Fixed Income: This is another word for bonds, and mutual funds that invest in bonds. While equity represents a small ownership stake in a company, with fixed income investments you are actually lending money to a company or a government in the form of a bond. They then pay you interest on that loan. For example, when the Government of Canada needs money to fund the construction of roads and bridges, it raises money by selling bonds and agrees to pay the buyers interest on those bonds. That interest, or income, is fixed.

There are two reasons why you would have fixed income in your portfolio: 1) you will need the income to live off during your post-paycheque phase, and 2) fixed income is lower risk than equity and so helps to reduce the volatility caused by the equity portion of your portfolio.

Cash: Cash can literally mean the cash in your bank account, or the assets that you could turn quickly into cash at low or no risk to your

investment. For example, anything you've put into a "money market" account is considered cash.

EACH INGREDIENT HAS ITS PURPOSE

Butter tarts need sugar to make them sweet, butter to make them creamy, and the pastry shell to hold it all together. Like the ingredients in butter tarts, each ingredient in your investment plan has a different purpose.

Equities are higher risk, but they generally perform better than fixed income over time. Over a twenty-year period you would expect equities to grow about 6% to 8% a year on average, with some big swings higher and big swings lower along the way. If you hold only equities, you will be hit harder when the stock market inevitably dips, as it did in 2008. If you were invested entirely in equity in 2008, your portfolio likely declined by 40%. In contrast, fixed income investments are lower risk, but they earn only 3% to 4% a year over a long-term time horizon. If you hold only fixed income, you'll be safer during market dips, but if the stock market jumps 40%, you'll miss the entire gain.

Butter tarts need sugar to make them sweet, butter to make them creamy, and the pastry shell to hold it all together. Like the ingredients in butter tarts, each ingredient in your investment plan has a different purpose.

This is why it's important to hold a mix of assets in your portfolio. This strategy is called "diversification," and it puts into practice the age-old advice, "Don't put all of your eggs in one basket." Having a diversified portfolio with a good mix of each asset enables you to take advantage of the great years on the stock market and to minimize the impact of the bad years.

INFLATION CAN TAKE A BIG BITE OUT OF YOUR BUTTER TARTS

People often wonder why everyone doesn't have a portfolio made up of all low-risk fixed income investments. The answer, in a word is this: inflation. Inflation refers to the increase in prices over time, and it's one of the main reasons why you need your money to increase more than the 3% to 4% return per year that you would get from investing in fixed income.

Ask anyone over the age of forty about how prices have changed, and they'll agree that prices definitely increase over time. When I first became addicted to coffee in 1989, I could buy a cup for about $1.00. Today, I'm lucky if I can get one for $1.89, and that isn't just because Starbucks has taken over the world. It is also because inflation has been running at about 2% a year for the last twenty years. That upward trend will likely continue, meaning that my cup of coffee will likely cost $2.51 twenty years from now. So if all your money is in fixed income investments earning only 3% a year, you'll barely be keeping ahead of inflation, making it more difficult for you to buy the coffee you want when you're seventy-five years old.

COMPOUNDING CAN MULTIPLY YOUR BUTTER TARTS

I first talked about compounding in Chapter 3. Let's say you invested $300 per month, every month over thirty years, from age thirty-five to age sixty-five, for a total of $108,000. If at the end of the thirty-year period your average annual return was 3%, about the average for fixed income investments, you would end up with $175,000, for a gain of $67,000. If your return was 7%, the long-term average for equity investments, you would have $368,000, for a gain of $260,000. That is a difference of almost $200,000.

So you will want to hold some of both fixed income and equity asset types in your portfolio. We'll get to how much of each in a minute.

ALL SUGAR DOESN'T TASTE THE SAME: WHITE, BROWN, AND TURBANDINO

Sugar can be white, brown, or turbandino. Butter can be salted or unsalted, and come from a cow or a goat. The "what" of butter tart ingredients can also be more precisely defined. And if you were teaching a Sherpa how to make my Aunt Marg's recipe, these details would be relevant.

As it relates to your investment plan, in addition to fixed income, the types of equity you'll have are Canadian equity, U.S. equity, and global equity. This means you'll own a little piece of various companies in each of those three regions. The idea again is "diversification." The stock market in Canada behaves differently from those in other parts of the world—markets go up and down at different times and with varying degrees. So by investing in other regions you won't have all your eggs in "one basket." The "what" of the butter tart recipe is just six ingredients: pastry shells, butter, brown sugar, cream, egg, and vanilla. The "what" of the Moolala DIY investment plan is just four ingredients. Yep, just four.

THE MOOLALA DIY INVESTMENT PLAN—THE RECIPE

WHAT	HOW MUCH	HOW
Canadian equity		
U.S. equity		
Global equity		
Fixed income		

WHAT ABOUT MY HOUSE? A NOTE ABOUT OTHER ASSET TYPES

Our focus has been on fixed income and equity investments, but you likely have other assets on your net worth statement. There are three in particular I'd like to highlight.

- **Real estate:** Your home isn't included in your investment plan because you won't easily be able to draw income from it during your post-paycheque phase. Sure, it is an important asset, and you've already included it in your net worth statement. But when it comes to planning for your long-term future, you can't really count on your home to generate income unless you're going to sell it and invest the proceeds. A lot of people talk about using this strategy, but not that many people actually do it because it isn't that easy. Selling a single-family home in the burbs and "downsizing" to a new two-bedroom condo downtown reduces the number of rooms you have to dust, but it might not free up that much money. Also, people get attached to their home and their neighbourhood and often aren't willing to move to another location when the time comes. There are other options for how you could use real estate to generate income—like getting a reverse mortgage or buying rental properties—but these are more complex and outside the scope of this book.

- **Jewellery and art:** For the same reason as real estate, your bling isn't included in your investment plan, because you aren't that likely to sell it to generate income.

- **Defined benefit pension plans:** Aren't you a lucky thing? Congratulations! Defined benefit pension plans are becoming rarer and rarer these days, but some people still have them. If you are one of those people, it means that you have a "defined" amount of income coming to you when you stop drawing a paycheque. It also means that you'll have less room to contribute to an RRSP. If you have a defined benefit pension plan, the question to ask yourself is whether or not the amount of income you're going to receive will fund the lifestyle that you want. If it will, great. Pour yourself a margarita. If it won't, it makes sense to develop an investment plan alongside your pension to give you more financial flexibility during your post-paycheque phase.

So, now you have a sense of "what" goes into the recipe for the Moolala DIY Investment Plan. Next we need to look at "how much" of each ingredient goes into your portfolio.

"HOW MUCH" OF EACH INGREDIENT GOES INTO THE RECIPE

12 pastry shells, ⅓ cup butter, 1 cup brown sugar, 2 tbsp cream, 1 egg, and 1 tsp vanilla.

As mentioned above, it is crucial for your portfolio to have some of both types of assets, fixed income and equity. *How much* of each ingredient you have is referred to as your *asset allocation*—and people will talk about how much you *allocate* to each asset type. Your asset allocation is determined, in part, by your age.

FIXED INCOME = YOUR AGE: A SIMPLE RULE OF THUMB

The most common benchmark is that the percentage of fixed income in your portfolio should equal your age. So if you're forty years old, you should have about 40% of your portfolio in fixed income and the remaining 60% in equities. The reason for this is that when you're younger, you can take more risk. If the stock market falls there is more time for your portfolio to rebound. But as you get older you'll want to have less risk—that means more fixed income and less equity—because you'll be needing access to the money sooner and relying more on the *income* in the phrase *fixed income*. You'll be less concerned about your portfolio growing and more concerned about it holding onto its value and how well it spins off income for you to pay your bills and fulfill your Moolala Goals.

In the case of someone who is forty years old, the Moolala DIY Investment Plan allocates 40% of the portfolio to fixed income. The remaining 60% equity portion is divided into three equal parts of 20% each. This recipe will give you exposure to the stock market here in Canada (20%), the United States (20%), and globally (20%).

THE MOOLALA DIY INVESTMENT PLAN—THE RECIPE FOR A 40-YEAR-OLD

WHAT	HOW MUCH	HOW
Canadian equity	20%	
U.S. equity	20%	
Global equity	20%	
Fixed income	40%	

If you don't happen to be forty years old, the chart below illustrates the percentages for a number of age brackets. If you are under thirty years old, you might go as high as 100% equity, remembering, of course, that this money is for the long term and not for a trip you want to take or a down payment for a house. For how to manage your money for these shorter-horizon Moolala Goals, refer to the sidebar "Save for the short term, invest for the long term" on page 238.

ASSET ALLOCATION BASED ON AGE

WHAT	AGE 30	AGE 40	AGE 50	AGE 60	AGE 70
Canadian equity	23%	20%	16%	13%	10%
U.S. equity	23%	20%	16%	13%	10%
Global equity	23%	20%	16%	13%	10%
Fixed income	30%	40%	50%	60%	70%

CALCULATE HOW MUCH OF EACH INGREDIENT YOU NEED

WRITE: Round your age up or down to the closest decade—and be honest—this is your financial future we're talking about, not filling out your online dating profile. Jot that number into the fixed income box on the table below.

CALCULATE: Subtract that number from 100, and divide what's left by 3 to find out the percentage of your portfolio you should invest in each of Canadian, U.S., and global equity, based on this rule of thumb. Then complete the table below, or you could just look at the above chart (but that would be cheating).

WHAT	HOW MUCH
Canadian equity	%
U.S. equity	%
Global equity	%
Fixed income	%

So, now you know *what* goes into the Moolala DIY Investment Plan, and *how much* of each ingredient. Now *how* do you actually do it?

"HOW" TO MAKE THE RECIPE

Beat all ingredients together and spoon into tart shells. Bake at 450 degrees for about 8 minutes.

Okay, I'll admit that the "how" of your Moolala DIY Investment Plan is more complex than the "how" of making butter tarts. But not more complex than banking online, once you get the hang of it.

THE HOW OF PASSIVE INVESTING

The "how" of the Moolala DIY Investment Plan focuses on something called *passive investing*. There is a passive approach to investing, and there is an active approach. Now these are industry terms, not a commentary on you as an individual. If you pursue a passive approach to investing it doesn't mean you're passive in life. In fact, reading this book means that you are *actively* getting a handle on your money. But the terms are the terms.

You're likely more familiar with the active approach than the passive one, even if you have never heard these terms before. That's because most mutual funds employ an active approach. Active investing is when someone *actively* makes a decision about which stocks to buy and which stocks to sell. With passive investing, no one makes any decisions about which stocks to buy and which to sell. Essentially, passive investments hold the entire contents of all the stocks in a given index, which allows them to simply mirror the index's performance.

GETTING TO WORK IN A NEW YORK MINUTE: THE SUBWAY VERSUS THE TAXICAB

You could say that passive investing is like riding the subway in New York City in rush hour. When we lived in Manhattan, our apartment was on the Upper West Side, one block west of Central Park and two blocks north of Jerry Seinfeld's private parking garage. I worked in Midtown, at the Nasdaq Marketsite, right in the heart of Times Square.

In the morning, there were two ways to get to work—the subway or a cab. I could choose the passive route, the subway, or the active route, the cab. The passive route would cost $2, required very little effort on my part, and delivered a pretty predictable result, getting me from home to work in about twenty minutes every day. The active route, the cab, was more comfortable, but less predictable. I would have to run out and hail the cab myself, and I could only hope that the driver would know how to weave through the traffic and get me to work fast—I could never be sure. And it cost a lot more for the cab than the subway, at closer to $10. The bottom line is that the passive route worked better for me.

The same might be true for you when it comes to investing.

Passive investing mirrors the performance of the index, and that means when the index goes up, your investments go up. And when the index goes down, your investments go down. While the dips can be really hard to stomach, at least you don't have to worry whether or not you should have bought or sold a particular stock or mutual fund, because there are no decisions to make. You are just following the index.

As I mentioned in Chapter 8, it is really hard for mutual fund managers to beat the index. With passive investing you aren't even trying to beat the index. You're just trying to match the performance of the index, at a minimal cost.

EXCHANGE TRADED FUNDS, OR "EXTRA TERRIFIC FUNDS"

When you pursue a strategy of active investing, you buy mutual funds or individual stocks. When you pursue a strategy of passive investing, you buy something called Exchange Traded Funds or ETFs.

Paul, a participant in an early Moolala workshop, understood the ETF concept, but couldn't remember what it stood for. So he coined his own phrase, and he has given me permission to borrow it. He calls them "Extra Terrific Funds." An Extra Terrific Fund is simply a way to match the performance of the benchmark index. ETFs hold the same stocks as the index they mirror, giving you diversification at a very low cost. Recall that I said the average mutual fund had a management expense ratio of 2.3%. These MERs are deducted from the performance of the mutual fund, and this is one of the main reasons why so few of them beat the performance of the index. The MER on an ETF is much lower, between 0.20% and 0.60%. An ETF's performance is the same as the index it mirrors, minus the cost of the MER.

ACTIVE AND PASSIVE INVESTMENTS: A COMPARISON

ATTRIBUTE	MUTUAL FUNDS	ETFs (EXCHANGE TRADED FUNDS)
STRATEGY	• Active: Fund manager decides which stocks to buy and sell	• Passive: Holdings simply mirror contents of a given index
INVESTMENT OBJECTIVE	• Beat the benchmark index	• Match the benchmark index

SUCCESS VERSUS THE INDEX	• 10% • Under 10% of actively managed mutual funds beat the index over time, and those that underperform sometimes miss by a large margin	• ~100% • ETFs consistently match the performance of the index, less the amount of the MER
AVERAGE MER	• 2.3% on average for Canadian equity mutual funds • MERs can be higher or lower depending on the type of mutual fund	• 0.3% on average for Canadian equity ETFs • MERs can be higher depending on the ETF, up to about 0.6%
PROS	• Mutual funds easily allow for small monthly purchases • Easy to buy from any bank • Provide a commission for financial adviser to provide advice	• Investment performance matches the benchmark index • Commissions to buy them are low, usually in the range of $9–$29
CONS	• Investment performance is usually lower than the benchmark index • Fees to buy are high • MERs on mutual funds are higher than ETFs and you might also be paying sales commissions	• Small monthly purchases are more expensive to make because of trading commissions • More difficult to buy because you need to set up discount brokerage account (see Chapter 14, "Do It Yourself")

THE BRANDS OF BUTTER

Walk the dairy aisle and you'll see there are many different brands of butter. There are a number of different brands of ETFs you can buy, as well. One of the largest ETF brands in the world is iShares. There are also Claymore and Horizon Beta Pro, as well as ETFs sold by the big banks. (Go to www.moolala.ca for an updated list.) For simplicity, I have used the iShares brand throughout, but you can easily make the same recipe using another brand of ETFs.

Each of these ETFs also has something called a *ticker.* It is sort of like the UPC code on the package of butter. Outlined below are the four ingredients you'll need for the Moolala DIY Investment Plan, followed by the index they follow and the ticker you'll need to buy them.

- **Canadian Equity ETF:** This one tracks the S&P/TSX 60, which is an index that represents sixty large Canadian companies. The ticker is XIU.

- **U.S. Equity ETF:** The S&P 500 is the index here. This ETF follows the performance of five hundred large companies in the United States, and its ticker is XSP.

- **Global Equity ETF:** This ETF tracks an index with a crazy name: MSCI EAFE, which stands for Morgan Stanley Capital Index—Europe, Australasia and Far East. It follows large companies in those regions. XIN is the ticker.

- **Fixed Income ETF:** And finally, this ETF tracks something called the DEX Universe Bond Index. Included in this index are bonds issued by Canadian governments and Canadian companies. The ticker is XBB.

→ **Other types of ETFs:** The Moolala DIY Investment Plan uses only the four types of ETFs listed above, but there are many, many more ETFs out there. Some mirror the performance of other sectors or regions, and others have features that are too complex for this discussion. Don't worry about those ingredients. Stick to the ones in this recipe. Remember, this DIY approach is all about keeping things simple, simple, simple.

BAKE UP A BATCH: THE MOOLALA DIY INVESTMENT RECIPE IN PRACTICE

In Chapter 14 you set up an online discount brokerage account. That is where you'll buy the ETFs. Assuming that you now have money in your RRSP account, you are next going to purchase ETFs according to the percentages in the Moolala DIY Investment "recipe." So, for example, if you are forty years old and are going to invest $10,000, you would buy 40% or $4,000 worth of the Fixed Income ETF, and 20% or $2,000 worth of each of the three equity ETFs (Canadian equity, U.S. equity, and global equity), for a total of $6,000.

THE MOOLALA DIY INVESTMENT PLAN— THE $10,000 RECIPE*

WHAT	HOW MUCH	HOW
Canadian equity	20%	Buy $2,000 in XIU through a discount broker
U.S. equity	20%	Buy $2,000 in XSP through a discount broker
Global equity	20%	Buy $2,000 in XIN through a discount broker
Fixed income	40%	Buy $4,000 in XBB through a discount broker

* There are many investment plans out there already that use passive investing. The Moolala DIY Investment Plan was put together with the help of Shaunessy Investment Counsel.

CALCULATE HOW MUCH OF EACH ETF YOU NEED

FIND: Figure out how much money in total you're going to invest into ETFs, with this first purchase.

CALCULATE: To calculate the dollar amount of each ETF to buy, multiply your total investment amount by the "how much" percentages that you came up with in the previous exercise on page 247.

WHAT	HOW MUCH (%)	HOW MUCH ($)
Canadian equity	%	$
U.S. equity	%	$
Global equity	%	$
Fixed income	%	$

Now that you know how much of each ETF you are going to buy, you can make your transaction. Log on to your discount brokerage account and follow the instructions to buy your ETFs.

I recommend that you do this when you have some time to fuss around a bit. If you have any questions as you go along, call the toll-free helpline for the discount brokerage. The customer service staff won't be able to give you advice on *what* to buy, but they will be able to tell you *how* to buy it.

GOING BACK FOR SECONDS (AND THIRDS): THE ONGOING PURCHASE OF ETFs

After you have set up your discount brokerage account and made your initial investments, you'll continue adding money to the account and then buying more ETFs. How many times per year you buy ETFs depends on how much money you have to invest. For starters, I recommend twice a year. In addition to being simpler, it might not be economical to buy ETFs more than twice a year. That's because you pay a trading commission each time you buy an ETF. The cost is about $29 per trade (or $9.99 per trade if you have more than $100,000 in total household assets, including those of your spouse). So it generally makes sense to purchase at least $1,000 worth of a particular ETF each time. See the sidebar "Almost ETFs" for an alternate approach.

ALMOST ETFs: THE E-SERIES FUNDS FROM TD CANADA TRUST

TD Canada Trust offers a selection of funds called the "e-series." The e-series funds mirror certain indices, just like ETFs, and have MERs that are almost as low as ETFs. (At the time of publication the iShares Canadian Equity ETF had an MER of 0.17%; the equivalent TD e-series fund had an MER of 0.31%.) The e-series funds are a really compelling choice for a number of reasons, particularly for investors who don't have thousands of dollars to invest at one time. First, the minimum purchase amount is $100, less than a fancy dinner for two. Second, there is no trading commission, so you can buy them every month without worrying about paying a $29 commission each time. Third, they have a pre-authorized purchase plan that allows you to set up a regular purchase of the e-series funds, directly from your bank account. You won't even have to put a reminder note in your calendar—it happens automatically. And fourth, you don't have to open up a separate discount brokerage account. Once you set it up, you can buy them online through your current TD bank account. Swing by a branch to get the skinny, and ask which e-series funds best match up with each of the ETFs in the Moolala DIY Investment Plan.

If you didn't already do so when you opened up your account, I recommend setting up monthly auto-withdrawals from your bank account to go into your RRSP account. Or put a reminder into your calendar to manually transfer money over. (To calculate what your monthly RRSP contribution should be, refer to the "Panic prevention: How to avoid the stress of RRSP season" sidebar in Chapter 11.) Then put a note into your calendar to remind yourself to buy more ETFs twice a year.

REBALANCING YOUR PORTFOLIO

In addition to buying more ETFs twice a year, you are going to revisit your account once every year to rebalance your portfolio. Some of your investments will have gone up and others will have gone down. Rebalancing returns your asset allocation—the "how much" of each ingredient in your portfolio—to the target percentages determined by the rule of thumb for asset allocation. You can choose the date, but I recommend New Year's Day, in the spirit of making a fresh start. We'll go over full details on how to rebalance your portfolio in Appendix D.

The Moolala DIY Investment Plan is simple enough for almost anyone to follow on their own. But many of you may prefer not to put in the time and energy to do it yourself, or you might already have a great financial adviser to bake those butter tarts with you. No worries. This next section will take you through some of the things you need to know to develop your investment plan together with a financial adviser.

THE "FINANCIAL ADVISER" INVESTMENT PLAN—THE RECIPE

The Moolala Investment Plan framework of *what, how much,* and *how* still applies if you're working with a financial adviser. Your adviser might suggest some different ingredients, and use them in different quantities, but the principles are largely the same. What I will outline here are a few questions to ask as you work with your adviser to develop your investment plan. You'll notice that some of these are the same you'd asked when "rejuvenating your relationship with your financial adviser" (Chapter 13).

QUESTIONS ABOUT THE "WHAT"

Your financial adviser will help you determine "what" you should have in your portfolio. They have knowledge about and access to a huge number of products that you might never have heard of. Here are some questions to ask as you go through the process.

What is the portfolio going to be comprised of?

Many financial advisers use mutual funds. But some use ETFs or individual stocks, or even a combination of all three. It is worth asking about the types of ingredients that will go into your portfolio.

How has this mutual fund performed versus its benchmark index over time?

If your adviser is recommending mutual funds, the key thing to ask is how they have performed versus the benchmark index over time. Now, it might be a new fund and therefore not have any history, but your financial adviser should be able to tell you about the track record of the mutual fund manager who will be picking the stocks for the new fund. They will warn you, appropriately, that past performance does not indicate future performance. Still, it is important to have a fund's past performance for context. One pitfall is that your adviser might recommend to you last year's "hot" fund. Investing isn't fashion, so beware of following the hot trends of the season.

What is the management expense ratio (MER) of each fund?

The higher the MER, the harder it is for the mutual fund to meet the performance of the benchmark index. The average Canadian equity mutual fund has an MER of 2.3%. If the MER of the fund your adviser is selling you is much higher than that, I would want to understand why. In some cases, it makes total sense: it could be a mutual fund that focuses on a very specific niche, like biotechnology companies, and therefore costs more to run. But it is certainly worth asking about the MER and why it is higher or lower than the average.

What is the strategy on diversification?

Your financial adviser will work with you to diversify your portfolio, allocating money to equities in Canada, the U.S., and globally. They may also sell you products that invest in emerging markets like India and China. These funds can do quite well, but they can be riskier. I always go back to the Priority Pyramid and recommend that you have covered off the basics of regional diversification—Canada, U.S., global—before you start trying to optimize your returns.

Your adviser might also recommend that you diversify across different sectors of the economy. Examples of sectors include financial services, biotechnology, mining, and retailers. There are many equity mutual funds that focus on those particular sectors, but of course my focus is on finding the right level of complexity for your particular circumstances. People with $20,000 to invest simply don't require the complexity that sector-specific mutual funds bring to a portfolio. As your assets grow, you might consider adding some investments that focus on a particular sector, but do so only after you have covered the basics of Canada, the U.S., and global.

STOVES GET HOT: UNDERSTANDING THE RISKS OF INVESTING

Investing is risky. Over the long term, the stock market generally goes up. But it also goes down—sometimes way down, as many of you will have witnessed first-hand in 2000 and 2008. That is why you shouldn't invest money you might need in the next few years in the stock market.

That being said, *not* investing is also risky. As we discussed earlier, inflation means that simply stuffing your cash under the metaphoric mattress will lead to a loss in purchasing power. A dollar today doesn't buy what a dollar bought in 1972.

No matter which approach you choose—DIY or working with an adviser—be aware that there are risks involved.

Do I have the right number of mutual funds?

There is no hard and fast rule for the number of mutual funds that you should have in your portfolio. But, setting aside Carrie Bradshaw's feelings about shoes, more isn't necessarily better. The starting point would be four funds that follow the Moolala DIY Investment Plan we talked about above: three equity funds (Canada, U.S., global) and one fixed income fund. If you have more than eight mutual funds, I would definitely be asking your adviser why that is. If you have fifteen mutual funds, I would be concerned. There is a risk that your adviser has gotten caught up recommending the "flavour of the month" and has added various funds into your portfolio because they are popular at a given time, regardless of whether they are a good fit for your plan in the long term. Sometimes, the number of funds you hold creeps up because the adviser doesn't like the fund you already have and so puts you into a new one without selling out of the old one.

The problem with having too many mutual funds is that you can become over-diversified, and the plan you put in place at the beginning can get muddy. You don't need four types of sugar in the butter tarts. It doesn't add anything to the recipe except needless complexity.

QUESTIONS ON "HOW MUCH"

How much of each asset type should I have?

Recall the rule of thumb on asset allocation: the percentage of fixed income you have in your portfolio should equal your age. So, if you're forty years old, you should have about 40% of your portfolio in fixed income. There are exceptions to this rule of thumb, of course, so ask your financial adviser to make it clear to you why your asset allocation might be different.

One of the biggest issues I see in my workshops involves people who have an asset allocation that is weighted much too heavily towards equity investments given their age. During the market declines of 2008 I had a number of participants who were over sixty, but who had only 10% to 20% of their investments in fixed income, instead of the rule of thumb of 60%. This meant that they were hit much harder by the market decline than they would have been if their fixed income percentage had been higher. Here again are the basic benchmarks according to your age.

ASSET ALLOCATION ACCORDING TO AGE

ASSET TYPE	AGE 30	AGE 40	AGE 50	AGE 60	AGE 70
Fixed income	30%	40%	50%	60%	70%
Equity	70%	60%	50%	40%	30%

How much should I have invested in different regions?

The starting point we talked about earlier was Canadian equity 20%, U.S. equity 20%, global equity 20%. One thing to watch out for is a portfolio with too much focus on Canadian equities. While Canada has lots going for it, it represents less than 5% of the value of the total world market, so holding a disproportionate amount of Canadian equity means that your portfolio is not well diversified. Said another way, too many of your eggs are in one basket.

What type of sales commission am I paying?

Remember that there are a number of different sales commission structures, depending on which kind of mutual funds you buy. These are: no-load, front-end load, and back-end load (also called *deferred sales charge* or *DSC funds*). You can refresh your memory about the different funds, sales commissions, and fees by referring to the sidebar "Checking the price tag" on pages 220–24.

Look for no-load funds if possible. And avoid back-end load or DSC funds if you can. As I mentioned earlier, they are a profitable product for a financial adviser, offering an immediate 5% sales commission, but they are not a great product for the individual investor because you are essentially locked into holding the fund for as long as seven years to avoid being hit with a big sales charge. If the fund turns out to be a poor performer, you might have little choice but to stay in it.

One thing to watch out for is when a DSC fund reaches the end of its seven-year period. Some advisers have been known to switch their clients into a different DSC fund, generating a commission for themselves and another seven-year waiting period for the investor. Other advisers switch their clients from a DSC fund to a front-load fund that the investor will have to immediately pay a commission on, which defeats the purpose of waiting the seven years for a DSC to run out.

Will this plan deliver the goals I outlined to you earlier?

This is a critical check-in point with your financial adviser. Since you have talked to them about a holistic set of goals—some short-term, some long-term—you'll want to check to see if the plan they have developed will get you what you want. If it doesn't, you can either change the plan or modify some of your goals. Either way, it is important to check to see if you are on track. This question also helps to keep your goals top of mind for both of you.

QUESTIONS ON THE "HOW"

You have worked with your adviser on the "what" and the "how much." The "how" is fairly straightforward from your perspective as the client. Still, there are a few questions I would recommend you ask.

How can we best keep this plan top of mind?

Ideally, your adviser will give you a written document that outlines your investment plan based on your current circumstances and future goals. I would recommend that you review this document every time you see your adviser, and certainly at least once per year.

How will our meetings go in the future?

Great financial advisers will come to your meetings with an agenda. Some topics it could include are:

- **Market commentary:** How are stock markets performing in Canada and around the world? Where are interest rates heading?
- **Portfolio performance:** How is your particular portfolio performing against the benchmark index over time?

- **Recommendations:** Where does your adviser recommend you put your money?

- **Expectations:** Is your relationship meeting the expectations you set for it in Chapter 13? Is there anything to deal with?

CONCLUSION

Developing your investment plan is critical to your financial well-being. Whether you work with an adviser or on your own, it is key to have a plan that will provide you with the life you want during your post-paycheque phase.

In Step 3 of the Moolala Method, you developed the plan to get what you want. You determined where you are today, looked at dealing with your weaknesses around money, developed a plan for achieving your Moolala Goals, assessed your cash flow, and then came up with some ideas for how to improve it. You considered how to get the most value out of working with a financial adviser and whether the Do It Yourself approach is an option for you. And now you have the basic "what," "how much," and "how" of your investment plan ready to go.

That being said, a plan is only as good as what you do with it. And you do actually have to do something with it. We now move to Step 4, where we take action on the plan.

MY ONE THING

The one thing that I learned from this chapter that is most valuable to me is ____

____.

STEP 4

TAKE ACTION

•••Chapter 16

"JUST DO IT"
How can you make sure you act on your plan?

My plan to change careers was developed and ready to go. After finally figuring out that I really did want to pursue a career in television, I had developed a plan to get me there. It was organized into a very nice little table, and I had started working on a few of the smaller tasks, like registering for a broadcasting course and buying a few relevant books. But there was one part of the plan that I was totally procrastinating on. And it was a big one. It was *the* big one.

Quitting my job.

So far, everything about my career change was theoretical. Until I quit my job. As soon as the words "I quit" tumbled out of my mouth, I would go from successful corporate guy to unemployed TV wannabe.

And that was terrifying.

In practical terms, I was ready. I had made all the right financial arrangements, like getting a line of credit from the bank and paying off my new couch. But in emotional terms, I didn't feel remotely ready. I just couldn't bring myself to make the move to quit my job, and I really couldn't figure out what the hurdle was.

My best friend Tammy and I went out to dinner one night in mid June, at the Bloor Street Diner. She was one of the key people I had turned to along the way for support, ideas, and accountability in achieving my career goal. I presented my problem to her this way: "I want to quit. I need to quit. I know it is time to quit. But I just can't bring myself to actually go in there and quit. What should I do?"

Tammy came to her advice in a roundabout way. She talked about how sad she had been to leave her colleagues behind when she quit her first real job. And as she spoke, the hurdle I faced presented itself clearly.

I had grown up at that company, and the people I worked with had become like a family to me. And while it was clearly time to leave the nest, I was really upset by the prospect of actually doing it.

In hindsight, it seems like a pretty basic "dollar store" realization: of course I would be upset. But at it the time it was gold.

Then Tammy asked me, "What is it going to take for you to quit your job?"

I thought about it for a minute and then realized that the answer was simple. Courage. It was going to take courage to quit my job and leave behind the safety, comfort, and familiarity of that environment.

Then she asked the killer question: "Are you willing to do what it takes to quit your job and pursue this TV thing?"

Ugh. Was I willing to be courageous? I had to think about that for a second.

Yes. The answer was yes.

The next morning I walked into my boss's office and quit my job. It took all of five minutes and then it was done. Taking that key action kick-started my plan to change careers.

DIGGING DEEP: WHAT WILL IT TAKE FOR YOU TO TAKE ACTION?

As you worked your way through this book you first developed some ideas about actions you *could* take that would make the biggest impact for you in the area of money. Then, as you moved along, you started to develop a plan and probably made some commitments to actions you *would* take. Now is the time to actually *take* action on that plan.

I know, easier said than done, right? That is why Step 4 of the Moolala Method is focused on taking action.

Very often, smart, capable people do dumb things with their money because they don't take action. We wait until we feel motivated, inspired, or confident. We wait for the fear to pass, the anger to dissipate, the disappointment to fade. We wait for it to be convenient, or for when we have enough time. We also wait until we've figured out *why* we aren't taking action. We analyze our issues, and talk to our friends, co-workers, and therapists about why we can't seem to take action.

Very often, smart, capable people do dumb things with their money because they don't take action.

"Why am I not taking action?" is a useful question, but only to a point. It has you focus on analyzing the past and, in a way, absolves you of being personally accountable for taking action on your plan because there is some other "thing" outside of your control holding you back.

"What is it going to take for me to take action?" is an entirely different question. This question is oriented to the future and puts you back in control. The question inherently asks you to be personally accountable for taking action on your plan, which can be both liberating and terrifying.

In my experience, I have found that "what it takes" is a combination of creativity, patience, discipline, and courage.

Creativity: For some of the goals you have, there will not be a clear and proven plan for how to achieve them. You'll develop a plan to get started, but as you move forward you might hit some surprising roadblocks and need to be creative so you can keep taking action.

"My plan to improve my cash flow was to cut back on household expenses. But I still wanted to have a life. So I started a babysitting co-op with a few friends who also have kids. Instead of paying for babysitters, we take each other's kids for sleepovers. That means we all get a semi-regular 'date night' with our partners, but it doesn't cost nearly as much."

–Devon, 38, entrepreneur. Married, with two children.

Patience: I am not a naturally patient person. I get antsy even when dealing with the gold standard in efficient service—the Tim Hortons drive-through. But taking action on your plan often requires patience, because some goals simply take a long time to accomplish.

"I came up with an idea to hold a Girls Conference focused on building confidence in teens at risk. I wrote out the vision for the conference and got people onboard. But the event got postponed twice because we hadn't done our research to know how to pull it off. Three years later, the Young Women of Power Conference came to pass with thirty-two students in attendance. I learned so much during the process, especially the importance of taking my time and starting small, to get some wins under my belt and take larger steps next time."

–Skye, 33, self-employed. Single.

Discipline: Most goals worth working towards include actions that aren't particularly appealing. To take action on your plan you will likely need to do things that you don't particularly want to do. It will take discipline to keep moving forward when you're bored, overwhelmed, defeated, or tempted by other things.

"It took a lot of discipline to not spend any of the money I had been saving for my new computer. It meant making sacrifices in the way I lived my day-to-day life, like not going out as much as I wanted to. It was tough sometimes to accept the fact that I couldn't afford to go on a weekend trip with my friends, even though I could see the money just sitting there in my bank account. But it was worth it. The new machine is awesome."

–Max, 23, marketing coordinator. Single.

Courage: In all likelihood, you will be moving outside of your comfort zone to achieve your goals. Even the idea of having a goal, let alone going after it, can be a lot for people to handle. You might succeed or you might fail, but having courage will make a big difference in getting you moving towards your goal. Here is my favourite definition of courage, from Mark Twain: "Courage is resistance to fear, mastery of fear—not absence of fear."

"Courage is resistance to fear, mastery of fear—not absence of fear."

"For years I have really struggled with the idea of having kids. I'm a total Type-A personality and run my own company. While I wanted children, I was really concerned about how it would affect all aspects of my life, including my ability to do the work I really love. I wondered how motherhood would change me as a person, and whether I'd be happy with the new me. And I was terrified of this new responsibility. But my husband and I moved forward anyway and we're expecting our first child any day now."

–Andrea, 34, consultant. Married, with one child on the way.

So let's get personal and look at what it is going to take for you to take action.

EXERCISE

IDENTIFY WHAT IT WILL TAKE FOR YOU TO TAKE ACTION

REMIND: Write down your Moolala Context to remind yourself why you need to take action.

My money is for ______________________________.

PONDER: At this point you likely have a number of different areas to focus on, including your plans to achieve your key Moolala Goals, to deal with your weaknesses around money, to improve your cash flow, and to get your investments on track. Think about these different areas and ask yourself what it is going to take for you to take action on your money.

- Where will creativity make a difference?
- Where will you need to be patient?
- What will you need to be disciplined about?
- Where will you need courage?
- What else is it going to take for you to get into action on your plans?

____

____

____

ASK: Now that you have a sense of what it is going to take, ask yourself this question: "Am I willing to do what it takes?"

- **YES:** If your answer is "yes," good for you. In a minute, we'll talk more about how to overcome some of the pitfalls associated with taking action on your plan. And later, in Step 5 of the Moolala Method, I'll give you some ideas on how to stay engaged with your plan over time.

- **NO:** If your answer is "no," thanks for being honest. "No" is a completely valid answer, and answering that way doesn't make you a bad person. In fact, being honest with yourself might ease some of the anxiety you have about your financial situation. There will be consequences associated with not taking action, but they might be consequences you're willing to deal with.

- **NOT SURE:** If you're not sure you're willing to do what it takes, ask yourself this supplementary question, "What will it take for me to be sure in my answer?" and see what pops into your head. Sitting on the fence is natural, for a short period of time. But stay there too long and the chain link can really start biting into your skin.

TALK: This is one of the most important exercises in the entire book to talk about with a few people in your community. That's because the rubber is now hitting the road. You have come so far already and now is the time to get moving. Your friends and family can provide you with the support, ideas, and accountability that will make all the difference in your achieving your goals. In fact, one of the most powerful things you can do right now is to declare to someone in your community the actions you are going to take.

DECLARATIONS: A REFRESHER ON PUTTING YOUR GOALS OUT THERE

We first looked at the importance of making a declaration in Chapter 10. To make a declaration is to articulate the achievement of a specific goal (what), by a specific time (when), to a specific person other than yourself (who).

The idea of making a declaration may freak you out a little bit, which I totally understand. It freaks me out a little too. But it works.

A declaration delivered in this way will significantly increase the probability of you taking action on your plan.

Here are a few examples of declarations from the Moolala Community:

Declaration: Take action on my plan to deal with my weaknesses

"I called my dad, who is really into working on his money, and let him know I was going to focus on learning more about my money, and asked him if he'd be willing to help. From his reaction, you'd think I told him I was pregnant. He was thrilled."

–Melanie, 33, lawyer. Married, with no children despite parental pressure.

Declaration: Take action on my plan to improve my cash flow

"I told my cubicle neighbour at work that I'm going to pull back on eating out at lunch to just twice a week, starting on Monday."

–Joan, 55, legal secretary. Married, with two children.

Declaration: Take action on my plan to rejuvenate my relationship with my financial adviser

"I called my financial adviser and booked a meeting for a week from now to go through the list of 'rejuvenate' questions. I told my wife that it was time to fish or cut bait with my adviser. If we can't get the relationship on track within three months, I need to find someone else."

–Geoff, 37, engineer. Married, with one child.

EXERCISE MAKE A DECLARATION TO TAKE ACTION

Earlier you made a declaration related to one of your Moolala Goals. Now that you have moved through the rest of Step 3 of the Moolala Method and have a more comprehensive plan to get a handle on your money, it is helpful to take another look at what declarations you could make. What action are you going to declare, by when will it be complete, and to whom will you make the declaration?

CHOOSE: Review the various areas that you're working on to get a handle on your money and choose one that is really important to you. Then pick one action from your plan that you are going to declare to someone else.

DECLARE: Tell two people in your community what the goal is that you're working on and what your specific declaration is. Be sure to tell them when you will have it completed by. And I would strongly recommend that you ask them to make a note of it in their calendar to follow up with you to confirm that you took the action.

REMINDERS: HOW TO KEEP YOUR DECLARATIONS TOP OF MIND

Given all the delicious distractions of a life well lived, it can be really tough to hold yourself accountable to follow through on your declarations. If you're like me, you make one and then, five minutes later, you either completely forget about it, or *wish* you could completely forget about it.

A few reminders will make all the difference. I define the word *reminders* very broadly. I mean anything that you can do to help keep your declaration top of mind, and to give it its own momentum even when you're not focused on it. An obvious example would be posting your written goals on your mirror. A less obvious example would be when I invited my parents to cheer me on at the marathon finish line. That invitation gave my declaration its own momentum, because they had already agreed to be there, so of course I had to show up.

Here are some of the reminders that I created for my career change declaration:

- Booked regular phone calls with my friend Peter to talk about my progress on the plan.
- Asked my friend Kelly to come over to my house and hang out while I made cold calls to TV stations, an idea that completely petrified me. We talked about what I was going to say, which reminded me why I wanted to make the change in the first place. Then I picked up the phone, dialled, and stumbled through my spiel, either live or to someone's voicemail. After each call was done I went back to my living room and debriefed with her, then made another call. By the end of the afternoon I had called every TV station in town.

Making a declaration to someone in your community, and having them ask you about your plan somewhat regularly, as you did in the exercise above, is one of the most powerful reminders you can use. Now we're going to look at a few others.

"I'm a visual learner so I have to see and experience. It helps me to picture the outcome, like posting pictures on dream boards and using a picture of a thermometer that goes up the more I've saved. I even use a piggy bank—I know it sounds strange but I've saved thousands that way. I will mentally say to myself, 'If I want to go kayaking in the Everglades, then I need to put this money in the piggy bank instead of spending it on a sweater.'"

–Marty, 49, consultant. Partnered, with two stepchildren.

REMINDERS: USING ONLINE RESOURCES

There are a number of online resources that can help you create reminders to encourage you to keep taking action on your plan. For the latest list, go to www.moolala.ca. Here are two of my favourites:

- **Futureme.org:** "Future Me" allows you to e-mail a letter to yourself, which will be delivered at whatever date you choose in the future.
- **Monkeyon.com:** "Monkey on your back" allows you to set simple reminders that will be delivered to you, or to someone else, encouraging you to follow through on whatever task you choose.

"I photocopied my goals list four times, put it in an envelope, and gave it to my admin assistant. She mails it to my home address at the start of every quarter."

–Barb, 42, marketing executive. Married, with three children.

"I put a note in my Outlook calendar that reminds me every three months to send my receipts to my bookkeeper. Sounds simple, but before that I wasn't doing it and was getting dinged with tax penalties."

–James, 35, business owner. Married.

"I signed up for the Moolala newsletter, just so I would have something coming into my e-mail box regularly that had me think about money."

–Marsha, 37, stay-at-home mom. Married, with three children.

"I promised a friend that I would e-mail him every week with an update of my progress against my income goal. I do it maybe three out of every four weeks, but

I really appreciate the structure it sets up . . . even if it sometimes makes me crazy that I haven't hit the goal yet."

–Kelly, 41, learning consultant. Single, with two children.

CREATE REMINDERS OF YOUR DECLARATIONS

BRAINSTORM: Grab the plan that you want to take action on and think about what reminders you could create to keep it top of mind.

ACT: Do something. Anything. It matters less what you do, and more that you do SOMETHING, anything, to keep your declaration top of mind. I know you don't have the time—smart, capable people never do.

REMINDERS: START A MOOLALA MONEY GROUP

One of the best reminders you can use to keep goals and actions alive is to engage your community in what it is that you're working on. When it comes to your money, there is precious little community already out there, so it might make sense to create your own. My challenge to you is to form a Moolala Money Group with a few friends or colleagues. For ideas on how to do it, check out the appendix or go to www.moolala.ca.

THE MOOLALA CHECKLIST

We use checklists for grocery shopping, or to pack for a trip. And yet we don't often use a checklist to help us get a handle on our money so we can live the life we want. One of the most powerful ways to remind yourself of your plan is a list. A simple checklist.

Sure, there are some people who really don't like lists. And then there are people who really do. If you're a member of the *no list* group, you might skim the section below so you can roll your eyes with disdain (while secretly hoping to pick up a tip or two). And if you *are* a list person, here is a checklist of every action we have talked about thus far. A printable version can be downloaded from www.moolala.ca.

COMPLETE THE MOOLALA CHECKLIST

Now, those of you who have been doing the exercises all along and taking action as you worked through the book will move fairly quickly through the checklist. And those of you who haven't been quite so keen will have some catching up to do. You know who you are. And I know who you are.

COMPLETE: Work your way through the checklist below, adding a satisfying "✓" when you have completed the task. You won't likely get it all done in one swoop, so keep it handy to update as you move through it.

THE MOOLALA CHECKLIST

ACTION	
STEP 1: Lay the Foundation	
Discover your family's default context for money	☐
Identify society's default contexts for money	☐
Create your Moolala Context	☐
Identify the consequences of your weaknesses around money	☐

Determine where you are on the Priority Pyramid ☐

Understand how your communities impact your behaviour around money ☐

Talk to 2 or 3 people about your Moolala Context ☐

STEP 2: Determine what you want

Brainstorm your Moolala Goals ☐

Talk to 2 or 3 people about your Moolala Goals ☐

STEP 3: Develop the plan

→ Determine where you are today

Calculate your net worth ☐

Assess the performance of your investments ☐

Identify your strengths and weaknesses around money ☐

Talk to 2 or 3 people about your strengths and weaknesses ☐

→ Deal with your weaknesses

Identify the hurdles standing in the way of your being accountable for your weaknesses ☐

Develop a plan to deal with your top-priority weaknesses ☐

→ Develop a plan for your Moolala Goals

Prioritize your Moolala Goals ☐

Declare one of your goals to another person ☐

Develop a plan to achieve this goal ☐

→ Assess your cash flow

Answer the following questions:

Q1 Are you earning more than you're spending? ☐

Yes/No/Not Sure

Q2 Have you eliminated credit card debt? ☐

Yes/No/Not Sure

Q3 Are you saving enough for your post-paycheque phase? ☐

Yes/No/Not Sure

Q4 Are you saving towards your Moolala Goals? ☐

Yes/No/Not Sure

Q5 Are you taking advantage of RRSPs and RESPs? ☐

Yes/No/Not Sure

→ Improve your cash flow

Analyze your cash flow ☐

Brainstorm ways to improve your cash flow ☐

Commit to 2 or 3 changes you will make to the way you spend ☐

Talk to 2 or 3 people about what you are going to change ☐

→ Working with a financial adviser (if applicable)

Assess your financial adviser ☐

Rejuvenate the relationship with your financial adviser or find a new financial adviser ☐

→ Do It Yourself (if applicable)

Set up a discount brokerage account ☐

→ **Develop your investment plan**

- [ ] Develop your Moolala investment plan, either by yourself or with your adviser

STEP 4: Take action

- [ ] Identify what it will take for you to take action
- [ ] Declare the action on actions you are going to take to get a handle on your money
- [ ] Create reminders for your declaration
- [ ] Complete the Moolala Checklist (this one, right here!)

STEP 5: Stay engaged

- [ ] Get restarted after you stall (ongoing)
- [ ] Complete monthly check-ins (ongoing)
- [ ] Complete annual check-ins (ongoing)

THE HURDLES: PITFALLS IN TAKING ACTION

You've identified what it's going to take for you to take action so you can get a handle on your money. You've looked at the declarations you could make and what reminders would give them their own momentum. You've even skimmed a groovy checklist that brings everything together in one place.

But before you charge off and start getting stuff done, I want to draw your attention to a few of the pitfalls that you might encounter along the way and what you can do about them.

Working on too much at once: Trying to work on everything all at the same time is rarely a successful strategy. Be realistic about what you can accomplish so you don't set yourself up for failure. Instead, pick two or three areas to focus on and take actions that will move your plans forward in those areas. Yes, being strategic will take discipline, and yes, it will take patience. But, trust me, it will pay off.

Getting caught up in your feelings: Many of us wait to "feel motivated" before we take action. According to the *American Heritage Dictionary,* to motivate means to "provide with an incentive; to move to action"—no mention of *feeling* there.

If your motivation is solely based on your feelings, you will lose momentum every time you don't feel like doing something. And if you're anything like me, there are a LOT of things you don't feel like doing, especially when it comes to money. We have this misplaced belief that things should be easy and should feel good, when often they aren't and they don't. Yes, it would be easier if we felt motivated all the time. But you might actually never "feel" like doing anything to get a handle on your money. In fact, you can be bored, annoyed, even despondent, and still motivated and taking action.

"Pain is inevitable. Suffering is optional."

As the great American philosopher Nike once said, "Just do it."

Forgetting that goals take work: Pursuing what you most want in life is rarely easy. And yet we sometimes delude ourselves into thinking that it is supposed to be easy and that something is wrong if it isn't. A lot of the goals worth working on involve challenges. Which reminds me of this quote from Haruki Murakami, the Japanese writer and marathon runner: "Pain is inevitable. Suffering is optional." Remember, achieving goals takes work, maybe even pain. But you really don't have to suffer about it.

Being inflexible about your goals: I am generally an "anything is possible" kind of person. But a dollop of reality can be really important. I often get asked in workshops, "How do I reconcile the fact that my income is just not going to deliver on my goals?" Great question. It isn't very motivating to live in a fantasyland about what you can and can't achieve. Here's what I'd suggest: be flexible about the goal you want to achieve, and then get creative about how you can best realize a part of it.

"My goal was to own a house in the south of France. But I was working in the not-for-profit sector, so I was pretty sure it was never going to happen unless I married rich. Then I figured that I could rent a small apartment instead of buying a house. I asked my boss if I could work from 'home' on grant applications for two weeks every summer. She agreed, and also approved my working an extended day for two months in spring to save up another two weeks in lieu. Then I added two of my three weeks of vacation and SHAZAM! I'm now spending six weeks in Provence every year. I sublet my place back home in the city, and when friends come to visit they contribute some money to offset the rent. True, it isn't exactly what I initially dreamed of. But it is still fantastique."

–Joyce, 45, outreach manager. Single.

Procrastinating: This one is probably the biggest pitfall of all, which is why I saved it for the last. Everyone procrastinates at some time or another, for different reasons: boredom, fear, indecision.

The fact is that you can never be sure if the action you take will be the right one. What you can be sure of is that taking *no* action guarantees *no* results. Taking action creates momentum, and that momentum will build on itself. We'll talk about strategies for combatting procrastination in the next chapter.

TISSUES TO TELEVISION: TAKING ACTION PAYS OFF

Quitting my job was one of the most difficult things I've ever done. But not surprisingly, it has also been one of the best. I started networking up a storm and soon got an interview for an entry-level job working on a new business show. With the on-air date looming, the senior producer read my resumé and offered me a job as a researcher five minutes into the interview. I was so stunned I actually didn't register what she had just said, so I launched into a long and detailed sales pitch on why I was perfect for the job. Thankfully she ignored my vacuousness and my career in TV was launched. I started work on August 24, which was well before my self-imposed October 31 deadline.

I worked my way up to chase producer, then reporter, then anchor of my own daily show. Soon I was my network's bureau chief in New York City. To put it mildly, taking action really paid off for me.

CONCLUSION

Taking action on getting a handle on your money is what will help you get what you want. I know it might take something for you to take action: creativity, patience, discipline, courage, or whatever it is for you. But here's the thing: you *do* have what it takes. It may not feel like it sometimes, but you really do. Remember that taking no action will deliver no results, but even the tiniest action, the smallest step forward, can get your momentum going.

Coming up next is the final step of the Moolala Method. Step 5 is about how to stay engaged with the plan. Before you turn the page, put a recurring note in your calendar to reread that section in particular every year. You think I'm kidding . . . I'm not kidding. Make a note in your calendar for one year from today to reread it because now that you're *getting* a handle on your money, staying engaged will help you *keep* a handle on it.

MY ONE THING

After working through this chapter, the single most important action that I'm going to take is ____

____.

STEP 5

STAY ENGAGED

•••Chapter 17

MAKE IT A LONG-TERM ENGAGEMENT

What can you do to keep a handle on your money?

It was brand new, bright red, and had cost me a fortune. For the unimaginable sum of $500, I was the proud owner of my very own Toro lawn mower. I was thirteen years old and had bought my brother's lawn care business earlier that spring, and so this new lawn mower became the centre of my universe. Almost every day after school I was out cutting lawns all around the neighbourhood. The work was as back-breaking as it was lucrative, and I quickly learned how to keep my lines perfectly straight and avoid beheading the begonias. But clearly I did *not* learn the basics of engine maintenance, something that soon became blindingly obvious.

What started as an innocuous groan from the motor as I finished the Trusslers' front lawn grew more dramatic by the time I moved around to the back. It wasn't that I didn't notice my poor Toro was wailing in pain, but it was my last job of the day and I was desperate to just finish and go home. I knew a stall was imminent, and so with only one fifty-foot strip of grass left to mow, I ran faster as the groans shifted from urgent and infuriated to weak and defeated. Then suddenly, like Violetta in *La Traviata,* my Toro let out one last desperate dry heave and was silent.

I pulled frantically on the starter cord, but it wouldn't move an inch. It turned out that that final sickening sound had come from a piston, which had seized inside its cylinder: this is what happens when you don't add any oil to keep the engine lubricated. It turns out that engines need oil. Oh.

Sure, it would be great if you could get a handle on your money just once and be done with it. But, as with many things in life, your money needs ongoing maintenance.

I learned the hard way that you can't add oil to your lawnmower *just once.* You can't fill the fridge with groceries just once either. Your marriage needs ongoing attention, as do your body and soul. Sure, it would be great if you could get a handle on your money just once and be done with it. But, as with many things in life, your money needs ongoing maintenance.

Step 5 of the Moolala Method is about how to stay engaged with your plan, so that your money gets the maintenance it needs. As we discussed in the last chapter, when there is no action, there are no results. And most of the goals you have in life will require you to take action over time.

In this chapter we'll look at The Stall that occurs to almost everyone at some point in the process, and what you can do to get moving again if it happens to you. I'll also provide you with some check-in questions that will help you keep track of and celebrate your progress.

THE STALL: WHAT IT IS AND WHY IT HAPPENS

You've probably had a car stall at some point, so you know the sinking feeling that occurs when the engine sputters to a halt, and turning the key produces a faint grumble but no roar. As you work at getting a handle on your money, you'll likely have to deal with The Stall at some point. It usually occurs about four to six weeks after you start taking action, and can occur again and again over time. It is a natural part of the process, and one you can more easily overcome the better you understand it.

In just a few minutes we're going to look at a few simple things we can do to get ourselves restarted when and if we hit The Stall. But before we do, it's worth taking a quick look at why The Stall occurs in the first place.

Life happens. It isn't easy to stay engaged in getting a handle on our money when the @#$% hits the fan. The baby needs a new stroller. The car breaks down. Work gets really busy. The stock market falls. Any of a thousand of different life events can disrupt our momentum, and send that context we created for money—the one that we were so excited about—flying out the window. Money is for "freedom"? Ha. Money is for a new $2,000 transmission on the car.

The novelty wears off: We've been working diligently at getting a handle on our money, then slowly but surely the novelty just wears off. The effort required to keep working on our goals somehow seems to outweigh the benefit of achieving them, and so we find it harder to stay engaged.

We can't see results yet: We have taken a bunch of actions. We're feeling really good about our progress, and expect to see some results from all our hard work. But the results don't come soon enough. We know intellectually that these things take time, but we are desperate for

"The biggest challenge in staying engaged is NOW. We are dedicating so much to paying off our mortgage that saving for the future—kids, our wedding, trips—is difficult. I sometimes feel like I don't have the time or energy to sort out the steps from Point A to Point B, and that I have other worries in life that take precedence, like my parents' health and getting pregnant. I consciously forgive myself for being stalled because I've got 'other more important things to worry about.' To get restarted after I stall, I look for someone or something that reminds me that I'm a lame-ass and I just need to take action. And I look at my list of goals every week to help me to break down big scary things into little tasks over a longer period of time. Then I just start chipping away at them. I also find that it really helps me to stay engaged with my goals when I make an effort to help others accomplish their goals, too."

–Melissa, 39, public sector executive. Engaged.

some sign that the effort will all be worth it. Without any results to show for it, we wonder why we're bothering doing the work.

Our expectations aren't met: No matter how realistic we try to be, we still have high expectations of ourselves and others. And pretty soon into the new plan, various shortcomings might become apparent. The conversations with our community don't go the way we thought they would. We don't follow through on what we said we would do on our investments, or our investments don't perform to our expectations (see Appendix E, "Keeping Perspective on Your Investment Performance"). And it is very hard to stay engaged when our expectations aren't met.

We have a bias towards the status quo: We *want* to get a handle on our money. We know we *need* to get a handle on our money. But even though our financial situation isn't the way we want it, we have a bias towards keeping it that way. *WHAT?!* Yep, it's true. It is called the "status quo bias," and behavioural economists have lots of proof to show that we often prefer to hold the course, even if the course we're holding is taking us in the wrong direction. We don't change our spending habits. We are loyal to the same bank, mortgage lender, or cellphone company even if the fees they charge seem egregious. All because we have a bias towards the status quo.

START ME UP: WHAT YOU CAN DO TO GET MOVING AGAIN

Given all these factors, is it any wonder that our progress stalls from time to time? Staying engaged with our plan is actually a process of getting restarted after The Stall, again and again.

When our car stalls, we call a tow truck or a friend. In most cases it is a temporary situation and our car starts again. When it comes to our money, even if it doesn't feel that way, The Stall is also temporary and we *can* get restarted. Here's how:

Recognize The Stall

The first step in getting restarted after The Stall is to recognize that you have stalled. Given how common it is, you'd think we'd be good at recognizing it. We aren't.

Everyone gets stalled at one point or another. It doesn't mean we're failures or bad people, or that we're never going to get a handle on our money. It just means that our momentum has stalled for the time being. If you ever watch the *Biography* profiles on TV you'll see that most of the iconic personalities they feature have stalled at some point. World leaders, artists, sports heroes, business tycoons—all of them went through a time when they almost quit. We might think successful people never stall. The truth is that they stall all the time, but then they manage to start up again.

So how can you tell if you've stalled? There are two things to watch for. First, you aren't taking action. You aren't moving forward on the plan you developed. And second, you are having self-defeating thoughts and feelings and making excuses.

Once we recognize that we've stalled, we can do something about it.

Remind yourself of your Moolala Context

When people stall, it can sometimes be really hard to remember why they wanted to get a handle on their money in the first place. This is why it's so crucial for you to remind yourself of your Moolala Context and the list of goals that you are so excited about working towards.

We might think successful people never stall. The truth is that they stall all the time, but then they manage to start up again.

Engage your community

The whole purpose of engaging your community is to allow you to access their support, ideas, and accountability in the areas that are important to you. When you stall, it is really important to remember that you aren't alone in this. Not only does everyone stall at some point, but the people around you can really make the difference in helping you get restarted.

Take action

Action begets action. The best way to get over The Stall is to take action. Any action. It doesn't matter what it is. It just matters that you do something.

A ROOM WITH A VIEW: TAKING SMALL STEPS TOWARDS A BIG DREAM

"My husband Mark and I decided to move to Nova Scotia so we could realize several dreams at once. We bought nine acres of land and planned to build our own modern, sustainable house, live near water, and still be within twenty-five minutes of a city that offered Indian food, café con leche, and bookstores. But our finances were really up and down, due partly to having our first baby and partly to the nature of running an entrepreneurial business. There were many times when we stalled—including a couple of years ago when we were behind on our winter service payments. All the neighbours were at a meeting and started to discuss 'The Delinquents.' We were so embarrassed that we used our two-year-old as an excuse to leave early.

"We check in with each other at least a few times a month because we know we need to remind ourselves why we're doing what we're doing, especially when the going gets tough. For us, the land is about magical and adventurous living. We visit it a lot and everyone knows our plan. A couple of months ago I had a women's circle on the land. It was so wonderful to 'have people over,' and they loved sitting in a circle with these huge granite rocks at their backs. We've also developed a great relationship with Grace, an adviser at the bank. She has walked us through a number of scenarios about buying houses, building on the land, and dealing with credit card debt. Going in to see her every six months or so has kept us on track to where we need to be.

"Mark is always working on the house plans and even took a course about how to incorporate solar design. I recently visited our accountant to ask about the tax implications of Mark's idea to sell off a piece of the property. We've owned it for seven years and still haven't put a shovel in the ground. But we have stayed engaged in the plan, moving forward, inch by inch, and I know it is all going to come together."

–Karen, 37, counsellor. Married, with one child.

GET RESTARTED AFTER THE STALL

Once you recognize that you've stalled in your plan to get a handle on your money, here is what to do to get restarted.

REMIND: Go back to what you wrote down at the very beginning of this book as your Moolala Context for money.

My money is for ______________________________.

Now review some of the Moolala Goals you came up with and jot down a few here.

My Moolala Goals are ______________________________

______________________________.

Remember that staying engaged in getting a handle on your money will help you achieve your Moolala Goals. Keeping these goals top of mind again should help you to get over The Stall. For tips on how you can remind yourself of your Moolala Goals, see pages 278–81.

ENGAGE: Who in your community of friends and family could you go to for some support, ideas, and accountability? What would you say to them? What support do you need? Where do you need help in brainstorming ideas? What could you ask them to hold you accountable for? Reach out to two or three people and talk to them about where you're at and what you need.

ACT: What is one action you could take that would move you forward in the area where you are currently stalled? ______________________________

____

SHAKE IT, SHAKE IT UP, BABY: OTHER IDEAS FOR RESTARTING AFTER THE STALL

You'll come up with your own ways to get restarted after The Stall, but here are a few other ideas from the Moolala Community.

→ Give yourself a reward for keeping going

"I reward myself with a small bouquet of flowers and a good bottle of wine after tax season is over."

–Claudine, 42, consultant. Married, with two children.

→ Take a break

"I got really frustrated setting up my discount brokerage account. I decided to put it aside for a week, but not before asking two friends to check in with me to ensure that I restarted the process. Turns out I just needed to clear my head and get my mojo back."

–Will, 35, business owner. Married.

→ Cut yourself some slack

"I was raised to believe that anything worth doing was worth doing right. But that has been crippling for me when it comes to my money. Sometimes I just need to pop an imaginary Quaalude, turn on Joni Mitchell, and tell myself that even the little bit that I've accomplished is better than nothing."

–Mathew, 48, lawyer. Married, with three children.

"We have a young child with very specific needs, so we weren't always totally driven by perfection. We had to move along with what life threw us—and sometimes we did that well; sometimes not so well."

–Sarah, 39, account executive. Married, with one child.

Yes, it can be really, really hard to stay engaged with your plan. Trust me, you're not alone. We all need to keep drawing on our creativity, discipline, patience, and courage in order to continue to take action, even when we don't feel like it.

Now that you have a few ideas on how to start up again if you stall, let's look at how to keep you engaged in your plan on an ongoing basis.

REGULAR CHECK-INS: A PROCESS FOR STAYING ENGAGED

It will make a big difference for you to check in regularly on your various plans. The frequency with which you check in on your plan will depend on what you're working on. In some areas—like improving cash flow, for example—monthly check-ins make sense. But in others—like your goal to teach in a developing country when you stop working—annual check-ins will suffice.

Keep your check-ins really simple, simple, simple. Outlined on the following pages is one check-in you can customize to use monthly, and another to use annually. Both are available in printable versions at www.moolala.ca.

To increase the probability that these monthly check-ins will actually occur, put a note in your calendar on the first of every month to remind you to complete them. For your annual check-in, you might want to do it in January, right after New Year's, or in September, as the fall school term gets underway again. Or even on your birthday. Choose the date that will work for you.

BACK TO SCHOOL: KEEPING TRACK OF THE BABY, THE BANK BALANCE, AND THE BOOKS

"We decided as a couple that Colin should really pursue his goal to become a lawyer. We felt that it was likely best to deal with this financial strain on our family while our daughter was young, when she would feel the pressure and material change less. It was very difficult financially to support the family on one (dwindling) income, especially in a city that was down in the dumps economically. We really struggled to find enough time with our daughter—who was our bright spot each and every day—and enough time for Colin to commit himself fully to his goal. We really had to balance the guilt, frustration, doubt, and conflicting priorities with the greater good of the whole project. And while it wasn't a lifetime, it was a long time. Four years of commitment to a wavering ideal. Law school is tough—and almost anyone who has been through it will say that at some point they just wanted to quit. Family and friends provided accountability simply by checking in regularly—by being a part of our journey, asking for updates, and offering support. But most of the accountability came simply from our own back and forth, ensuring that when we got derailed, we got back on track, figured out what was important in the short and longer terms, re-jigged expectations where necessary, and 'Kept Moving Forward.'

"And now, here we are: School is done and we're back to the big city, living in a shoebox-sized apartment. Our lives are on a new path and we're hoping—always hoping—that this one will offer the right trajectory for us."

–Jen, 39, teacher. Married with one child.

COMPLETE THE MONTHLY CHECK-IN

SCHEDULE: Book thirty minutes into your calendar once a month to go through this quick check-in.

REVIEW: Remind yourself of your Moolala Context, then pull out your Moolala Goals and read through them. First, look to see if you've made any progress that you would like to celebrate. Then, focusing on the goals you prioritized, ask yourself if there are any actions you could take in the next month that would move you further towards achieving those goals.

CHECK: Skim through the questions below to see if there are any actions that you could take in the next month in the areas that are relevant to you.

- **Q1** Are you earning more than you're spending?
- **Q2** Have you eliminated credit card debt?
- **Q3** Are you saving enough for your post-paycheque phase?
- **Q4** Are you saving towards your Moolala Goals?
- **Q5** Are you taking advantage of RRSPs and RESPs?

ASK: What support, ideas, or accountability could you benefit from, from your community? Who could you ask to provide it? Who could you talk to about your check-in?

____

____

COMPLETE THE ANNUAL CHECK-IN

Below is a list of questions for the annual check-in. Feel free to pick and choose what is most relevant for you and skip over what isn't.

SCHEDULE: Book three hours every year to complete this annual check-in.

STEP 1: LAY THE FOUNDATION

→ CONTEXT

Does your Moolala Context still resonate for you? If it does, great. If it doesn't, how would you answer the question, "What is my money for?"

____

____

→ CONSEQUENCES

Refer back to the table of behaviours you said didn't work for you, on page 51. What is one area where you feel you have addressed the consequences?

____

____

What is one area where you feel there is still work to do?

____

____

→ COMPLEXITY

Review the Priority Pyramid (see pages 65–71). Based on your current circumstances, where would you say you are now?

____

____

What would you say worked about your efforts to find the right level of complexity for your financial situation?

What didn't work as well as you'd have liked it to?

Where do you need to reduce the level of complexity you have with your money?

Where do you need to increase the level of complexity you have with your money?

→ COMMUNITY

What worked about your efforts to engage your community in helping you get a handle on your money?

What didn't work as well as you'd have liked it to?

What could you do differently this coming year to improve how you engage with your community?

STEP 2: DETERMINE WHAT YOU WANT

→ COMING UP WITH YOUR MOOLALA GOALS

Review the table on page 101 or what you wrote down in your notebook, focusing on the goals that you prioritized. Where did you have progress on your goals? What would you like to celebrate?

____

____

Where did you feel that you didn't have the progress you wanted?

____

____

Are the priorities you set still valid? Or would you re-prioritize your goals?

____

____

STEP 3: DEVELOP THE PLAN

→ DETERMINE WHERE YOU ARE TODAY

Calculate your net worth based on current numbers (see page 118). Now compare it to your earlier assessment. How has it changed from last year?

____

____

Review your investment performance (see pages 128–33). How did your investments perform? And if you own mutual funds, how did they perform relative to the benchmark index?

____

____

Review the table of your strengths and weaknesses around money on page 137. How would you update the list?

____

____

→DEAL WITH YOUR WEAKNESSES

Based on what you identified above, are there any actions you are going to take to deal with your main weaknesses?

____

____

→DEVELOP A PLAN FOR YOUR MOOLALA GOALS

Based on your review of your Moolala Goals, what actions are you going to take to move you closer to achieving your goals?

____

____

→ASSESS YOUR CASH FLOW

Answer each of the following questions:

Q1 Are you earning more than you're spending?
(See pages 185–89.) Yes / No / Not Sure

Q2 Have you eliminated credit card debt?
(See pages 167–68.) Yes / No / Not Sure

Q3 Are you saving enough for your post-paycheque phase?
(See pages 168–77.) Yes / No / Not Sure

Q4 Are you saving towards your Moolala Goals?
(See page 177.) Yes / No / Not Sure

Q5 Are you taking advantage of RRSPs and RESPs?
(See pages 178–79.) Yes / No / Not Sure

→IMPROVE YOUR CASH FLOW

What changes did you implement to improve your cash flow? How did those changes work?

____

____

Overall, how was your progress on improving cash flow?

____

____

What more could you do to increase income or decrease expenses to allow you to reach your Moolala Goals faster?

____

____

→FINANCIAL ADVICE

- Reassess your financial adviser based on the criteria that is most relevant for you. Book time with him or her to discuss your results, and discuss any changes you would like to make in how you work together to ensure you're getting the most value from that relationship. (See pages 205–11.)
- If applicable, consider whether you need or want to rejuvenate your relationship with your financial adviser, find a new adviser, or take a Do It Yourself approach.
- If applicable, consider whether the DIY approach is working for you. Does it still fit with the level of complexity you're comfortable with, or do you need to find a financial adviser?

→DEVELOP/REFINE YOUR INVESTMENT PLAN

- If you're working with a financial adviser, based on your review of your investment performance above, is there anything that needs to be done to improve the performance of your investments?
- If you're following a DIY approach and using ETFs there is really

nothing to do to refine your investment plan. You aren't trying to beat the benchmark index. You're just trying to match it, so keep doing what you're doing.

- Rebalance your portfolio to get the proportions of your "ingredients" back to their target quantities. If you're working with an adviser, your adviser will do this for you. If you're taking the DIY approach, see Appendix D, "Rebalance Your Portfolio" for details on how to do this.

STEP 4: TAKE ACTION

→ DECLARATIONS

Based on the review of your results above, are there any new declarations you would like to make? And to whom?

____

____

→ REMINDERS

Which reminders have been most effective for you? Which have been the least effective?

____

____

What reminders about your plan are you going to put into place this year? (See pages 274–77.)

____

____

→ THE MOOLALA CHECKLIST

Review the Moolala Checklist on pages 278–81. What do you need to take action on?

____

____

STEP 5: STAY ENGAGED

→CHECK-INS

Is there anything you could do—or anyone you could speak to—to help you stay engaged in getting a handle on your money over the course of the next year?

____

____

A SECOND CHANCE: WHAT HAPPENED TO THE TORO

I learned my lesson about the importance of lawn mower maintenance the hard way. No, I really mean the hard way. I decided that I would fix my Toro myself and so I registered in a small-engine repair course at Fanshawe College. Every week for twelve weeks I took the bus across town to file down that piston and get the motor running again. Yes, it was brutally hard to stay engaged and I hated doing the work, but I was successful in getting the old Toro running again. While I moved on in life, that bright red Toro stayed in the family. My mom maintained it carefully and used it to cut her lawn for the next twenty-one years.

CONCLUSION

Step 5 of the Moolala Method is to stay engaged. Even though this is the final step, it isn't really the end of the process. We'll continue to focus on staying engaged over time because it is to getting a handle on our money what oil is to the smooth running of a lawn mower—critically important to ongoing maintenance. That said, while staying engaged is a journey, you have travelled a long way. Good for you. Working through this book was a big investment of your time, so I hope you feel pretty happy with yourself. Very few people put such energy into getting a handle on their money, but you have. So live a little. Celebrate. Maybe even indulge in your favourite vice. (As long as that vice costs under fifty bucks, with tax and tip. Kidding. Totally kidding.)

MY ONE THING

The one thing that will make the biggest difference for me in getting restarted if I stall is ____

____.

The one thing that will help me stay engaged in getting a handle on my money is ____

____.

Epilogue

It was my lifelong dream to become a TV news reporter. It took me twenty years of starts and stops, detours and self-doubt, but there I was finally living it. I had developed the plan, taken action on it, and now I was in the Big Apple.

On a sunny fall afternoon, I was standing outside the Waldorf Astoria on Park Avenue, finishing up a report on a game-changing corporate merger that had just been announced behind me. The street was packed with pedestrians, frantically dodging the satellite truck and all the accompanying lights and cables. And as the camera rolled, I delivered my sign-off: "Reporting live from New York City, I'm Bruce Sellery."

And then I did a little jig. It was certainly imperceptible to anyone else, but that jig perfectly captured how excited and grateful I was that I had achieved this lifelong goal.

Now it's your turn.

My objective in writing *Moolala* was to give you new clarity in your thinking about money, to help you develop a simple plan, and to inspire you to take action so that you can achieve your own goals and live the life you want. And as you've made your way through the five steps of the

Moolala Method, I know that you've already accomplished a lot. You've created a context for money that is empowering, personal, and consistent with your values. You've declared some Moolala Goals that reflect your interests in many different areas of life, and not just the purely financial. You've bravely addressed the consequences of your weaknesses around money and come up with some strategies to deal with them. And you've identified areas where you could increase or decrease the level of complexity you have in dealing with your money, so you can find the level that's right for you and your circumstances. You've even reached out to people in your community and talked more openly and frequently about money than perhaps you ever have before. Sure, you probably haven't followed through 100%, but you have taken steps—big steps—in moving from being a smart person doing dumb things with money to being a *smart person doing more smart things with money.*

And you've done this not because managing your money is your new full-time hobby, but because you've kept in mind what you love in life. If you recall, I said that this is a book about what you love, and I hope you have found it to be true. I have seen again and again that when people connect the task of working on their finances to what they love—and what they want more of in life—they're inspired to do what needs to be done to get a handle on their money.

I have seen again and again that when people connect the task of working on their finances to what they love—and what they want more of in life—they're inspired to do what needs to be done to get a handle on their money.

Congratulations on the amazing things you've already done, and on the amazing things that I know you will do in the future.

Now go out there and TAKE ACTION.

Now?

Yes, right now!

What are you still reading this for? We're done. You have better things to do.

Go!

Appendix A

CHECK OUT MOOLALA'S ONLINE RESOURCES

As mentioned throughout the book, there are additional resources available online at www.moolala.ca. Readers of the book will find many free downloads, including worksheets to help you come up with your Moolala Goals, spreadsheets for calculating your net worth and analyzing your cash flow, and printable versions of questions for your financial adviser. There is also a blog, a free Moolala newsletter you can subscribe to, details about upcoming Moolala workshops and events, and a discussion guide for those of you who would like to bring Moolala to your book club.

You'll also find a link to the Moolala membership website. For a small fee you will have access to our entire Learning Centre. It features video tutorials where I will take you through the entire Moolala Method step by step, plus additional worksheets, exercises, and calculators to help you get a handle on your money.

Appendix B

CREATE A CONTEXT FOR THE HOLIDAYS

I no longer leave out cookies and milk for Santa. I don't know who feeds him these days, but it sure isn't me. Leaving out treats for the bearded one was always a part of how my family celebrated Christmas as I was growing up. But as I got older, the way I marked Christmas changed. Santa lost out on his snack and I slept in later, in part because my context for the holiday had changed.

When I was a kid, Christmas was for celebrating traditions—trimming the tree, opening presents, warbling through the carols, eating a big meal, and of course feeding Santa. As an adult, Christmas has become more about being with family. While we still do some of the key things—cue the big meal—we've simplified the rest and focused on just being together.

You might not celebrate Christmas. Your big holiday might be Kwanzaa, Chinese New Year, or your birthday. So when I say *holiday,* insert one that is relevant for you, and then ponder this question:

What are the holidays for, for you?

This question can be a fruitful one to answer before you start your holiday shopping because your context might impact your behaviour. The holidays could be for celebration, spirituality, family, gift-giving, relaxation, tradition, generosity—or a combination of these ideas. If I were to ask fifty different people, I would likely get fifty different answers, even if the people I asked were from the same family.

Context is so important because it gives shape to events. Some of the "events" that occur over the holidays include taking time off from work, shopping for gifts, going to parties, watching classic movies, resting and relaxing. If you aren't clear on what the holidays are for, for you, it can lead to a lot of stress. You might overspend on credit cards, buy and receive gifts you don't really want, exhaust yourself with preparations at home, or spend too much time with people who drain you.

Once you've answered the question of what the holidays are for, you can look at your behaviour during that period to see if you're doing anything that is inconsistent with your context. For example, if you say the holidays are for relaxation, and yet you are running around to ten parties, then cooking and buying gifts for thirty people, you could say that your behaviour is inconsistent with your context for the holidays.

That behaviour, even once identified, can be difficult to change. You have expectations of yourself. Family members have expectations of each other. And there can be a whole emotional undercurrent that runs through the holidays, before, during, and after, too. But sometimes we get stuck in tradition for tradition's sake, even if it doesn't work for us any more. It's worth thinking about what you might do differently this year so your behaviour is aligned as closely as possible to the context you've created for the holidays.

Here are a few questions to get the creative juices flowing on how you can create a fantastic holiday—one that is consistent with what you say the holidays are for, and one that doesn't leave you with an emotional and/or monetary deficit at the end of it.

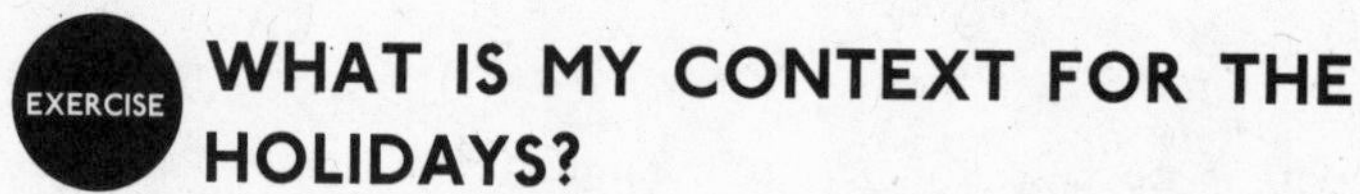

WHAT IS MY CONTEXT FOR THE HOLIDAYS?

PONDER:

- What are the holidays for?
- Where is your behaviour consistent with this context?
- Where is your behaviour inconsistent with this context?

BRAINSTORM: What would you like to continue to do during the holidays that you have always done? What would you like to change about what you do?

TALK: Who do you need to talk to, to make this happen?

Here is how one member of the Moolala Community answered these questions.

- **What is Christmas for?** Family.
- **Behaviour that is consistent:** Spending time with extended family. Eating a great meal together.
- **Behaviour that is inconsistent:** Worrying about buying gifts for everyone. Trying to see everyone on the 25th.
- **What I'd like to continue to do:** Give gifts to my young cousins.
- **What I'd like to change:** Set spending limit of $50 on gifts for cousins. And don't exchange gifts with other family members. Invite family over to my house on the 26th, instead of travelling around to see everyone on the 25th.
- **Who I need to talk to:** Parents and siblings. Make a request to talk about changing the plans.

Appendix C

START A MOOLALA MONEY GROUP

One of the best ways to remind yourself of your goals and the actions you need to take to achieve them is to engage your community. As you know, I'm a big believer in the power of community to help you get a handle on your money, and given that there is precious little community out there in the area of personal finance, it might make sense for you to create your own. My challenge to you is to form a Moolala Money Group with a few friends or colleagues. Outlined below are some steps you can take to make it happen. More details and exercises are available at www.moolala.ca.

START A MOOLALA MONEY GROUP

PONDER: What sort of people would you like to have in a group like this? What characteristics are important to you? Who do you know that fits your criteria?

INVITE: Put the invitation out to one or two people to start with. Then you can ask them to find one or two other people. Four or five people in the group is a great number. It can be tough to schedule meetings if you have more than six people—and tough for everyone to have enough air time. Here is a suggestion about what to say in the invitation: "I've been reading this book called Moolala. It's about getting a handle on your money so you can live the life you want. I'd like to get a small group of people together so we can help each other do just that."

SCHEDULE: Find a date when you can have an uninterrupted three-hour time slot—at least for the first meeting. Meet wherever you'll be comfortable having what may be a fairly personal conversation.

DISCUSS: A Moolala Money Group doesn't have to be a formal meeting, but I do find it helpful to have an agenda or plan to guide the conversation. I've included on the following pages some sample agendas your group could use for its first and subsequent gatherings, including ballpark time estimates. Your group might decide to take a completely different approach, and that's fine. What's important is that you meet regularly to talk openly about the process of getting a handle on your money.

SAMPLE AGENDAS FOR YOUR MOOLALA MONEY GROUP

First Gathering

Introductions (30 minutes)

- Tell us a bit about yourself (about your family, work, passions, etc.—whatever you think we should know).
- Why did you decide to join a Money Group?

This is a good icebreaker, whether people know each other or not. And it's important for everyone to talk about why they are attending, so you can begin to build the trust you need to make the group successful.

Objectives (30 minutes)

- What do we want this group to be about?

You can come up with whatever objectives you'd like for your particular group. Of course, support, ideas, and accountability top my list. Groups like this can provide a huge amount of support to their members, regardless of what the individuals' goals are. They can also brainstorm some great ideas and provide different perspectives on how to approach the goals you already have. And finally, a community like this can hold its members accountable for taking action on what they say they want in life.

Working together (30 minutes)

- How often will we meet? Once a month, once every three months?
- Who is going to lead the discussion, or will we leave it free form?
- What will we have for beverages or snacks?
- How will we keep confidentiality within the group?
- How do we foster open communication?

This is the time to figure out how you'll work together as a group, both in terms of the tangibles of meeting frequency and the intangibles of keeping confidentiality. You might not be able to answer all these questions right away, but it will be helpful to put them out there to start the discussion.

Context (50 minutes)

- What are some of your earliest memories of money?

- Looking ahead to the future, what would you say money is for, for you? (What do you value? What do you enjoy? What is important to you in your life that money enables? What role do you want money to play? How do you want to use it?)

Your members might not have read *Moolala* yet, but everyone can still participate in a conversation about context, with a bit of background from the book. I suggest having someone paraphrase or read aloud from the "Context is the backdrop for everything" section beginning on page 24.

The first question is designed to have members start to identify the default context they have from their family. The second question is a kick-start to having them create their own context for money.

Declarations and Requests (20 minutes)

- What is one action you could take between now and the next time we meet to help you get a handle on your money?
- What requests would you like to make of the group?

I find it makes a really big difference for each member of the group to declare an action they will take or a result they will deliver by the time the group meets again. Have one person write all these down so that you can bring them to the next gathering. Over time, these declarations will relate to the topic you just discussed.

This is also the time when each member can make specific requests of the group—for support ("Can you come to my house and ply me with wine as we shred old tax returns?"), ideas ("Who knows of a great financial adviser?"), or accountability ("Can you call me on the sixth of every month and check in on my progress cutting credit card debt?").

Wrap-up (15 minutes)

- What are the specifics of our next gathering?
- What is the one thing that you're taking away from tonight? (It could be an insight, an action, a tip, etc.)

You might determine the date, time, location, and topic for your next gathering or set it up later by e-mail. Just make sure one of your members is accountable for making it happen.

Finally, save some time at the end so everyone gets to share one thing they are taking away from the conversation to draw the meeting to a close.

Ongoing Gatherings

Check-in (50 minutes)

- What is one recent high and one recent low you've experienced as you have been getting a handle on your money?
- What was the declaration you made at the last gathering, and how did it go?

It is important for the members of your group to know what is going on with each other. The "one high and one low" approach is a way to do that quickly, by focusing on a few significant updates.

This is also the opportunity for the group to debrief on the declarations that everyone made at the prior get-together. This might mean celebrating others' accomplishments or being supportive when things didn't go as hoped. One pitfall of the declaration debrief is that people often move right into problem-solving mode. Be sure to ask the person speaking what they need from the group before you offer it—sometimes they will need problem solving but often they'll just need you to listen. They may have other requests to make of the group later in the gathering.

Topic (80 minutes)

- What is relevant to you about this topic?

Using the book as a guide, you can work through the chapters sequentially, or pick a topic that is of particular relevance to your group. Often the topic is determined in advance, and you can have members read the chapter and then come together to discuss it. Or you could have one person summarize the topic for the group and then do the exercises collectively.

One of the most important steps to share as a group is "Step 2: Determine what you want." I would definitely recommend you do this within your first few meetings so everyone knows each other's long list of Moolala Goals.

Declarations and Requests (20 minutes)

- What is one action or result that you're declaring you'll complete or achieve by the next meeting?
- What requests would you like to make of the group?

Wrap-up (15 minutes)

- What are the specifics of our next gathering?
- What is one thing you're taking away from tonight?

Mid-year Check-in

- What is working well about the group?
- What about the group is not working as well as it could be?
- What, if anything, would we like to do differently?

After you've been meeting for a while, I've found that it's really helpful to check in with the members of the group to see what is working well and what isn't working so well. I'd recommend that you revisit what your group said about its objectives and plan for working together to see if there is anything you need to add, subtract, or revise. You might also brainstorm things the group could do differently—such as add a guest speaker, add new members, hold a full-day meeting to give you more time to delve into questions, etc.

Appendix D

REBALANCE YOUR PORTFOLIO

Butter tarts need the right amount of each ingredient to taste delicious. Any baker will tell you that changing "how much" of each ingredient you use to make them is generally not such a good idea. Well, you need to keep an eye on "how much" of each ingredient you have in your investments, too.

Stock markets rise and fall in any given year so the percentage of each type of asset in your portfolio might have changed. When the percentages have shifted by more than 3% to 5% you should "rebalance" your portfolio. This will return "how much" of each asset type you have back to its target level, as set out in your Moolala Investment "recipe." It will also allow you to take into consideration your increasing age—because, remember, as you get older you'll want more fixed income in your portfolio.

Here's an example of how to do just that.

Rebalancing Sebastien's Portfolio

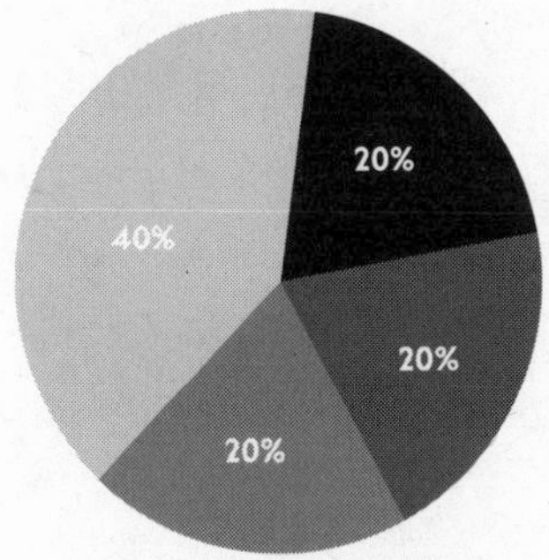

LAST YEAR: Sebastien's portfolio was worth $50,000. He's 40 years old, so he had 40% or $20,000 in fixed income, with the remainder divided equally among Canadian, U.S., and global equity (20% or $10,000 invested in each).

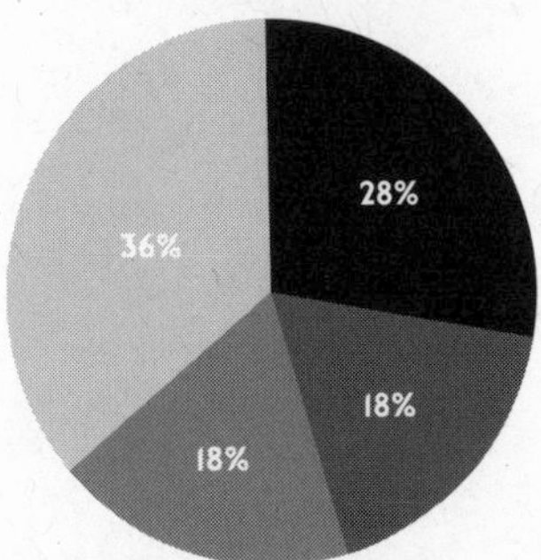

THIS YEAR: Sebastien's portfolio is now worth more. His Canadian equity has done quite well, growing to $15,000, while everything else remained at last year's levels. Canadian equity now represents 28% of the portfolio, which is more than the 20% target.

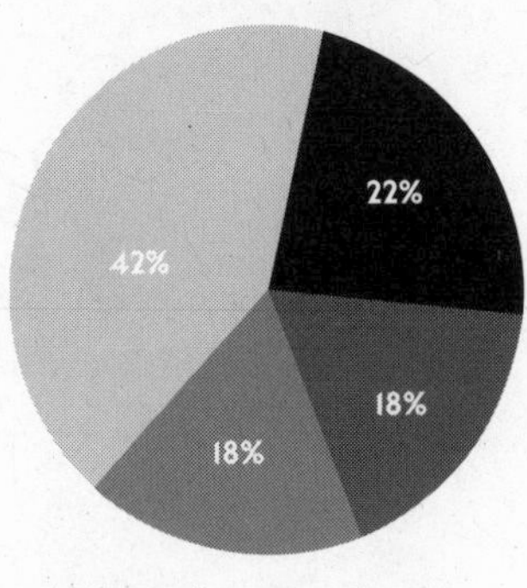

ACTION REQUIRED: To get the percentages back in line with his target levels, Sebastien needs to reduce the amount of Canadian equity he has and to increase the amount of fixed income. To do this, he would sell $3,000 worth of the former and buy $3,000 worth of the latter. The new percentages aren't exact, but they are close enough.

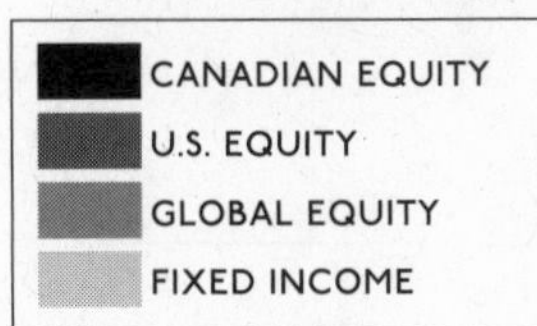

You can also rebalance your portfolio when you add new money to it. Divide the money you have to invest among the assets so that your new percentages are as close to the target percentages as possible.

It might seem crazy to sell some of your winners and buy more of your laggards, but rebalancing is a key part of the investment process because it will have you "sell high" the investments that have done well, and allow you to "buy low" the investments that haven't done as well and so are cheaper to add to your portfolio. It is akin to "not putting all your eggs in one basket."

Appendix E

KEEPING PERSPECTIVE ON YOUR INVESTMENT PERFORMANCE

The ups and downs of the stock market

"I try not to look at my iShare ETFs every morning, but they're there on my bank's homepage. And the value has been going down consistently. I know investments like these are long-term, and one shouldn't eyeball the day-to-day, but I just wanted to ensure that I've put money in the right things and that indeed, yes, this is a bit of a slow time. Should I worry? Because I'm now worrying."

–Barry, 42, director. Single, with two children.

This is an email I received in 2008 from a member of the Moolala Community. Here's the gist of my response: The stock market goes up and the stock market goes down. That said, it is one thing to understand this pattern intellectually and another to watch your investments lose one-third of their value in three months. Stock market declines can be crushing emotionally, so it is important to put things into perspective. We've talked about how, historically, the stock market goes up about 7% per year on average. But along the way, you can see boffo years, and some disastrous years. Below is a look at the year-by-year returns for the TSX Composite Index over a twenty-year time period. In its worst year it was down a devastating 35%, but the very next year the TSX Composite Index was up a euphoric 31%, delivering its best year-over-year gains in twenty years.

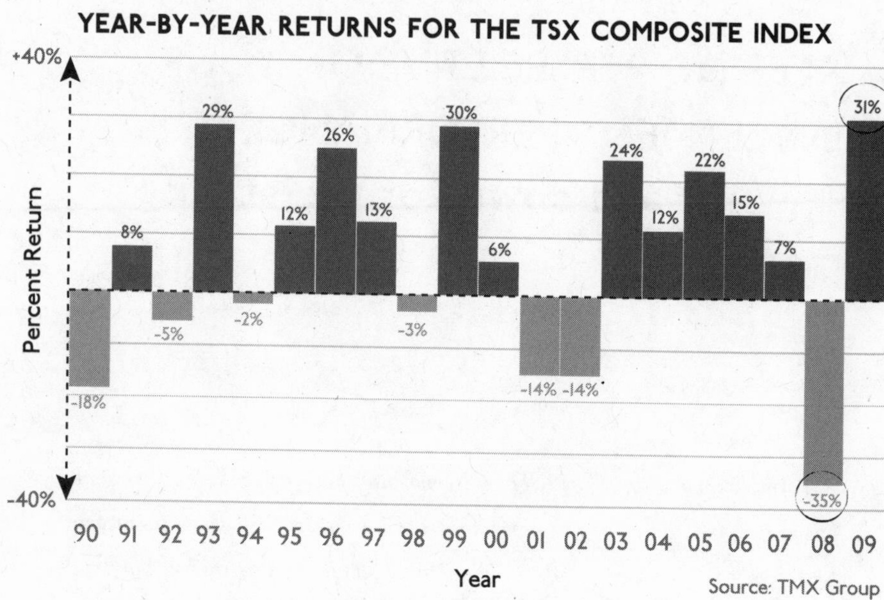

But when you look at performance from a longer-term perspective, the swing in the numbers won't be nearly so significant, and neither will the swing in your emotions. The graph on the next page shows the historical performance of the TSX Composite Index over the same twenty-year time period, during which the TSX rose 8% per year on average—a solid, respectable return.

HISTORICAL PERFORMANCE OF THE TSX COMPOSITE INDEX

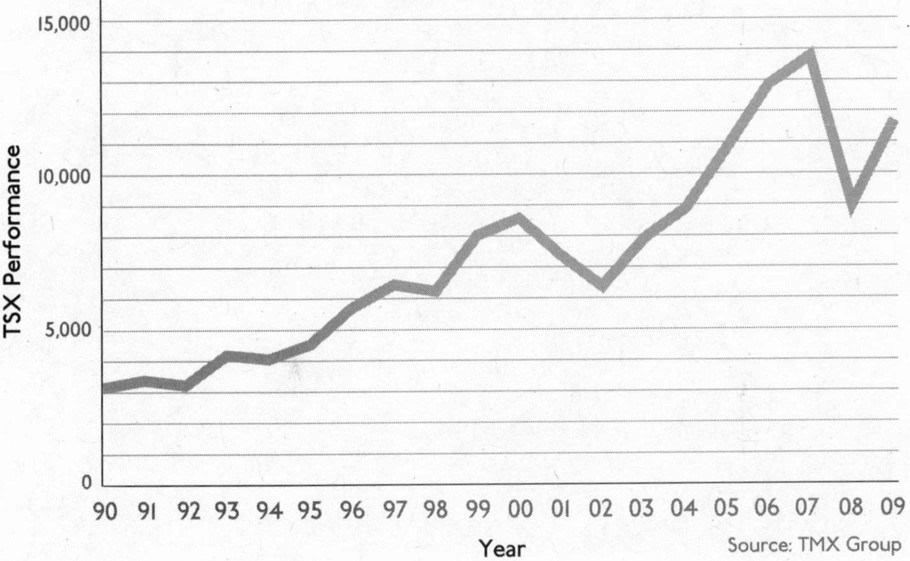

So if you're investing for the long haul, it makes no sense to focus on the day-to-day, or month-to-month moves in the stock market. Get your drama from reality TV instead.

Acknowledgements

I have benefited immeasurably from the support, ideas, and accountability of my community in the writing of this book. I would like to thank many of them here.

First and foremost, I am indebted to the many members of the Moolala Community who have participated in my workshops over the years, especially those who have allowed me to share their stories in the book. Without their openness and insight, I would never have been able to develop the Moolala Method in the first place.

I'd also like to thank the people who read through various drafts of the book and provided their insight and encouragement, including Melissa Thompson, Leah McMullin, Megan Peart, Heather Hudson, Jennifer Westhoven, and Beth Hamilton-Keen.

Colleagues in my Springboard entrepreneurs group provided their counsel through the highs and lows of the book writing process. Thanks to Karen Ward, Jeff Straker, Ron Tite, Trevor Currie, Michelle Cederberg, Andrea Holwegner, Sue Jacques, Vicki Young, and Marty Avery.

Thanks as well to my many loyal and vocal cheerleaders: Danny Nashman, Kelly Cowan, Guy Beaudin, Claire Sakaki, James Fotheringham,

Pam Bond, Bretta Gerecke, Evelyn Ackah, Gina Mollicone, Carol Brickenden, Shelley Ambrose, Lori Burwash, Marcel Jacob, Jen Evans, Gord Ray, Dan Wilton, Craig Kelly, Dave Zietsma, Paul Gardner, Pam Cushing, Patti Pon, Deb Hagen, Shira Gilbert, as well as the Garnhum family, and the Sellery siblings, Janet, Alan, Ruth, Julie, and Maria.

Jennifer MacTaggart was the very first person in the publishing industry to listen to the idea for this book. Her seeds of encouragement, planted almost ten years ago, and her ongoing support were invaluable in keeping me committed to it. Trena White was the book's first champion at McClelland & Stewart, and I am grateful for her passion and partnership as I wrote the first draft. Anita Chong, my editor at M&S, did all the heavy lifting to get the manuscript into shape and into your hands. She is whip-smart, hugely insightful, and completely unflappable under pressure.

Thanks to Dianne Rotteau for giving me my first job in journalism, and to Jack Fleischmann for putting me on TV. To Mark Kryzan and Terry Shaunessy at Shaunessy Investment Counsel for their perspective on investing. To author Karen Schaffer for her experience on navigating the emotional journey of writing a book. To my mentor Debbie Wood for teaching me most of what I know about creating a community. And to my best friend, Tammy Sturge, for never being more than a phone call away, day or night.

Thank you to my dad, Gord Sellery, for instilling in me strong values about the importance of understanding money, and to my stepmother, Cathy Sellery, for helping all of us in the family celebrate spending it once in a while. And to my mom, Helene Sellery, for being the best example I have ever seen of a life well lived.

And finally, I would like to thank my partner, Dennis Garnhum, and daughter, Abby Sellery. Dennis's vision, creativity, and tenacity have allowed us to live our life of adventure. And Abby has made all the work that that entails completely and totally worth it.

BRUCE SELLERY is a business journalist and professional speaker. As one of the founding staff members of CTV's Business News Network (BNN), he has anchored thousands of hours of programming from both Toronto and New York since the network went on air in 1999. In addition to his work on BNN, he has appeared on *Canada AM,* CTV News Channel, CBC News Network, and CityTV's *Breakfast Television.*

More recently, Bruce founded *Moolala,* a personal finance training company focused on inspiring people to get a handle on their money so they can live the life they want. In addition to overseeing Moolala's online Learning Centres, he is a regular keynote speaker on the topics of investing and personal accountability.

Prior to his move into business journalism, Bruce worked at Procter & Gamble, where he held leadership roles in both sales and brand management. In addition to his line management responsibilities, he was head of the company's training programs in both Strategic Thinking and Diversity.

Bruce is an alumnus of the Governor General's Leadership Conference and a member of the Canadian Association of Professional Speakers. He has an Honours Bachelor of Commerce degree from the Queen's School of Business in Kingston, Ontario.

Born and raised in London, Ontario, he now lives in Calgary, Alberta, with his partner, Dennis, and daughter, Abby.